Postmodernity, Sociology and Religion

Edited by

Kieran Flanagan
Reader in Sociology
University of Bristol

and

Peter C. Jupp
United Reformed Minister

palgrave

Published by
MACMILLAN PRESS LTD
Houndmills, Basingstoke, Hampshire RG21 6XS
and London
Companies and representatives
throughout the world

First edition 1996
Reprinted (with a new preface) 1999

ISBN 0–333–63009–2 hardcover
ISBN 0–333–75198–1 paperback

A catalogue record for this book is available
from the British Library.

This book is printed on paper suitable for recycling and
made from fully managed and sustained forest sources.

Printed and bound in Great Britain by

Antony Rowe Ltd. Eastbourne

Published in the United States of America by
ST. MARTIN'S PRESS, INC.,
Scholarly and Reference Division
175 Fifth Avenue, New York, N.Y. 10010

ISBN 0–312–16109–3

POSTMODERNITY, SOCIOLOGY AND RELIGION

Kieran Flanagan dedicates this book to his brother Brian, his wife Joan, and David, Orla, Julie and Martina who felt they should be mentioned too

Peter C. Jupp to his wife Elisabeth and sons Edmund and Miles for their support. If postmodernity proves to be the correct interpretation of contemporary culture, may this book help them cope with it

Contents

Acknowledgements

Postmodernity, Sociology and Religion is the third in the series of books proceeding from the conferences of the Sociology of Religion Study Group of the British Sociological Association. Its predecessors were *Religion and Power: Decline and Growth* and *Religion in Contemporary Europe*, both edited by John Fulton and Peter Gee. We are grateful for the support of the Study Group and of its officers in the production of this volume.

This book originates in the conference on 'Postmodernity and Religion' held at the University of Bristol in March 1993 and organised by Kieran Flanagan and Peter C. Jupp. This was one of the most well-attended of the Study Group's annual conferences in recent years. This compilation represents a selection of the papers first presented at Bristol, all of which have been substantially re-written for this volume. The contributors were also asked to make constructive comments on issues discussed in other chapters. The editors wish to acknowledge the good humour and endless patience of all the contributors as they responded to requests for re-drafting and clarification.

We are very grateful to Ms Annabelle Buckley, our editor at the publishers, for her support. She has been continually constructive, encouraging and patient. We thank also Keith Povey for the diligence of his copy-editing. We are grateful to Mrs Jackie Bee at the Department of Sociology at the University of Bristol for dealing with accents, printing and numerous other forms of assistance that greatly facilitated the production of this volume.

In the planning of the book, the editors wish to record their own pleasurable pilgrimage around the fringes of postmodernity in culinary transactions at an Indian restaurant in Windsor, the Reform Club and Brown's in Bristol, all of which enhanced a fruitful and enjoyable collaboration in editing this volume.

September 1995

KIERAN FLANAGAN
PETER C. JUPP

Notes on the Contributors

Rex Ambler is Lecturer in Theology at the University of Birmingham. His previous publications include *Global Theology: the Meaning of Faith in the Present World Crisis* (1990). He was editor of *Agenda for Prophets: Towards a Political Theology for Britain* (1980). Currently he is working on a book on faith and the crisis of modernity.

Lewis Ayres is Lecturer in Systematic and Historical Theology at Trinity College, Dublin. He has published in a number of areas of modern theology and early Christian thought. He is the author of a book on Christology (1997), editor of the *Trinity Reader* (1996) and co-editor of the Blackwell series, *Challenges in Contemporary Theology*.

James A. Beckford is Professor of Sociology at the University of Warwick. His publications include *The Trumpet of Prophecy* (1975), *Cult Controversies* (1985) and *Religion and Advanced Industrial Society* (1989). He is editor or co-editor of *New Religious Movements and Rapid Social Change* (1986), *The Changing Face of Religion* (1989) and *Secularisation, Rationalism and Sectarianism* (1993). He is currently Vice-President of the International Sociological Association and is President-Elect of the International Society for the Sociology of Religion.

Maxine Birch is a research student at Oxford Brookes University. Her essay is drawn from a wider research topic: 'The Quest for Self-Discovery: A Sociological Exploration into the Construction of Self-Identity in the Alternative Health Setting'. She teaches part-time in social policy and sociology of health for the Open University and Oxford Brookes University. Her research interests are concerned with issues of reflexivity in social research and sociology itself.

Grace Davie is Lecturer in Sociology at the University of Exeter. Her publications include: *Inner City God: the Nature of Belief in the Inner City* (1987) co-authored with Geoffrey Ahern; and *Religion in Britain since 1945: Believing without Belonging* (1994). She is General Secretary of the International Society for the Sociology of Religion (SISR) and is a member of the Research Committee 22 (Sociology of Religion) of the International Sociological Association.

Kieran Flanagan is Reader in Sociology at the University of Bristol. He has written widely on theology, sociology and culture. His publications include *Sociology and Liturgy: Re-presentations of the Holy* (1991) and *The Enchantment of Sociology: a Study of Theology and Culture* (1996). Currently, he is writing a book on *The Social Construction of Virtue* which deals with habitus, holiness and reflexivity amongst young Catholic and Anglican males in relation to religious vocations.

Paul Heelas is Reader in Religion and Modernity and is a member of the Department of Religious Studies at the University of Lancaster. He is also Director of the Centre for the Study of Cultural Values. Specialising in the study of cultural change and religion, he has written extensively on issues of the self, capitalism and postmodernity. His latest book is: *The New Age Movement: Celebrating the Self and the Sacralization of Modernity* (1996); and he has co-edited with Scott Lash and Paul Morris, *Detraditionalization: Critical Reflections on Authority and Identity* (1996).

Peter C. Jupp is a Visiting Fellow in the Department of Sociology, University of Bristol. A United Reformed Church minister, he was Director of the National Funerals College, 1992–97. His doctoral thesis investigated the development of cremation in England. He was Convener of the Sociology of Religion Study Group of the British Sociological Association, 1991–94. With Glennys Howarth, he is co-editor of *Contemporary Issues in the Sociology of Death, Dying and Disposal* and *The Changing Face of Death* (1997) and the journal *Mortality*.

David Lyon is Professor and Head of the Sociology Department at Queen's University Kingston, Ontario, Canada. His publications include *The Steeple's Shadow: On the Myths and Realities of Secularization* (1985); *The Information Society: Issues and Illusions* (1988); *The Electronic Eye: the Rise of Surveillance Society* (1994); *Postmodernity* (1994) and *Living Stones: St. James' Church, Kingston 1845–1995* (1995). Currently, he is researching for a book on religion and postmodernity and for a sociological biography of Robert Rogers.

Stephen Sharot is Professor of Sociology in the Department of Behavioural Sciences, Ben-Gurion University of the Negev, Israel. His publications include: *Messianism, Mysticism and Magic: a Sociological Analysis of Jewish Religious Movements* (1982) and *Ethnicity, Religion and Class in Israeli Society* (1991) co-authored with Eliezer Ben-Rafael. His research areas are in the sociology of religion and the sociology of ethnicity. Currently, he is engaged in a comparative study of popular forms of religion in the context of world religions.

Michael York, King's College, London, is Director of the Amsterdam Centre for Eurindic Studies and, with Elisabeth Arweck, is also Co-Director of the Academy for Cultural and Educational Studies. He has written widely on New Age movements. His publications include *The Emerging Network: a Sociology of the New Age and Neo-Pagan Movements* (1995) and *The Divine versus the Asurian: an Interpretation of Indo-European Cult and Myth.*

Graham Ward is Dean and Fellow of Peterhouse, Cambridge, where he is Director of Studies for Theology and Religious Studies. His essays have appeared in *Modern Theology*, *Theology*, *The Heythrop Journal* and *New Blackfriars*. His two books are: *Barth, Derrida and the Language of Theology* (1995); and *Contemporary Critical Theory for Theology* (1996). He is the editor of *Literature and Theology.*

Preface to the 1999 Reprint

Incredulity, fragmentation, pastiche and contextualisation, the domain properties of postmodernism, have percolated into almost every aspect of culture and economy. Postmodernism is the tag that still can launch a thousand sociological conferences. Every branch of the discipline has its own problem with the term which has come to denote the uncertainty of living in an intensified, commodified culture where attachments, so easily unsecured, undermine the making of commitments. Even if made, they relate to no moral purpose; there is no galvanising consensus as to what this ambition might be. Thus, postmodernism denotes a term of change and decay, of fear and resignation now exasperated by the onset of the millennium. Yet, since 1993 postmodern matters have changed.

The deaths of Lyotard and Foucault have effectively removed the cult of personality from the notion of postmodernism. Without their charismatic presences, there is less faith abroad in the incredulity they propagated about knowledge and structure. Somehow, the self and issues of identity have crept back from the fringes of postmodernism. Now these occupy the centre stage of domain concerns with culture. The popularisation of postmodernism has not so much deconstructed the term as demystified it. As the emblem of the human condition it has lost its reverential distance in the text. Because it has no rules of definition, postmodernism can mean what one wishes, hence its appropriation into myriads of cultural orders and disorders. It has now become an instrument of belief and liberation. Definitional pliability facilitates endless appropriations, a point well captured in Lemert's book, *Postmodernism is not what you think* (1997). It has become domesticated into an instrument of liberation, faith and enlightenment unexpectedly opening out vistas for new ideals.

There are also reasons to believe debates on postmodernity have moved on in a way that endorses the basis of this collection. Bauman's inestimable contribution to the viability of the notion points to an evolution from the definiteness of legislation within modernity to the indefinite state of being a pilgrim in postmodernity. In turn, postmodernity has evolved into a concern with ethics, the face of the Other and the question of securing identity in conditions of fragmentation where the mental life of the city has become even more fatiguing. Despite the exhaustion, there is still a yearning, to use Simmel's term, to be something other than the mere self and in this quest religion has become more rather than less attached to the issues now generated by postmodernity.

xiii

There is, however, an ambiguity within postmodernity, one which sociology rather than philosophy can decipher, for it points to matters of perception and reception in present culture. Does postmodernism facilitate the entry of the marginalised into the cracks in culture? Given the pastiche, the fragmentation and the plenitude of surface meanings, many avenues are opened for those engaged in identity politics to stake their claim. But this facet of liberation might be illusory, for postmodernity wears an ideological mask that disguises a mechanism of perpetuating the displaced in their marginality. As a game of the weary, it marginalises those fresh and idealistic about modernisation, for whom the venture is still replete with possibility.

For those in the Islamic world, modernisation without secularisation can occur without the seemingly fated transformation into postmodernism, with its attendant blindness to morality and its fracture of idealism. Thus, non-Western societies seek a maturation of modernisation in a manner that rehabilitates and sustains tradition, so that selectivity over the tenets of postmodernity operates. Globalisation rests alongside tradition and the commodification of images persists alongside the forms of resistance to secularisation oddly, yet, so definitely embodied in a notion – postmodernity – that exemplifies a condition of indefiniteness. Thus, the future of this debate is definitely guaranteed.

KIERAN FLANAGAN
PETER C. JUPP

Introduction
Kieran Flanagan

Interesting conferences capture shifts in academic mood. Participants gather to discover new agendas, concepts and galvanising intellectual fashions to take back to their settled small academic worlds. Like retreats, ideal conferences also legitimate contours of thought and affirm the participants in new paradigms and orders of faith in their discipline. But, sometimes it is unclear what the paradigm is or, indeed, what the puzzle is that underlies a shift in modes of sociological appreciation, a case in point being the link between postmodernity, sociology and religion.

The conference, upon which this collection is based, sought papers on the impact of postmodernity on traditional religions, the New Age, the self, aesthetics and on sociology of religion itself. It gathered to hear a sociological tale untold on this matter. The resultant flood of interest was gratifying to the conveners, indicating there were others wondering what was going on in the cultural marketplace as it affected religion. Clearly, the issue belonged to sociology of religion, but somehow lay outside the image of its conventional territory of sects and secularisation. Questions raised about religion and postmodernity also belong to the wider sociological discipline. But they beg questions as to what its specialism, sociology of religion, has to say, hence the calling of the conference.

Even sociologists reading the quality newspapers cannot but notice that times are changing. There is a worry abroad in the cultural milieu in which sociology operates. These worries relate to unsettlements of self and identity that betoken a cultural angst, a condition known by the elastic phrase, postmodernity. It denotes a mood of ending, of privatisation and of removal from traditions, an opportunity expressed in globalisation and technology, but also a denial, a feeling of excess and emptiness that nullifies the gift of commodification.

Postmodernity denotes a condition of ambiguity with implications for religiosity. Unexpectedly, it has placed issues of religion back on the agenda of mainstream sociology. This return of religion to sociology might surprise. As an issue it seems disconnected from society, a corpse modernity buried with a tombstone called secularisation. But now comes a resurrection, the seeds of which can be denoted in the issues that have come to signify postmodernity. A searching, an escaping, a rootlessness of image and affiliation, the effects of technology and globalisation, mark an unsecured

self, now forced to ask questions of metaphysical identity inconceivable
on the agenda of a radical sociology of critical concern two decades ago.
Why has this come to pass? As sociology re-centred its interests in culture, it brought in a theological baggage, resources of tradition and memory,
to ameliorate another condition emerging at the same time: postmodernity.
Not unexpectedly, the interests in culture and postmodernity became confused in a way which this collection seeks to clarify. This ambiguity has
caught a sociology of religion by surprise, it being more geared to calibrat-
ing issues of disbelief rather than belief, as Lyon suggests in his chapter.
It seems as if sociology is forced into a contest with religion, a game postmodernity now makes it play.

Increasingly sociology is dealing with a commodified culture, with the
products of the service industry that manufacture images with metaphysical impunity, that entangle artifice with authenticity in a way that has put
issues of ethics back on the sociological agenda. This ethical turn, this concern with self, points to the ingredients of an implicit religion, properties
that could be turned into matters of a more definite spiritual affiliation.
This agenda of the mid-1990s points to a new beginning, one where religion seems to play an unexpected part. There is a dabbling, a New Age
of spiritual eclecticism, that marks the concerns of a new generation of
cultural pioneers, who forge their own identities in an era characterised by
postmodernity. These are the unapparent heirs of the counterculture, those
Romanticists of the late 1960s who found Enlightenment in the East.

There are distinctive signs of religion being on the cultural agenda,
but in an condition of ambiguity which postmodernity signifies. Inversions
of religiosity are clear in the supposed postsecularity of postmodernity. At
one level, they can be considered the fickle fiddling of moronic pop groups
given to blaspheme with impunity, plundering past spiritual traditions in
the hope of shocking the clime of indifference that marks the postsecular
condition. But at another level, fringe groups of culture, dealing with ecology, feminism, New Age, are hallowing such traditions, seeking spiritual
roots to ameliorate a felt emptiness that seems to characterise a culture
of postmodernity. Neither of these two polarities seems possessed by the
indifference to religion which secularity prophesied would come to pass
in postmodernity, in the maturation of modernity.

In some inchoate way, there is a worry abroad amongst academics,
sociologists and theologians that matters have taken an ironic turn. It
seems that religion has not gone down some positivist plughole; rather,
it would appear that postmodernity suggests that the Enlightenment, and
the modernity to which it was linked, have been themselves drained
away. If so, this seems to account for the metaphysical thirst that afflicts

contemporary sociology as it gazes more closely at the landscape of a culture of postmodernity.

Like forms of dry rot, postmodernity, once invasive, becomes the ubiquitous condition of sociology. It means everything and nothing; it encapsulates a mood, but also denotes its elusiveness; it is the proverbial polo mint of the discipline – enough to go around but with no centre. It has surfaced in almost every other branch of the discipline. Feminism, medicine, class and culture, to name a few, have all tagged postmodernity to their deliberations. It was only a matter of time in this academic mood of pluralism, fragmentation and surface before the implications of its link with religion would be explored; hence the convening of the conference at Bristol.

Unfortunately, the relationship of postmodernity to sociology of religion is peculiarly problematic. An ambiguous term at best, postmodernity is seen sometimes as the property of the cultural fringe, of New Age and ecological movements and of the self-made spiritualities of feminism and therapeutic groups. These have a property of 'pick and mix' spirituality, the manufacture of a religious smorgasbord characterised by endless choice. As Clifford Longley, that astute English religious affairs journalist, noted:

> in religion, long standing and fundamental differences over belief are boiled down, in this Post Modern perspective, to mere cultural styles, all of them deemed equally 'valid'. The one measurement that matters is the quality of the spiritual high they give, as if worship was something you snorted through your nose.[1]

Sociology might not be able to arbitrate on the spiritual highs and lows which postmodernity signifies for mainline and fringe religions but it can assess and characterise the life-styles they spawn, their social construction and cultural forms of realisation. The needs postmodernity embodies are as interesting as the consequences it effects, especially in sociological approaches to religion.

Postmodernity signifies a radical contextualisation, a grounding in cultural forms, whose changes affect and effect sociological understandings of religious belief. In dealing with postmodernity, sociology has its own agenda. This emerges from the writings of Bauman, Beck and, in his own formulation of a late modernity, Giddens, who (with Gellner) are given a rigourous appraisal in Beckford's essay in this volume. Religious considerations emerge in their writings, not least in the recognition of the sociological significance of fundamentalism in the later writings of Giddens and Gellner. If postmodernity is a cultural moment, it draws attention to its producers, its ideal site of social construction: in short, a sociology of

Introduction

knowledge. Some forms of postmodernity are more user-friendly to sociology than others.

As a discipline, sociology finds it less than easy to handle the rather imperialising text-bound nihilism and deconstruction that comes from Derrida and, in some unresolved way, Nietzsche. Spiritual issues do lurk in this somewhat pretentious postmodernity, all text and no context. A negative theology can be found in Derrida, and the dalliance of Foucault (like Althusser) with Thomism and Catholicism is only becoming apparent. A need to mark this shift in awareness of spirituality lay behind the convening of a conference at King's College, Cambridge, in July 1990, on the theme 'The Shadow of Spirit: Contemporary Western Thought and its Religious Subtext'. But the conference made little reference to sociology, which did not make an appearance even in the index of the book that resulted.[2] What is and has been missing, which this volume seeks to supply, is the sociologist's account of postmodernity and religion. Admittedly, the product risks merely bearing anxious tales from Babel. Yet the assessment of disaster impact – as of deception – is a necessary and honourable task.

Initially, postmodernity might seem to confirm the destruction of traditional forms of religious belief. But the definiteness of the postsecular agenda implicit in postmodernity seems at odds with its claim that all narratives had collapsed. Postmodernity lacks the authoritative capacity so to rule on the basis of reason. A pluralism and heresy now afflict post-Enlightenment culture itself, where no means of transcending judgement are possible. The destructive forces of secularity which slew religion and which characterised modernity, in postmodernity have been turned inward in an implosion of images and opportunities for self-actualisation.

The indefiniteness of postmodernity, and the endless non-judgemental contextualisation it permits, suggest endless analytical opportunities where nothing is to be excluded, even religious belief in its most traditional forms. This raises questions of interrogation and of hermeneutic considerations that emerge from incommensurability in the comparison. These echo earlier methodological dilemmas to which zealots of postmodernity make little reference. These were apparent in anthropology in the rationality and relativity debate. There is an untapped hermeneutic aspect to postmodernity, which Lyon notes in his contribution.

An unfettered approach to contextualisation permits the admission of any practice into sociological view. Complications emerge from questions of context in dealing with religion. The puzzle governing the debate on rationality and relativity arose over the incommensurability of belief systems and practices between Western scientific thought and the cultural assumptions of a primitive society. But issues of incommensurability within religions, for instance between the rituals of a New Age sect and those of Catholicism, suggest an equivalence in description that seeps into a language of incompatability when contextualised. Adherents of a New Age ritual would resist having their activities classified in terms of Catholicism, and vice versa. To their adherents, these rituals do *not* have an equivalence and this is a sociological *and* a theological issue which postmodernity masks, but which this collection uncovers. There is an unresolved tension in the collection, between theological notions of truth and the study of religion as social forms and manifestations of any spiritual imperatives, particularly signified in the notion of the New Age. Is sociology a discipline that postpones its theological judgements, or should it offer none?

This issue of judgement arises inconveniently in current disputes about culture and religion. These leave sociologists divided against themselves, like other intellectuals who try to draw conclusions. Sociologists have little choice but to recognise the persistence of religious belief in the civil war in Bosnia, where religious affiliations are tied into ethnicity in a manner without European equivalent, save perhaps in Northern Ireland. These tribal disputes hardly mark the end of history, but rather the inexhaustible grip of the past on the present. They give mocking witness to the notion of a postmodernity married to a postsecularity. Furthermore, the most conspicuous revolt against modernity has come from Islamic religious fundamentalists. Postmodernity has deposited an ambiguity on to sociology, not of its own making. If postmodernity is about ambiguity, should sociology take the condition seriously?

Unlike other contributors in the volume, Beckford does not take postmodernism seriously, but fears he may have to, should the fashion persist. In his systematic consideration of Bauman, Giddens and Beck, Beckford shows the nugatory place of religion in their accounts of postmodernity. He subjects their writings to close scrutiny and in their dealings with religion finds them analytically wanting. He finds more satisfaction in Gellner's approach to postmodernity, which is vigorous and furious in its denunciation of postmodernism and all it obscures in Western culture. Gellner's Durkheimian solution of a 'constitutional religion', however, gives Beckford little sociological satisfaction as a corrective to the fractious effects of postmodernity which, for him, threaten to engulf the capacity of the discipline to reason. But sociology often has to deal with issues in circumstances not of its own making, a point that illuminates the link between postmodernity and religion.

Keynes wrote that the scribbling of the academic on the blackboard becomes part of public parlance a decade later. In sociology, matters are more complex, for the very culture in which it is implicated and which it seeks to constitute can also change its agenda. A case in point is the turmoil that achieved great publicity in late August 1995 (when this introduction was being written) surrounding an Anglican liturgy that sought to relate to a culture of postmodernity, ecology, feminism and the New Age. This experiment collapsed in a welter of charges of cult leadership and abuse of power, and led to the tragic dispersal of its followers.

This Anglican experiment suggested some fatal form of contact between postmodernity and theology over religion's social shape and credibility. Again, it also said something about the ambiguous nature of postmodernity itself in relation to religion. Far from confirming the indifference to religious belief which a postsecular postmodernity affirms, a desperate urge for spiritual expression was revealed amongst the congregation of young professionals who believed this form of rite made a spiritual difference in their lives. There are other reasons why postmodernity is less indifferent to religious belief than it might seem.

Postmodernity has given rise to two contradictory movements in religion that are difficult to reconcile: first, the quest for a New Age spirituality; and, second, the imperative to rehabilitate tradition in mainstream religions that has given rise to the term fundamentalism. Far from confirming an indifference to religious belief, postmodernity reveals a search for spiritual differences. This suggests that if postmodernity is about postsecularity, it also represents a revolt against apparently settled notions of indifference which secularisation cultivated in its marriage with modernity. These polar opposites, which the debate on postmodernity brings into focus, expose another point: the absence of a middle ground which more traditional theologies could exploit. Debate on postmodernity has also overturned a convention of liberal theologians, itself deriving from modernity, that tradition is both incredible and incompatible with the age. Postmodernity points to a rehabilitation of tradition and forms an important plank of the contributions of Heelas and Davie. A value of Davie's chapter is the significance of memory in Hervieu-Léger's approach to sociology of religion. Tradition also has a role in Sharot's contribution on religious developments amongst Jews in Israel. He notes that although the fragmentation and pluralism signified by postmodernity has affected religious developments in Israel, as a society, it has been largely unaffected by any postmodern forms of religion. Religious tradition ameliorates a need to explore some postmodern formulations.

It is clear that a sociological assessment of the link between religion and postmodernity has thrown up some singular issues. These represent a diversity of views which this collection signifies. Any introduction on the issue of postmodernity of religion cannot square the circle of contributors.

This would impose a consensus on their narratives that does not exist. As in the case of postmodernity itself, they all have differences in their reading of the link between religion and postmodernity. For some contributors, the link is of spirituality being harnessed to issues of self-realisation in the context of a galaxy of elective affinities with New Age sensibilities that reach for their own traditions (York, Heelas and Birch); for others it relates to a shift in sociological thought about the basis of religion within culture (Lyon, Beckford, Davie and Sharot); whilst another contributor persuasively traces issues of self and postmodernity back to Martin Luther (Ambler); and finally, the issue is a matter of theological opportunity to which sociology gives unexpected prophecy (Lyon, Flanagan, Ayres and Ward).

All the contributors seem to feel that postmodernity has facilitated a change in approach to religion and spiritual matters, as unexpected as it is difficult to theorise. Why has this shift come to pass, such that spirituality has unexpectedly entered the soul of sociology as an analytical consideration in a way that must cause Comte's remains to rotate?

Perhaps the primary reason is the dawning sociological realisation that, in the words of the Irish poet Seamus Heaney, 'a search for images and symbols adequate to our predicament' in present culture necessitates the recognition of spiritual considerations.[3] The secularisation of sociology itself has cultivated a tradition of blindness towards spiritual concerns lodged in its memory, but forgotten in the writings of Simmel and Weber. The issue of postmodernity has changed this sightlessness. Spiritual considerations, of the self, the body, and the reflexive community are embedded in the politics of life-style, in New Age sensibilities and needs which by default lead back to theological considerations of Christianity and Judaism, and also of Eastern religions. Postmodernity signifies the inadequacy of sociological instruments, amongst others, for dealing with the predicaments of the times. As noted earlier, the rise of religious sensibility now calls for what Lyon aptly terms a sociological recalibration.

In this collection of essays, a number of contributors recognise the way that Bauman, Beck and Giddens have changed the agenda of sociological approaches to issues of postmodernity (or late modernity) in a way that has profound implications for questions of religion. Their concerns with ambivalence, risk, anxiety, the self and what is known as a reflexive modernisation point to issues of cultural introspection that relate, however tangentially at times, to spiritual considerations.

As a term, postmodernity appears to signify a conceptual moment, a gathering point for characterising a contemporary culture that is globalised, commodified, de-traditionalised and de-contextualised. The power endlessly to make images and cultural artefacts excites sociological interest in postmodernity. But this interest has its dangers. To some extent, the term hoists sociology on a petard, for it too is caught, as Baudrillard suggests. Postmodernity risks rendering sociology impotent, as a condition of unresolvable fragmentation enters its theoretical gaze. Yet sociology has to examine postmodernity, for it is a ubiquitous condition of present culture. There is a sense that the term captures a loss of a capacity to be original, to re-invent, that society runs on tramlines, on ringing grooves of change, laid down in the mid-1960s and from which it has lost even the capacity to fall off. What was then original has become profoundly unoriginal; there are no new gripping forms of belief, no avenues of relief; all is dead and deadening, hence relief for sections of a lost generation in drugs. Even sex has taken on a property of the moribund in a way that would furrow a Jansenist brow.

Postmodernity is the tag of the times that speaks much of the condition it represents but says little that is memorable. It galvanises to the degree to which it demolishes; it unifies to the degree to which it signifies fragmentation; and it permits any play, but without rules, so that games seem pointless. Yet postmodernity has its uses. It enables a theoretical consensus to exist within sociology that there is no consensus.

The notion has further uses. One might think of postmodernity as a perambulator for the conveyance of present perplexities that afflict sociology. It lacks a fleshly occupant, but then the absence of an heir apparent justifies its use. The label 'postmodernity' stuck on the side advertises a suitable carriage for transportation of a lot of unexaminable analytical baggage. As it trundles along the sociological highways, it seems a serviceable vehicle for gender, economics, accountancy and medicine to deposit their doubts. Nobody knows who pushes it, where it came from or where it is going. But then, nobody really noticed its arrival and few will attend to its departure. It is a perambulator that is pushed only down First World roads.

The term postmodernity conveys a brilliant diagnosis of a fated process of opportunity that paralyses choice and which ultimately might render sociology redundant, for it can never find a transcending basis to assimilate the implosion postmodernity signifies. As a cultural moment, it bears sociological investigation in terms of a sociology of knowledge. Only sociology can offer a diagnosis of the diversity postmodernity signifies, but only the discipline can offer a means of escape, even if this leads into some unexpected theological directions (Lyon, Flanagan and Ayres).

At a trivial level, postmodernity abolishes fear of commodification of culture, by describing a diversity of possibilities. But this freedom carries its own dread, one that dehumanises before limitless choice. A retreat from the social, from the communal, from imperfect ties that cannot be constituted perfectly, draws sociology into a common interest with theology, for it is in the nature of both their traditions to seek to bind and to heal that which postmodernity seems to cast asunder. This is why there is a property of salvage in sociological approaches to issues of postmodernity. The self has become an unexpected central part of the agenda of the sociological discourse on the culture of postmodernity. It characterises the prospect that everyman can be an island in a sea of technological possibilities. Internet signifies this capacity to make images in any likeness in a manner divorced from social accountability. The communal has become archaic and if found is an artificial construction of type, of gender, ethnicity and sexuality. In this setting the self floats with impunity. The seeking of instant gratification in an eternal present marks properties of having but not possessing, and therein lies a disquiet, a lurking metaphysical dread that all is not perfect.

This sense of unsettlement, of choosing to escape from forces of dehumanisation, represents a strand of postmodernity that relates to spiritual questing in a diversity of forms which characterises particularly New Age thought. These form the focal point of concerns of York, Heelas and Birch. These contributors give a thorough analysis of the implications of postmodernism for New Age beliefs.

Some of these issues emerge in York's contribution on the implications of a pluralism in postmodernism for New Age thought. He provides a defence of new religious networks as offering a means of challenging the traditional stance of religion. In substance, his contribution is nearest to Heelas in its general reach of the literature on postmodernism and the New Age, but in style, in the seeking that characterises his chapter, he comes nearer Birch. The implied theology of his study, dealing with Pagan and New Age beliefs, again offers grounds of dialogue with traditional religions: but on whose terms? A magical-mystical reality is recognised as emerging in issues of postmodernism, which a neo-Pagan movement perceives, but which traditional theologies do not seem to grasp. His concern is that if postmodernity does mark an ending, the creation of new forms of religious life is required. He sees too much of 'the same old thing' in Ambler's account of the self and modernity, that operates within a traditional theology.

However, this places sociology in an awkward dilemma, of arbitrating in a way it cannot, on which cultural form best domesticates the spiritual and contains the tribulations of the self in the clouds of unknowing which swirl around postmodernity. If York, Heelas and Birch, are right – that postmodernity has masked an expressivism and an individualism that seeks new forms of realisation from their own traditions – they expose themselves to the question of by what authority? Movement in itself, in what York concedes to be a range of beliefs that characterise New Age and Pagan religions, hardly suffices. At some point it has to collide with a question of truth, for there is a tautological property to these three contributions, an endorsement of what is expressivist that comes near what MacIntyre criticised as emotivism, which raises particular questions for sociology.[4] Anyhow, Catholic theologians could respond to all three by asserting that self-made spirituality is but an illusion, a deception. But that is a theological point, and one that marks that very thin line it shares with sociology in dealing with matters of culture. How does one know?

In a radical re-interpretation of the literature, Heelas argues against the notion that the New Age and postmodernism are coterminous. New Age belief embodies its own tradition in a way that sets it at odds with the de-traditionalising process that characterises postmodernism. He argues that although the New Age positively encourages the collapse of cultural meta-narratives, it also involves the 'amplification of an experiential meta-"narrative"' that precludes de-traditionalisation. Thus, New Age thought seeks to rehabilitate tradition, and not to demolish it. Furthermore, he suggests this expressivism goes against the notion that the New Age is in some ways postmodern. His conclusion is that 'it becomes difficult to see what could be postmodern about religion as a whole'.

His chapter complements some themes in Birch's. The particular originality of her contribution lies in her fieldwork, in her account of how these individualised and expressive meta-narratives are constructed. The focus of her fieldwork is the therapeutic group and the facilitators who enable the self to seek health and holism. These self-help groups seek to affirm and to empower the realisation of the 'god/goddess within'. The value of her study also lies in its rare illumination of passages of self-realisation as a social process. This understanding governs her notion of self-disclosure but also what postmodernity permits. The groups she studies are of postmodernity but, as in the analysis of Heelas, they do not quite belong to it. For both writers, as for Ambler and Flanagan, the self has become the site of postmodernity. This is an unexpected development, as postmodernity seems to be about cultural movements and a response to globalisation, where the local becomes obscured, never mind the issue of detail of the self. But *pace* York's comment, Ambler could accuse those flirting with New Age philosophies of re-inventing the theological wheel.

Ambler provides a fuller account of the tradition from which issues of the self flow into postmodernity that marks an interesting contrast also to the chapters of Birch and Heelas. He is concerned with the theological roots of self-assertion in Luther and Kant and with the evolution of the self in the humanities. This account shows the way many facets of postmodernity are not peculiar to it, but are to be derived from antecedent traditions that stem from the Reformation, but also from the Enlightenment. The contribution of sociology lies in understanding the cultural conditions of self-actualisation which the debate on postmodernity has uncovered. For Ambler, the way forward lies in the acceptance of difference and mystery, and in the interpretation of tradition for changed circumstances.

The strength of tradition in ameliorating the worst excesses of modernity in late or post form is explored in Sharot's study of religious developments in Israel. In the light of the Jewish contribution to the formulation of modernity, his comments on postmodernity are of especial interest. The religious movements he notes relate to the revival of pilgrimage, the increased strength of ultra-Orthodoxy, the religious Zionist movement and new religious movements. But these new religious movements are small and marginal, although human potential movements attract large memberships. The *flâneur* of modernity has ended up as the pilgrim of postmodernity. Both Heelas and Sharot discount the notion that postmodernity has dispatched tradition to the history of ideas. It still matters and it very much counts in the settings of religion both authors deal with (the New Age and Judaism). Indeed, in their writings one senses that postmodernity has expanded interest in religion in a distinctive way, a point that emerges in Davie's assessment of Danièle Hervieu-Léger.

This is perhaps one of the first general assessments of an important but largely untranslated French sociologist of religion. Themes in her work, of community, pilgrimage, secularisation and memory (or rather a collective amnesia), relate to a central interest in French Catholicism. Her interest is in the survival of belief, and for her certain forms of religious life are the distinctive products of modernity. This demands a fresh reading of the impact of secularisation. Like Sharot, her notion of religion has a strength of tradition, however broken, that sets its own agenda in relation to modernity and postmodernity. An agenda of resistance to modernity is evident in her work, a point that relates to a number of other contributors. This is a point liberal theologians fail to understand and is perhaps a discomforting message from this collection.

Lyon's contribution has been placed first because it gives a general account of postmodernism. But this polemic of Lyon against a necessary disbelief relates to the last batch of papers, those of Flanagan, Ayres and Ward. Their interests relate to the link between theology, sociology and postmodernity. Lyon deals with the persistence of religion, despite recent theories of secularisation. He argues that religion, with little thanks to sociology of religion, is recovering its place within mainstream social theory.

He draws on Beckford for this view. Like Davie, Lyon seeks a reappraisal of the assumptions of secularisation, which the 'postmodern turn' necessitates. Lyon would welcome a change away from a hermeneutic of suspicion to one of retrieval, a turn necessitated by the concerns with reflexivity and enchantment that characterise postmodernity.

Some of these themes lurk in the background of Flanagan's chapter. It deals with the implications of the self in theological terms, arguing that the ambiguity of postmodernity has resuscitated Pascal's wager within sociology. Suggesting that there is an unacknowledged theological facet to sociology, evident in Blondel's approach to action, he argues for a re-siting of concerns of the self in the context of the theo-drama of the Swiss Catholic theologian, Hans Urs von Balthasar.

Ayres offers a critical reflection on this contribution from the position of a theologian. He provides a remarkably clear account of Milbank's approach to postmodernity in the latter's much discussed book, *Theology and Social Theory*. Like Milbank, and to some extent Ward, Ayres seeks to free the structure and distinctive narrative of theology from the clutches of an imperialising sociology. He argues that sociology cannot hover around the foothills of theology but has to recognise the autonomy of its discourse if an authentic dialogue on theological terms is to proceed. Unfortunately, the terms of reference between the two are not clear. Because sociology recognises a sacramental aspect to theology, it is implicated in its discourse when deciphering social transactions which deal with grace and holiness. It could be said that theologians, such as Milbank and Ayres, need to recognise the constraints of the narrative of sociology, and not just swat them with rolled-up textual exegesis, if debate with theology is to proceed. In his chapter, Ayres also refers to *Theo-Drama*, but in a very different way from that of Flanagan. There is an interesting contrast between the two readings.

Debts to von Balthasar lie more recessed in Ward's account of the French lay theologian, Jean-Luc Marion, whose approach to postmodernity works more at the interface of philosophy rather than sociology. Ward seeks to locate Marion in a French intellectual milieu, giving a clear reading of his significance. Ward's essay underlines the degree to which debate on postmodernity can be taken into philosophical depths that threaten to leave sociology gasping for breath. But Ward, by making use of Bourdieu, provides a relevant and useful siting of Marion within considerations available to sociological scrutiny. The conservative aspect of Marion's Catholicism seems to baffle Ward.

The return to the issue of re-enchantment is a suitable ending for this collection, whose contributors have sought to divine what the link between postmodernity and sociology means both for religion and for each other. The collection will have succeeded if the issues it has faced are re-thought in an enhanced reflexivity that underlines the distinctive contribution sociology makes to the interplay between religion and postmodernity. Upon this interplay, the proceedings which prompted this book raise a curtain.

Notes and References

1. Clifford Longley, *The Daily Telegraph*, 1 September 1995.
2. Phillipa Berry and Andrew Wernick (eds), *Shadow of Spirit: Postmodernism and Religion* (London: Routledge, 1992).
3. Quoted in Richard Pine, *Brian Friel and Ireland's Drama* (London: Routledge, 1990), p. 13.
4. Alasdair MacIntyre, *After Virtue. A Study in Moral Life* (London: Duckworth, 1985).

1 Religion and the Postmodern: Old Problems, New Prospects

David Lyon

The connections between religion and postmodernity are as yet quite unclear. In general, sociologists of religion have not exhibited much enthusiasm for postmodernity. Theorists of postmodernity often seem equally lukewarm about religion, an issue that does not figure prominently in their accounts. If modern sociology, appealing to secularisation theory, seemed to marginalise religion by assuming it was a dying phenomenon, then theorists of the postmodern have performed little better.

On the cusp of the twenty-first century, religion shows few signs of fading away. Implicitly acknowledging this, thoroughgoing secularisation theories are being quietly abandoned, and theorists are casting round for some means of incorporating religion into contemporary social analysis. The question is, what if anything is offered by the debate over postmodernity? The old 'legislative' mode of sociology, which seemed to require that religion wither, has lost ground. But despite this, theorists of the postmodern seem unable to go beyond similarly negative analyses of religious phenomena.

Old problems reappear. Religion is either relegated to the status of a reflex *of something else*, or is accorded what seems to be an old-fashioned functionalist treatment. In contemporary discussions, the old difficulty of recognising religion as a phenomenon *in its own right* resurfaces. However, at just this point the debate over postmodernity offers new prospects. Religion need not be viewed epiphenomenally, or as some kind of social pathology, as in some modern accounts. The alternative is to see religion as having its own integrity, historicity and capacities.

Of course, this does not make problems disappear. The approach proposed here encourages theorists to be candid about the ways in which religious perspectives themselves impinge upon theory. While much common ground exists for analysis, in the end, different forms of theory may be incommensurate for religious reasons. At the same time, theorists with particular religious commitments may not assume that their views have any more right to be heard than others. It is up to theorists who wish to connect religion and postmodernity to show that the new limitations on sociology are preferable to the old.

Three major tasks confront anyone wishing to explore this area. First, to retrace the path taken by social theorists, following their nineteenth-century forefathers, that led away from serious, integrated accounts of religion. The result was threefold: religion came to be studied as a contracting phenomenon; or as a channel that could easily be marginalised from the mainstream; or it was assumed that one should not take 'religious' accounts of religion seriously.

The second major task is to highlight the ways that interest in religion is being revived in the wake of the debate over the postmodern in social theory. To anticipate, this also leads to three tasks. The first is to see how social theory, under pressure from postmodern theorists, is reconsidering its general neglect of the 'cultural'.[1] The second is to reassess the secularisation thesis in the light of events such as renewal and growth in Islam and Christianity, the burgeoning of fundamentalism and the rise of spiritualities such as 'New Age'. The third is to question the epistemological assumptions on which previous accounts of religion were based.

The third major task – 'ravelling' – is more difficult. Yet some hints about the implications of the breakdown of old paradigms can be made. Again, with apologies to the classic sermon or to Habermas, three may be outlined. One is that social theory should be more accommodating to religious assumptions once excluded by definition from social explanation. The next is the recalibration of how the social role of religion is understood today; reductionism, it seems, is not an exclusively 'modern' failing. Third, this would facilitate the theoretical reintegration of the religious as a perennial feature of social order.

According to some classic sociological accounts, religion increasingly fell victim to modernising pressures. The process of secularisation meant that religion would be at best a marginal and ineffective force. Today, religion reappears in accounts of the post- or late-modern social condition. Anthony Giddens, for instance, states that 'religion not only refuses to disappear but undergoes a resurgence'.[2]

The evidence for this is of various kinds. Some evidence focuses on the dramatic or the exotic, but some on religion as a crucial dynamic of social change. For example, the Islamic revolution of the late 1970s has obliged serious reconsideration of how religion relates to modernity. The paradox, in that it seems to turn Max Weber on his head, is that modernity came to countries such as Iran as a largely exogenous force, and that its arrival seemed to prompt religious change in a conservative direction.[3]

In the USA, over the same period, the so-called religious right has gained tremendously in power and influence, to the chagrin of sophisticated East Coast liberals and the puzzlement of many European intellectuals. The 'Moral Majority' phenomenon of the 1980s seems to have become a self-fulfilling prophecy. The 'culture wars' of the 1990s are waged on terrain divided by tradition, religion and morality.[4] Meanwhile, all this has happened within America, the supposed acme of modern societies. Equally, cultic movements seem not to have lost any of their potency. The fiery end of a religious commune at Waco, Texas, at the hands of the National Guard, shows to what lengths the powers-that-be will go to repress cultic activity. And in Japan, a 'cult' group, Aum Shinrikyo, is, at the time of writing, under strong suspicion of perpetrating sarin-gas attacks that killed seven people in Matsumoto in 1994, and twelve in the Tokyo subway system in 1995.

For whatever reasons, then, the palpable persistence of religion obliges sociologists and historians to think again about secularisation. Anthony Giddens is one such, in whose recent work an account of fundamentalism prominently features. The phenomenon of fundamentalism provides a useful analytic foil for attempts to theorise contemporary religion–society relations, not least because such analysis is premised on the persistence rather than the passing of religion in modern conditions. Religious themes have thus begun to retrieve their place within mainstream social theory. This owes little thanks to the sociology of religion.

After decades, if not a century, during which social theorists all too often assumed religion was a shrinking, collapsing or dying phenomenon, the place of religion is now being reconsidered. But this is not just because religion has somehow pushed itself into the academic agenda. At the same time, modernity itself is being rethought within the current debates over postmodernity, reflexive modernisation, and so on. Do these fresh theoretical excursions in themselves open the way for the reappraisal of religion's role?

On the one hand, it would seem appropriate if the general questioning of modernity's 'grand narratives' led to the relaxing of certain secular strictures about religion's limited future. If modernity is not the invincible force it was once touted to be, then perhaps religion could read in its own right, and not just as an epiphenomenon of other social processes. On the other hand, while some accounts of the postmodern condition do appear, wittingly and unwittingly, to make more space for the religious, it is still a fairly circumscribed notion of religion, and not necessarily one that recognises its intrinsic irreducibility.

While the prospects for religion are not somehow limited to what social theory might predict or permit – although there is an important sense in which social theory affects these prospects – social theorists are obliged to rethink the role of religion in their accounts. To do so requires considerable unravelling of threads, some of which are badly tangled. The best guide to the ways that religion was marginalised in classical and mid-century sociology is James A. Beckford, in his *Religion in Advanced Industrial Society*.[5] The present argument depends on his work, although it also goes beyond it. On the one hand he wishes to show – rightly – how the sociology of religion has been insulated from wider sociological debate, but a further case can be made for sociology which takes account of religious presuppositions. On the other hand – and again, one applauds this – he picks up ways that Marxist theory has become more accommodating to religion. Here a similar case is made regarding some so-called postmodern theory.

Beckford observes that early modernisation theories framed sociological aspects of religion in three ways. Functionalist arguments suggested that though religion itself was outmoded and obstructive of progress, religious institutions still performed socially as means of integration. More Marxian accounts insisted that not only religious ideas but also religious institutions prevented full human development. In each case, human beings were advised to abandon immature concern with the 'spiritual' in order to take responsibility for their own fate and to dismantle the social conditions that produced religious responses. A third approach – seen in, among others, Weber, Troeltsch and Simmel – was to view religion as a means of making sense of the world, as a symbolic resource for meaning.

Thus, understanding religion – however negatively – was integral to the task of understanding the nature of modernity. Frequently, this happened under the rubric of an ill-defined process of secularisation.[6] Nevertheless, religion did not retain this central place within social theory. Why? For one thing, as increasing differentiation occurred, and modern social institutions such as education and welfare were split off from their religious roots, so sociology had less to say about religion as such. For another, religion tended to be seen as a monolithic entity rather than as having a diversity of aspects, such as organisation, knowledge, belief, emotion, ethic, ritual and so on.

Against the backdrop of the kind of sociology that actually became dominant – the 'orthodox consensus' of functionalism – religion did retain a place within social analysis. Some sort of religious functions were needed in any society, it was implied, even if the content of religion altered. But functionalism began to falter and fail during the 1970s, at just the same time as some public and academic attention began to refocus on religion.

While Western mainstream Protestantism seemed to show signs of terminal decline, Roman Catholicism started to loosen up, fundamentalist
groups (and the so-called Moral Majority) became more prominent, new
religious movements flowered and one or two varieties of Islam flexed
political muscle. Simultaneously, the centre of gravity of Christianity shifted
to the southern hemisphere; churches were growing in African countries,
Latin America and in parts of the Pacific Rim. Of course, these are not
'purely' religious phenomena, as if such were ever available. Some 'conversion' related to an equation of Christianity with technological progress.
To see religion as a mere reflex of economic change in these countries
would, however, be to fly in the face of the evidence.

In a defensive move, sociology often continued to explain these shifts
in generally functionalist terms, but with an eye to increasing complexity.
But plainly religion was not merely the quiescent, status-quo-buttressing
institution it had been supposed to be. Critical, controversial, subversive:
these were the kinds of adjectives used for everything from liberation theology to the Ayatollah. Even the concept of secularisation seemed inadequate for this new situation, although many tried to make the politicising
of religion into further evidence of the secular or to talk of simultaneous
processes of 'sacralisation' and 'secularisation'.

As Beckford observes, the sociology of religion was both insulated and
isolated from broader trends in sociology, with the result that very few
really interacted with the mainstream. Despite some vigorous activity within
the sociology of religion, paradoxically it was theorists working outside
the sociology of religion who were to stimulate current interest in the relation of religion to modern – and 'postmodern' – social conditions.

As far as secularisation is concerned, while the concept still generates
debate in itself, and frames other kinds of debate, there is little doubt that
its use is contracting. Peter Berger noted a 'crisis of secularity' in the early
1980s, and since then that crisis has if anything deepened.[7] Berger had
also spelt this out in *The Heretical Imperative*. In a pluralist situation, who
is to say what counts as 'orthodoxy', even what counts as orthodox secularity?[8] In any case, what is secularity without some concept of the sacred?
In the 1990s, the question of 'heretical discourse' has become central to
the whole social-cultural debate over postmodernity.[9]

Confusion has reigned for decades as to just what is covered under the
rubric of 'secularisation'. One aspect of this is the suspicion that secularisation could be as much policy as process. From David Martin's (1965) proposal that the concept be dropped due to its rationalist and anti-religious
connotations,[10] to Jeffrey Hadden's (1987) charges that secularisation expresses 'ideological preference rather than a systematic theory,'[11] some

have argued that secularisation is sociologically compromised by its association with anti-religious sentiment. However, there is confusion within *this aspect* of the debate, as well. Martin went on to write his brilliant *A General Theory of Secularization* (1978) which, simply, limits what can be said about secularity.[12] Secularisation, he affirms, is about religious institutions, not religion – or Christianity – in general. Hadden's contention cannot be generalised; many prominent users of the secularisation concept have been religiously committed, usually Christians. But this does not rule out the possibility that religious assumptions are embedded within versions of secularisation theory, or that these assumptions may affect the social situations that secularisation theories purport to describe. We shall return to this in a moment.

Without a doubt, sociologies of religion have been framed by theories of modernisation. But what if modernity itself is failing or undergoing transformation? Is secularisation theory merely a modern idea and itself ripe for reappraisal in the light of both social-cultural change and of theories about such change?

Before proceeding further, the meaning of the 'postmodern turn' must be clarified. Despite the overblown rhetoric of some proponents of the postmodern, the concept of postmodernity does good service in drawing attention to certain crucial transformations of modernity. Central to these is globalisation, in turn stimulated by and articulated with two crucial processes, the diffusion of information technologies and the spread of consumer capitalism. That there is no fully-fledged postmodern condition anywhere does not mean that no inklings, no portents, of the postmodern exist. Indeed, one could also argue, the USA notwithstanding, that no fully-fledged modernity exists either, if that phrase is taken to mean that no traces of the premodern persist.

The postmodern turn need not be construed as a turn away from sociology. On the contrary, it can be interpreted as a return to the classic quest for social understanding in times of rapid social change, and to some of the classic themes of the relation between the social and the cultural, of human agency and its historical structuring. The postmodern turn is, however, a turn away from assuming that modernity, with its typical foci on work as economic activity and on calculation as the acme of reason, will continue to form the matrix for social interaction. In a sense, then, the postmodern turn *sharpens* the focus on modernity, just because it involves above all a *reappraisal* of modernity.

Secularisation is limited in specific ways.[13] It is not so much a universal process as one that relates to the European disintegration of what Martin calls the religious monopoly. Just those very 'modern' factors that fostered secularisation – heavy industry, class differences, and so on – are of diminishing social significance in contemporary 'advanced' societies. While there is no reason to believe that this alone could foster a religious resurgence, it does at least behove sociologists to be cautious in delineating the *kind* of secularisation that is occurring.

On the other hand, factors sometimes underplayed by sociology, especially in the cultural sphere, are increasingly seen as crucial components of social reproduction.[14] Consumerism, with its emphasis on taste, and the accompanying aestheticisation of social life, along with the new centrality of what might be called a 'sacred self'; these may signal not only a new appreciation of the symbolic realm but also offer opportunities for considering these 'religiously': that is, as evidence of a quest for transcendant meaning.[15] Doubts about the monolithic and abiding character of classic modernity, together with the evidence of fresh forms of symbolisation, could contribute to releasing the sociology of religion from the gratuitous constraints of some theories of modernity and secularisation.

Outside the sociology of religion, increasing sociological interest in religion has sprung from several sources. One comes from the growing reality of multiculturalism within the advanced societies, with its attendant questions of education policy (should Muslims have separate schools?), dress (may Sikhs wear turbans in the Royal Canadian Mounted Police or in Canadian Legion buildings?), and so on. These are not so much new questions as old questions with a new twist. For example, 'separate' schools in anglophone Canada are normally Catholic, and legal allowance has been made in times past for the traditional dress, transport and even the decision to opt out of the welfare state by groups like the Old Order Mennonites.

Interest in religion emerges as a result of the impact of Islamic revival in the Gulf region, as well as its diverse forms of growth in North America, Africa and Europe. Another secularisation anomaly lurks here in that it is precisely the *modernising* Iran that exhibits more 'fundamentalist' varieties of Islam.[16] Other, more conventionally Christian, forms of fundamentalism are also forcing themselves onto the analytic agenda in the late twentieth century. This is what Giddens has in mind in the quotation used earlier, that religion has not disappeared. He seems to return to traditional religious confidence as one response to the chronic doubt characteristic of late modern situations.[17]

Another area of concern, mentioned above, that impinges on the question of religion in the late or postmodern world is globalisation. Both universalistic tendencies, and particular local responses to them – such as new church–state relations – suggest to Roland Robertson that the globalisation process itself 'raises religious and quasi-religious questions'.[18] Robertson argues that in the later twentieth century concern with what it means to be human is stimulated in two ways. On the one hand, while many feel alienated from the state, the state has more and more to do with 'deep' features of life, its definition and quality, the regulation of religion and so on. On the other, relations between societies lead to doubt that we know what is a 'good' society. Thus questions of what a human *telos* might be now extend into international dialogue, seen in fields such as human rights discourse. Globalisation helps to relativise both 'selves' and 'societies', thus foregrounding questions once considered in the more 'religious' realm.

Linked with this is a broader trend within sociology towards cultural analysis. So, far from seeing cultural processes as some kind of epiphenomena of supposedly deeper social-economic processes, the postmodern turn in social thought highlights the role of culture in social reproduction. While style, fashion, architecture, music, literature and especially television feature within this shift, 'religious' matters are no less under scrutiny in fresh ways. This now derives as much from an interest in popular culture as in the more conventional history of ideas approach that has often predominated within sociologies of religion, and especially of secularisation. This move could well encourage 'bottom up' rather than 'top down' analyses of contemporary religion.

Perhaps the most prominent aspects of this are New Religious movements – including 'self-religions' like New Age – and the growth of fundamentalisms.[19] New Age 'fits' with the so-called postmodern condition in some significant ways, centering on the self, being undogmatic, involving networking rather than an established institutional base and so on. But this does not mean that New Age relates only to the postmodern: far from it.[20]

New Age may be seen as a cultural resource that is mobilised in response to the spiritual vacuum of modern administered, technological societies, but which in many ways offers escape rather than engagement with or critique of them. Seen in this way, it is also a response to modernity. But the fluidity, 'tolerance' and self-oriented nature of New Age renders it peculiarly attractive in postmodern times. Other sorts of religious symbolism may be developed in quite different directions.

To comment on the 'escapism' of New Age, however, may be to minimise ways in which just such 'escapism' contributes to issues of how contemporary societies are organised. This paradoxical way of seeing things may be attributed to the insights of Michel Foucault, among others. For Foucault, the 'individual' of privatised and self-religion is no less a cultural artifact than, say, religion itself. Foucault's 'discourses' of medicine, psychiatry and incarceration individualise people who previously experienced power of a 'pastoral' kind that emanated from medieval religion.

Such discourses of self, the body, well-being, and human rights are still informed by religious ideas which may thus continue to play a part in creating the individual 'private' subjects who must collude with the overall patterns of domination of today's society. If Foucault is right, supposedly autonomous individuals of modernity are simply individuals who have been constructed differently from those of previous times. How we view such individuals depends on the distribution of power and domination obtaining at any given time.

How far we can go along with Foucault is an open question, but the interesting thing about his work and that of others such as Derrida and Lyotard is that basic epistemological assumptions are up for grabs. Neither individuals nor religion are in any sense fixed entities. The only apparently universal feature of human life, in Foucault's world, is power. Of course, Foucault tends to see his subjects in the thrall of one sort of power or another. And he certainly shows little sympathy for what he calls the 'pastoral' power that originated within Catholic churches. But in his view, that the Reformation was a 'struggle for a new subjectivity', perhaps lie grounds for conceptualising religion in fresh ways.

Religion, then, is reappearing in sociological accounts of post- or late-modern societies. As yet, however, those accounts themselves do not appear to be a big improvement over earlier sociological treatments. For Bauman, as for Giddens, religious questions reappear mainly in the guise of moral and existential dilemmas. Bauman, for instance, thinks of 'the revival of religious and quasi-religious movements' as part of a renewed attraction to 'agencies claiming expertise in moral values'.[21]

Of course, recognition of a social role for religion could be viewed in a positive light, in that a window is opened for dialogue about the actual part that religion might be playing in a postmodern context. One could be forgiven for asking, 'Is that all there is?' The collapse of the dogmatic secularisation thesis, the new appreciation of the cultural sphere, the need to deal theoretically with New Religious Movements and fundamentalisms: these all seem to call for a more basic recalibration of religion in social thought than a response that merely falls back on a semi-functionalist argument about religious revival as a symptom of the late modern malaise of relativist doubt or ethical aporia.

Earlier we suggested that the prospects for religion are not limited to what social theory might predict or permit. While this may be true, how religion is viewed within social theory *does*, potentially at least, have an effect on its prospects. After all, the plausibility of religious accounts depends in part on what sort of status they are perceived to have. For many decades the so-called 'warfare' between religion and science was a plausible way of seeing things because, given the editorial policies of relevant journals, few alternative opinions were available.

Social theory that remains in the library stack journals is unlikely to play any role here, but theory that works its way into popular imagination – as 'religion is the opium of the people' or 'religion is the projection of a father-figure' once did – may have social consequences, including some that produce a modification in the social conditions that inspired the theory in the first place. Of course, in certain circumstances popular scepticism about official accounts of religion's demise itself acts as an implicit theory of religion, as in post-1989 Eastern Europe.[22] So the kind of social theory available may be highly significant.

While classical sociologies of religion may have recognised religion as socially important, various notions were built into them that led to religion's marginalisation within theory. Today, with the empirical evidence on religion slapping us in the face, and the demise of modern*ist* theories creating space for 'new' cultural phenomena, social theorists are – perhaps begrudgingly – finding a place for religion once more. But it tends to be a restricted place, maybe limited still by the presuppositions of the theorists in question.

This is why some of Beckford's suggestions are so attractive, especially that religion be considered sociologically once more as a 'cultural resource' and not just something tied to social institutions.[23] As such, it is highly flexible and unpredictable, appearing in a plethora of guises and forms with a variety of consequences. It may seek to conserve but, equally, to challenge or to change. When religion has lost its once necessary ties to formal religious organisations, it is likely to be controversial. As Beckford says, 'the deregulation of religion is one of the hidden ironies of secularization. It helps to make religion sociologically problematic in ways which are virtually inconceivable in the terms of the sociological classics.'[24]

One phenomenon now receiving increased sociological and historical attention is fundamentalism. This makes a good final case-study for the relation of religion, postmodernity and social theory. Fundamentalism may be seen as a cultural resource, drawn upon to meet critical issues of a fast-changing modernity. But it has two important features. First, it has significant historical connections with the conditions against which it now reacts. Second, it cannot but highlight the ultimate irreducibility of religion.

Fundamentalism originally referred to an American defence of conservative Christianity against a theological 'modernism' that refused to negotiate over certain matters of biblical doctrine. Today, Giddens thinks of fundamentalism as 'tradition defended in the traditional way – but where that mode of defence has been widely called into question'.[25] He sees it not as a long-term response to modernity but as a recent one, reacting to de-traditionalisation, globalisation and 'diasporic cultural interchange'.[26] He argues for using 'fundamentalism' to refer not only to the ostensibly religious but also, for example, to 'sexual fundamentalism'.

Paradoxically, however, Giddens thinks that lessons may be learned from fundamentalism, at the very least that contemporary nihilism is wrong to proclaim that 'nothing is sacred'. While one might object that this a simplistic reading of Nietzsche, it is clear that what Giddens dreads is a world of multiple fundamentalisms, disintegrating through the 'clash of rival world-views'.[27] But what he discerns is emerging universal values, including 'the sanctity of human life and the universal right to happiness and self-actualisation'.[28] Robertson's prediction that globalisation requires new 'religious' values is fulfilled in Giddens' (analytical) attempt to supply them.

Giddens is right to see current fundamentalisms appearing as responses to apparent crises of contemporary modernity, and it would be myopic to imagine that in present conditions they will somehow go away. But religious responses to modernity are manifold. In Christianity alone, there is a range of varieties from ritualistic revivers of ancient liturgy to adaptationist evangelicalism. The latter has been marked by its ability to keep abreast of scientific and social change without losing sight of the pristine gospel of God's grace. Of course, it may occasionally fall over itself in keeping up with the times. Accepting too readily the empirical method in science has produced some curiously rationalistic versions of Christianity, while adopting the tactics of television advertising for evangelism has in some eyes cheapened the gospel. But evangelicalism is more generally found 'in but not of the world', attempting to adapt without sacrificing essentials.

The further paradox here, as Weberians are well aware, is that at least in the North Atlantic regions (if not elsewhere) evangelicalism has grown symbiotically with modernity. In Canada, for instance, William Westfall has shown how the notion of 'God's dominion' always had a forked thrust. Under this banner was sought both continental compliance with the ways of God *and* economic mastery 'from sea to sea', by the same people.[29] In this case religion and modernity are bound up with each other in ways that a simplistic analysis of 'religion against modernity' just could not capture. While the 'two worlds' of religion and modern life have in some limited ways split off from each other, itself one definition of secularisation, the process is far from complete or irreversible.

The reasons for this are no doubt varied, but one has to do with the 'manufactured uncertainty' of modern life.[30] While refuge was at first sought from the negative effects of de-traditionalisation within the new 'traditions' of modern life, it is now clear to many that deepening scepticism demands a reappraisal of the place of values. At the same time Giddens shies away from commitment to a world-view that might carry the dangers of fundamentalism, where an unacceptable fanaticism and potential violence lurk. But can one really have one's cake, 'ultimate values', and eat it by avoiding religious commitment in this way?

It is a vitally important project to consider the role of contemporary fundamentalism within social theory. The danger is that of polarising some supposedly a-religious values and a belligerent, heel-digging fundamentalism. That there might be possibilities of non-fundamentalistic religious modes of meeting modernity is not considered by Giddens, but just this possibility appears from a study of such modes, such as evangelicalism. Positive contributions to social theory and to politics could be – and are being – made by such alternatives, which recognise the need for shared visions of balanced ecosystems and justice in the distribution of the earth's resources.[31] But such social and political theory also recognises that a 'non-adjudicable battle of human creeds' lies beyond all talk of 'values' and 'narratives'.[32]

The presumption that religion would wither and fade was part and parcel of the Enlightenment arrogance that infected social theory in the nineteenth century. Whether or not the concept of secularisation featured significantly as a tool of 'counter-religious ideologies'[33] the fact remains that the assumptions built into social theories of religion were frequently detrimental to understanding its place in the modern world. This was sociology in what Bauman calls its legislative mode.

The postmodern turn in social theory could well help to open the door to much more constructive ways of understanding religion today. Above all, the study of religion could become a site of interest in its own right – as its own centre of intelligibility – rather than a dependent reflex of something else. From this starting point, for instance, it would be quite legitimate to see one set of religious phenomena in terms of another, without the mediation of some criterion of functionalist, rationalist or empiricist dogma.

While the 'hermeneutics of suspicion' should still be permitted to probe the interests and power relations of religious institutions, influences and movements, this does not exhaust the possibilities for a contemporary sociology of religion. A hermeneutics of retrieval – the term is Paul Ricoeur's – would permit us not only to see religion as a set of resources on which people in general draw, but as providing resources for sociological and other forms of analysis. Scott Lash, who raises the question of retrieval, argues against a 'postmodern' tendency to 'chronically defer and deny meaning'. Rather, he says one might 'modestly "look beneath" [signifiers] to gain access to the shared meanings which are the conditions of existence'.[34]

On the one hand, a hermeneutics of retrieval might allow the descriptions of the religiously committed to enter the process of concept formation and theoretical development. In the case of evangelicalism, mentioned above, items derived from self-definitions are fruitfully being used in analysis, such as a quadrilateral of foci, on the Bible, conversion, the cross of Christ and on activism, as ideal types.[35] At least this approach takes seriously what people say about their own commitments.

On the other hand, a hermeneutics of retrieval serves as a reminder that, ultimately, no separation is possible between religious commitments and (in this case social science) epistemology. Recognising the pervasive and unavoidable phenomenon of reflexivity could encourage what is desirable from a religious – and particularly a Christian – perspective: the *responsibility* of knowing. Indicating how theorists allow their religious assumptions to show would then be a reason not for continuing to pretend that such assumptions can be excluded but for acknowledging them, insofar as they are perceived, and indicating their contribution to theory.

The 'postmodern turn' need signal neither a drift towards an abyss of self-referentiality nor a commitment to some view that 'postmodern society' is a description of contemporary conditions. Rather, it indicates a willingness to reappraise modernity radically, analytically and ethically. This would emphasise two things in particular: one, a more careful analysis of religious situations within the broader sweep of sociological studies, which might for instance include dialogical evangelicalism as well as fundamentalist retrenchment and second, an acknowledgement that if creeds are worth anything, they will certainly engender disagreement and perhaps hostility. Modern conditions militate both against open analysis of religion and understanding religion as a phenomenon not ultimately comprehensible to 'science'. Today's shifting conditions may open doors to new modes of analysis.

If, as has been argued, religious background influences theory formation and modes of analysis, then clear acknowledgement of faith orientation would make for more honest, open scholarship. It often makes a qualitative difference to outcomes whether the stance of a study is rooted in neo-providentialism, sympathetic agnosticism or whatever, and this can be stated candidly. On the other hand, there may be much common ground in the details of analyses with different origins, even if there is religious incommensurability between them in the end. The important thing is that the sociology of religion be willing to admit that its limitations are not just 'methodological' but may well be 'theological' as well. Bracketing the one from the other is at best only a logical device.

At the same time, having encouraged believers and unbelievers alike to come clean, no space is left for privileging particular perspectives. Jungian psychology, planetary theology, poststructuralism or phenomenology should simply be seen for what they are. Summoned to emerge from behind the philosophical fig-leaf of unacknowledged presuppositions, scholars may take their place within the academic arena armed only with argument, supported by the best available evidence. Of course, what counts as evidence is also a matter of ongoing debate, as poststructuralists in particular will be quick to observe.

In conclusion, the context of contemporary debates over the postmodern offers new prospects for the sociology of religion, even though, paradoxically, the treatment of religion is somewhat weak in most postmodern accounts. Those new prospects include an opportunity to see religion outside the frequently constricting frames of 'modernity' and 'secularisation', frames that themselves are often tinged with religious unmusicality or even hostility. This entails a new reflexivity regarding the religious roots of different forms of theory and method and thus an awareness that differences are inevitable between alternative faith-perspectives. This seems far better than a bland and specious tolerance that keeps its head firmly in the sand.

In this way religion can be seen afresh – not just in the sociology of religion but in general social theory – as an irreducible aspect of being human in its specific and manifold contemporary manifestations, and as having its own integrity, historicity and capacities, several examples of which have been alluded to above. Religion may well be more, but it certainly is not less, than this.

Notes and References

1. Sociology has often neglected the cultural, but this has been far from a total neglect. For instance, phenomenology stressed cultural factors and so, classically, did theorists like Weber and Simmel.
2. Anthony Giddens, *Modernity and Self-Identity* (Cambridge: Polity Press, 1991), p. 195.
3. Ernest Gellner, *Postmodernism, Reason and Religion* (London: Routledge, 1992).
4. James Davison Hunter, *Culture Wars: The Struggle to Define America* (New York: Basic Books, 1994).

5. James A. Beckford, *Religion and Advanced Industrial Society* (London: Unwin-Hyman, 1989).
6. David Lyon, *The Steeple's Shadow: On the Myths and Realities of Secularization* (London: SPCK, and Grand Rapids: Eerdmans, 1987).
7. Peter L. Berger, 'From the crisis of religion to the crisis of secularity', in Mary Douglas and Stephen Tipton (eds), *Religion and America: Spirituality in a Secular Age* (Boston, MA: Beacon Press, 1983).
8. Peter L. Berger, *The Heretical Imperative* (New York: Doubleday, 1980).
9. See Barry Smart, *Postmodernity* (London and Boston, MA: Routledge, 1993).
10. David Martin, 'Towards eliminating the concept of secularization', in *Penguin Survey of the Social Sciences* (Harmondsworth: Penguin, 1965).
11. Jeffrey Hadden, 'Towards desacralizing secularization theory', *Social Forces*, vol. 65, no. 3, 1987, pp. 587–610.
12. David Martin, *A General Theory of Secularization* (Oxford: Blackwell, 1978).
13. Kenneth Thompson, 'The secularization debate', in Peter Gee and John Fulton (eds), *Religion and Power, Decline and Growth* (London: British Sociological Association, Sociology of Religion Study Group, 1991), pp. 7–14.
14. David Lyon, *Postmodernity* (Minneapolis: University of Minnesota Press, 1994).
15. David Lyon, 'Jesus in Disneyland: the church meets the postmodern challenge', *ARC: The Journal of the Faculty of Religious Studies, McGill*, vol. 23, 1995, pp. 7–36.
16. Ernest Gellner, *Postmodernism, Reason and Religion*, op. cit.
17. See also Anthony Giddens, *The Consequences of Modernity* (Cambridge: Polity Press, 1991), pp. 103–11 and Ulrich Beck, Anthony Giddens and Scott Lash, *Reflexive Modernization: Politics, Tradition and Aesthetics in the Modern Social Order* (Cambridge: Polity Press, 1994).
18. Roland Roberston, 'Humanity, globalization and worldwide religious resurgence', *Sociological Analysis*, vol. 46, no. 3, 1985, pp. 219–42.
19. See Martin Marty, *The Fundamentalism Project*, vols 1–4 (Chicago: University of Chicago Press, 1991–4); David Lyon, 'A bit of a circus: notes on postmodernity and New Age', *Religion*, vol. 23, no. 2, 1993, pp. 117–26; and Jonathan Sacks, *The Persistence of Faith* (London: Weidenfeld & Nicolson, 1991).
20. Paul Heelas, 'The New Age in Cultural Context: the premodern, the Modern and the postmodern', *Religion*, vol. 23, no. 2, 1993, pp. 103–16.
21. Zygmunt Bauman, *Intimations of Postmodernity* (London: Routledge, 1992), pp. 202–3.
22. Ivan Varga, 'Modernity or pseudo-modernity? Secularization or pseudo-secularization: reflections on east-central Europe', in Richard R. Roberts (ed.), *Religion and the Transformations of Capitalism* (London: Routledge, 1994), pp. 231–47.
23. James A. Beckford, *Religion and Advanced Industrial Society*, op. cit., p. 171.
24. Ibid., p. 172.
25. Anthony Giddens, *Beyond Left and Right: The Future of Radical Politics* (Stanford, CA: Stanford University Press, 1994), p. 6.

26. Ibid., p. 84.
27. Ibid., p. 252.
28. Ibid., p. 20.
29. William Westfall, *Two Worlds: Nineteenth Century Protestantism in Ontario* (Kingston and Montreal: McGill-Queen's University Press, 1991).
30. Anthony Giddens, *Beyond Left and Right: The Future of Radical Politics*, *op. cit.*
31. For example, Bob Goudzwaard and Harry de Lange, *Beyond Poverty and Affluence: Towards an Economy of Care* (Toronto: University of Toronto Press, 1995).
32. John Milbank, 'Problematizing the secular: the post-postmodern agenda', in Phillipa Berry and Andrew Wernick (eds), *Shadow of Spirit* (London: Routledge, 1992), p. 43.
33. David Martin, 'Towards eliminating the concept of secularization', *op. cit.*
34. Ulrich Beck, Anthony Giddens and Scott Lash, *Reflexive Modernization*, *op. cit.*, p. 146.
35. David Bebbington, *Evangelicanism in Modern Britain* (London: Unwin-Hyman, 1989), pp. 2–17.

2 Postmodernity, High Modernity and New Modernity: Three Concepts in Search of Religion

James A. Beckford

The aim of this chapter is to explore some of the paradoxes that occur in attempts to relate recent changes in religion to the advent of postmodernity, high modernity and new modernity.[1] The starting point is that relatively few accounts of postmodernity and its variants have paid much attention to religion.[2] This observation may appear to be a strange basis on which to build claims about postmodernity and religious change, but it is actually essential to the main theme of the chapter. For the argument will be that advocates of the idea of postmodernity and its variants face formidable difficulties if they attempt to make sense of religion. It is not therefore surprising that, in all the speculations about postmodernity, serious interpretations of religious phenomena are rare birds.

The main objective is to examine what tends to happen to sociologists' understanding of religion when they use 'postmodernity' and variants on the concept. Three recent contributions which take very different stances towards the relationship between religion and prevailing socio-cultural conditions will be analysed. Each of the three characters in search of an explanation for religion in conditions of post-, high or new modernity will be seen to experience difficulties. Ironically, as the penultimate section will argue, one of the most outspoken critics of the notion of postmodernity also finds it hard to explain the survival of religious institutions in late twentieth-century Britain.

Postmodernity is supposed to involve the eclipse of grand theory, foundational knowledge and narrative histories. Yet one of the ironies of the postmodern view of the world is, paradoxically, that it claims that a series of long-range and wide-ranging changes has occurred in society and culture. So this turns out to be one more narrative despite its claim that narrativity is finished.[3]

If this problem of logical inconsistency is put to one side, however, a good example of theorising about postmodernity which centres on the dynamics of modern, rational capitalism can be examined. Bauman's *Intimations of Postmodernity* brings together several arguments which amount to a concerted claim that postmodernity has arrived and is a distinctive phase of socio-cultural development.[4] The ethical implications are further elaborated in his *Postmodern Ethics*.[5] Its main arguments can be summarised around three themes.

The first is that *wage labour* has been displaced from the centre of social life and is no longer the linch-pin of the whole of individual and social existence. The second is that *consumer freedom* has replaced wage labour as the driving force and guiding thread of the social and cultural system. In other words, the struggle for control has shifted from the capital/labour relationship to the sphere of distribution where pleasure in consumption supposedly holds society together, motivates individuals and ensures that the system will be reproduced in an orderly fashion. Not surprisingly, then, Bauman chooses tourism as a metaphor for life in postmodernity since, 'ideally, one should be a tourist everywhere and everyday. In, but not of. Physically close, spiritually remote. Aloof . . . Ideally, with the moral conscience having been fed a sure-fire dose of sleeping pills.'[6]

The third main argument is that capitalism can continue to thrive on the basis of what Baudrillard called 'seduction' rather than production.[7] There is no longer any need for political legitimation, dominant ideologies or central values. Instead, the vision of untrammelled personal consumer choice and, therefore, *variety* of tastes is supposedly enough to make the capitalist market thrive and to integrate all consumers into a spending utopia. Moreover, Bauman suggests that, 'postmodernity (or whatever other name will be eventually chosen to take hold of the phenomena it denotes) is an aspect of a fully-fledged, viable social system which has come to replace the "classical" modern, capitalist society and thus needs to be theorized according to its own logic'.[8]

According to Bauman, these underlying sociological changes in the form of capitalism are responsible for the socio-cultural characteristics of postmodernity: namely, the decline of certainty, objectivity and authority as well as the rise of neo-tribalism. This is apparently why intellectuals have been demoted from the status of legislators to that of 'interpreters'.[9] Postmodern culture tends therefore towards pastiche, collage, decentring, chaos, ambiguity and polyvalence.

The prospects for religion do not appear very bright if Bauman's depiction of postmodern society and culture is correct. He might consider the playfulness of some New Age beliefs and practices as instances of postmodern religion, contrary to the interpretation that Paul Heelas puts on them elsewhere in this volume. He would almost certainly see confirmation of his views in the rise of a postmodern theology which tries deliberately to move away from ideas of textual authority, historical narrativity or ethical foundationalism. Indeed, Bauman seems to welcome the re-enchantment of the world that postmodernity supposedly brings in its train as well as the re-personalisation of morality.[10] Both processes involve the release of the putatively autonomous moral conscience from the 'stiff armour of the artificially constructed ethical codes'.[11]

Yet Bauman *does* leave a small opening for religion in his postmodern world driven by a consumerist pleasure principle and reflected in a kaleidoscope of competing cultures. He recognises that, despite the decline of institutionalised repression, regulation and control, *ethical* questions have not disappeared. In fact, they have become even more acute at a time of conflicting authorities, multiplying choices and declining principles. For Bauman,

> the ethical paradox of the postmodern condition is that it restores to agents the fullness of moral choice and responsibility while simultaneously depriving them of the comfort of the universal guidance that modern self-confidence once promised. Ethical tasks of individuals grow while the socially produced resources to fulfil them shrink. Moral responsibility comes together with the loneliness of moral choice.[12]

Bauman therefore attributes 'the revival of religious and quasi-religious movements' to the 'increased attractiveness of the agencies claiming expertise in moral values'.[13] This sounds suspiciously like an argument about the appeal of authority and moral principles at a time – postmodernity – when such things were not supposed to be important. In other words, there is a tension between the claim that postmodernity has somehow dispensed with ethical foundationalism and the claim that religion is becoming increasingly attractive to people who seek assistance from experts in moral values. In places this argument seems to imply a position of stalemate or mutual paralysis between moral dilemmas and moral resources. Since Bauman writes confidently of the *revival* of religious movements, however, he presumably wishes to imply that growing numbers of people actually succeed in resolving moral dilemmas by applying religiously sanctioned moral codes. Nevertheless, this implication sits uneasily with Bauman's reluctance to accept that codified morality can ever be effective, because it stifles autonomous moral conscience.[14]

At best, then, Bauman consigns religion to a residual realm of little importance where ethical issues can be handled in a relatively mechanical fashion by reference to fixed ethical codes. This has the ring of special pleading in an attempt to fit the persistence of religion into postmodernity.

A less charitable interpretation of Bauman's reasoning is that, in keeping with many other intellectuals who until recently had found little reason to study religions carefully, his claim that there has been a revival of religious movements in postmodernity merely signifies a failure to appreciate the *continuous* importance of religion throughout history, including the modern period. It is as if he has only just noticed that, despite the effects of the Enlightenment, many generations have continued to find religion attractive and powerful; it is also as if he has inferred that religion's attractiveness must therefore be a recent (and aberrant) phenomenon. A better understanding of the history of religion would have shown that the appeal to sources of religious authority for expertise in morality has been more like a constant feature than a failure of modernity or a postmodern innovation. In other words Bauman's recourse to an argument about the supposed link between the 'increased attractiveness of the agencies claiming expertise in moral values' and 'the revival of religious and quasi-religious movements' betrays a weak understanding of the history of modern religion.

In fact, it is perverse that Bauman's history of ethical theories in the modern and postmodern eras makes virtually no reference to religion at all. In his eagerness to emphasise the alleged failure of the Enlightenment project to provide a reasoned basis for universalisable ethical codes he totally ignores the much older and, arguably, more far-reaching systematisations of religiously inspired, even revealed, ethics. This striking omission facilitates the contrast that he wants to draw between the universalising aspirations of everything modern and the neo-tribal thrust of everything postmodern. But it totally fails to do justice to the much more complex interplay of universalism and particularism that is characteristic of every world religion.

This is definitely not to say, however, that religion has not undergone changes in the twentieth century. There is abundant evidence of changing forms, expressions and themes of religion in most parts of the world. One of the notable achievements of Anthony Giddens, the next of the four commentators on religion, is that he avoids the temptation to infer the presence of postmodernity from the observation that religion is unexpectedly important to some people. Nevertheless, his very distinctive explanation of the 'creation of new forms of religious sensibility and spiritual endeavour' also gives rise to its own problems.[15]

There is a good measure of agreement between Bauman and Giddens about the experience of life in late twentieth-century Western societies. But Giddens rejects the notion of postmodernity, preferring the term 'late modern age' or 'high modernity'; and the seductions of consumerism play little or no role in Giddens' scheme. His explanations turn, instead, on the implications of distinctly *modern* types of knowledge and technology for everyday life. Two of his recent books, *The Consequences of Modernity*[16] and *Modernity and Self-Identity*[17] spell out the social and cultural features which allegedly set the present age apart from earlier phases of modernity. In a nutshell, these features comprise:

(a) the *re-organisation of time and space* so that events and actions occurring in different places and/or different times can be precisely coordinated (e.g., world-wide stock markets, simultaneous broadcasting, Women's World Day of Prayer, International Year of the Child, etc.);

(b) the *disembedding of institutions* in the sense of abstracting sets of social relationships from their local contexts and recombining them with other relationships at a different time and place (e.g., 'ethnic' foods becoming international standard menus; or Hawaiian *huna* – indigenous healing practices – being re-packaged for Californian New Agers);

(c) the thoroughgoing *reflexivity* of advanced modernity in the sense of constant monitoring and adjustment of ideas and practices in the light of newly acquired information. This generates uncertainty and instability; not the kind of secure knowledge envisaged by Enlightenment rationalists and positivistic scientists (e.g., types of therapy premised on social science findings; or *anorexia nervosa* as a pathological form of the high modern reflexivity of the body).

These three characteristics of advanced modernity are all extensions of the forces of differentiation and rationalisation which produced early modernity. But Giddens believes that, in combination, they signal a distinctive phase of development which contains special problems for self-identity. For example, he argues that it is now more difficult for individuals to cultivate a continuous thread of self-identity in the face of the endless mutability of time/space connections, the constant recombinations of social relationships out of context and the perpetual exposure of the self to fresh information about itself. There is also pressure to make life-style choices all the time in order to impose a narrative thread on events and to get closer to the theoretical ideal of a 'pure relationship' or a completely self-actualised self. Even the calculation of risks becomes ever more unsettling as it becomes more 'scientific' in the hands of experts. According to Giddens, this culminates in a process which *sequesters* experience to the point where whole areas of life which are resistant to high modernity can be shunted into a siding. Any issues which raise existential or strongly moral questions are institutionally sequestered. Examples include madness, sexuality, criminality, death and incurable disease. They are defined as deviant or disturbing because they challenge the belief in transformability-through-reflexivity, thereby leaving ethical and existential questions unanswered.

In other words Giddens does not claim, with Bauman, that high modernity renders moral choice simultaneously more urgent and less feasible but he insists, by contrast, that it *generates* significantly new moral problems. He suggests that:

> abstract systems help foster day-to-day security, but trust vested in such systems . . . carries little psychological reward for the individual; trust brackets out ignorance, but does not provide the moral satisfactions that trust in persons can offer . . . The loss of anchoring reference points deriving from the development of internally referential systems creates moral disquiet that individuals can never fully overcome.[18]

Indeed, Giddens goes even further than Bauman in claiming that the doubt and insecurity inherent in high modernity actually favour a resurgence of religion because, 'in modern times some forms of traditional authority continue to exist, including, of course, religion. Indeed, for reasons that are to do precisely with the connections between modernity and doubt, religion not only refuses to disappear but undergoes a resurgence.'[19] In a further refinement of his explanation Giddens argues that this resurgence of interest in religion is apparently likely at 'fateful moments' of birth, marriage and death because it connects 'action to moral frameworks and to elemental questions about human existence'.[20]

Giddens does not confine his argument to traditional forms of religion but is sensitive to the

> creation of new forms of religious sensibility and spiritual endeavour. The reasons for this concern quite fundamental features of late modernity . . . New forms of religion and spirituality represent in a most basic sense a return of the repressed, since they directly address issues of the moral meaning of existence which modern institutions so thoroughly tend to dissolve.[21]

Giddens' explanation seems to be that high modernity has reached its outer limits and that this is why 'moral/existential questions thrust themselves back to centre-stage'.[22] Limits have been reached in the 'invasion of the natural world by abstract systems',[23] the medical control over life and death, the globalisation of everything, and the colonisation of self and body by therapeutic experts. As a result, pressure grows for a 'remoralising of daily life'.[24] Traditions play a major part in the process of remoralisation. There is a firm connection in Giddens' thinking between religion and tradition, even in 'post-traditional' societies and cultures. This is because he believes that tradition helps to mediate morality, emotion and solidarity by means of a 'formulaic notion of truth'.[25] Traditions can apparently operate in one of two frameworks. On the one hand, traditions can be articulated discursively as a set of values in pluralistic competition with others. On the other hand, traditions become fundamentalist when they assert 'formulaic truth without regard to consequences'. Now, while Giddens correctly acknowledges that 'there is nothing mysterious about the appearance of fundamentalism in the late modern world', his argument that fundamentalists assert their beliefs without regard to consequences could be misleading.[26] In fact, fundamentalisms are preoccupied with the translation of formulaic truths into *practices* which embody and preserve the truths' purity. The consequences are therefore taken very seriously indeed.

In comparison with Bauman, then, Giddens regards the survival of religion as a central consequence of high modernity rather than as an awkward or incidental residue of early forms of pre-modernity. Moreover, Giddens allows for the creation of new forms of religion: not just residual forms. And he explains both the survival of old religion and the creation of new forms of religion as integral aspects of modernity's dynamism: not just freak shows on the side. Yet it is also paradoxical that high modernity, which is supposed to be responsible for the continuous application of objective information to the monitoring and amending of everyday life, should turn out to be the site of a resurgence of religion. The claim that religion re-emerges when people perceive a need for reassurance has a distinctly functionalist ring about it. This is one of the reasons for being sceptical about the account that Giddens provides of religion in conditions of high modernity.

Another difficulty inherent in Giddens' approach to religion is that he seems to posit the existence of a 'real' self, which is resistant to the pressures of high modernity and which comes to the surface only at times of acute existential anxiety. The implication is that high modern institutions can eclipse, sequester or conceal moral issues only up to the point where individuals have to face up to 'elemental questions about human existence'. This is the point at which the 'repressed' morality asserts itself. This 'volcanic' or emergent version of moral agency is inadequate insofar as it runs the risk of implying that the real moral agent is pre- or even non-social. It is difficult to avoid the suspicion that 'the return of the repressed' is a rabbit pulled out of the theoretical hat when all other tricks have failed to make sense of the persistence of religion at a time when, according to the theory of high modernity, religion's chances of survival are extremely slim. The reason for criticising Giddens' notion of the resurgence of a repressed morality is therefore similar to the reason for objecting to Bauman's notion of an autonomous moral conscience which is somehow immune from socialisation and sociality. Both cases seem to represent attempts to reach beyond the socio-cultural realm in the search for an entity which is activated by non-social and non-cultural resources.

There is a further problem with the meaning attributed to religion by both Bauman and Giddens: they both account for religion in terms of the response allegedly shown by *individuals* to purely moral dilemmas. They do not seem to envisage any possible reason for the survival of religion other than its presumed capacity to provide a transcendental basis for reassuring moral values and judgements. It is as if they present narrowly individualised and rationalised accounts of religion which leave no opening to, say, a Durkheimian appreciation of the force of collective consciousness or collective effervescence.[27]

Ulrich Beck has provided a third possibility for making sense of what Bauman and Giddens tend to explain in surprisingly functionalist and individualist terms as a need for ethical and psychological reassurance.[28] In comparison, Beck does not hold out any prospect of a revival, or even survival, of religion. In fact, he has very little to say about religion directly, but he does offer some insights into the 'self-politicisation of modernity' which definitely contain at least spiritual significance. His insights tend to support the contention[29] that what he calls 'the new culture of politics' to be found, for example, in new religious and healing movements and alternatives to mainstream medicine, politics and technology, contains a spiritual quality.[30] Beck has the great advantage over Bauman and Giddens of being able to explain the 'remoralization' of 'new modernity' without recourse to functionalism or to a questionable psychology.

Beck's widely read book *Risk Society: Towards a New Modernity* has no place for the notion of postmodernity. Instead, it proposes that the dynamics which started in the 'old' industrial society of the early nineteenth century are continuing to operate in the 'new' modernity of the late twentieth century but with startlingly different consequences. His argument is that the nature of social life has changed drastically and, in many respects, ironically as a result.

The central theses are that scientific and political modernisation processes 'dissolved the structure of feudal society in the nineteenth century and produced the industrial society', and that the same processes are now 'dissolving industrial society and another modernity is coming into being'.[31] The accumulated side-effects of the principles underlying industrial society have apparently created a new reflexive modernity which challenges faith in progress and undermines many of the taken-for-granted features of industrial society such as the nuclear family form, sexual division of labour, social class conflict and the centrality of paid work.

According to Beck, the shift from old to new modernity is powered by contradictions at the heart of early modernisation between *universal* principles (human rights, equality, functional differentiation, critical reason) and the *partial* character of the institutions which supposedly embodied them (politics of privilege, rigidly hierarchical class structures, exploitative family forms). These contradictions have allegedly continued working themselves out over the past century and have now thoroughly disturbed the central axes of gender, family, occupation and faith in science. In other words, the acids of Enlightenment liberalism which succeeded in dissolving feudalism have more recently dissolved the semi-modern forms of industrial society as well. In its place have emerged 'new' modern forms of society and culture which reflect the production of risks alongside wealth and a self-reflexive critical outlook instead of faith in science, economic growth and progress.

Beck is insistent that 'risk' in this context does not mean the same thing as chance or danger. Humans have always faced chances and dangers of various kinds, but the distinctive feature of the new modernity is that it is founded on the *systematically produced* risks (not unforeseen accidents or uncontrollable circumstances) which accompany technological modernisation. Moreover, the risks that are inseparable from scientific and technological development are potentially catastrophic not just for particular groups or nations but for the whole of humanity. Yet the rationality of science can only conceive of these risks as side-effects or errors, overlooking the point that it is scientific knowledge, not ignorance, which generates them as a matter of routine.[32]

Nevertheless, Beck claims that people have begun to recognise the new risks for what they are. These involve: ' "side-effects" speak up, organise, go to court, assert themselves, refuse to be diverted any longer . . . These are the dynamics of *reflexive politicisation* producing risk consciousness and conflict.'[33] Environmental problems, for example, are no longer regarded as solely a matter of the physical conditions of life but also as thoroughly political and social problems concerning control over decisions affecting the quality of people's lives. Beck's view is that, through the agency of citizens' protest groups and alternative institutions, the critical reason which was originally essential to science is now being applied reflexively to the social consequences of scientific and technological dominance.

The protests are not a Luddite backlash, a Romantic rebellion or an atavistic nostalgia. On the contrary, according to Beck, they represent only the latest application, albeit paradoxically, of the very same critical reason which launched the earliest phases of modernisation. They represent continuity of development at the same time as they attempt paradoxically to force modernisation on to different tracks.

One of the most interesting aspects of Beck's analysis of 'new modernity' is the space that it creates for spiritual and moral developments which, contrary to the diagnoses of Bauman and Giddens, do not involve a regressive search for existential security in particularistic identities in opposition to, or outside the dynamic of, modernity. On the contrary, Beck emphasises that the scope and intensity of the risks systematically produced in industrial society are so great that 'a new type of community of the endangered' comes into being.[34] This new community cuts across boundaries of social class, gender, generation, ethnicity or nationality. It supposedly gives rise to a solidarity of self-conscious victims on an increasingly global scale. It may even generate a 'solidarity of living things'[35] that would 'undermine the dualism of body and spirit, or nature and humankind'.[36] Beck can therefore be said to advance a religious or at least spiritual argument about the emergence of a new collective consciousness of what Paul Tillich called 'the felt whole'. For example, Beck's language is consonant with the tone and content of the declaration entitled *Toward a Global Ethic* which was ratified by representatives of the major world religions at the Parliament of the World's Religions in Chicago in 1993.[37]

According to Beck, conventional politics are not the appropriate vehicle for conveying this new self-reflexive criticism of modernisation because the imperative of economic growth has already corrupted political parties, legislatures and states. The new twist of critical reason is to bypass mainstream politics and to repoliticise society by operating through subpolitical channels such as citizens' initiatives and new social movements. But, again, this does not represent a break with modernity. In fact, Beck claims that these developments are merely the 'amplification' of processes set in train when basic political rights were in principle granted to all people in liberal democracies but actually diverted into liberal and socialist party systems.

Despite his insights into the spiritual character of the new 'solidarity of living things', religion seems to play a mainly negative role in Beck's scenario. The new risk consciousness supposedly creates 'a kind of new "shadow kingdom", comparable to the realm of the gods and demons in antiquity, which is hidden behind the visible world and therefore human life on this Earth . . . Everywhere, pollutants and toxins laugh and play their tricks like devils in the Middle Ages.'[38] In short, the factor which precipitates the 'solidarity of living things' is *fear*. Thus, 'new communities and alternative communities arise, whose world views, norms and certainties are grouped around the center [*sic*] of invisible threats'.[39] According to Beck, the response to this fear of intangible threats may take the form of scapegoating, denial or the formation of 'radical and fanatical reactions and political tendencies'.[40]

Insofar as religion has any place in Beck's characterisation of the 'new modernity', it seems to consist of (a) the symbolisation of threats to civilisation in the form of malevolent spirits, and (b) radical and fanatical reactions to these intangible threats. This may seem rather bleak; but at least the predication follows logically from his analysis of 'new' modernity. In other words, Beck does not need to do any special pleading to explain religion in terms of an exceptional need for psychological security or moral assurance.

On the other hand, Beck's approach to religion and spirituality is a throwback to some of the most *deterministic* aspects of Karl Marx's and Friedrich Engels' materialism. He credits religion with virtually no autonomy. His argument is that the conditions of life in a world of high risk simply call forth threatening symbols and images. Redemption allegedly lies elsewhere: namely, in the capacity of the new cultural politics to challenge and resist political and economic trends towards further exploitation and oppression. Nevertheless, as has been remarked of environmentalist mobilisations,[41] a distinctly spiritual significance can be attributed to the kind of causes which typically occupy the heart of cultural politics. Issues which emphasise the embeddedness of individuals or groups in more comprehensive collectivities are particularly likely to give rise to a politics of identity[42] with spiritual overtones. Beck's work is suggestive of just such spiritual possibilities in connection with protests against the calculated risks allegedly taken in 'new' modernity with people's health, well-being or even chances of survival. He stops short of exploring these possibilities, but his theoretical framework can be interpreted as an invitation or a challenge to examine the religious and/or spiritual aspects of the positive and negative responses to risk society.

Ernest Gellner, a merciless critic of the very idea of postmodernity, offers a better appreciation of the capacity of religion to symbolise collectivity in a positive sense. Yet he also has problems fitting religion into his interpretation of the present day.

Gellner has gone at least one step further than Giddens and Beck. Not content with merely doubting the appropriateness of labelling today's western societies 'postmodern', he anathematises the term. His *Postmodernism,*

Reason and Religion contains a blistering attack on what he sees as the philosophical-cum-methodological capitulation of social science to hermeneutics.[43] He excoriates the notions of postmodernity and postmodernism as an 'ephemeral cultural fashion'[44] which is 'too ethereal and volatile to be captured and seized with precision'[45] but which favours philosophical relativism and 'a kind of hysteria of subjectivity'.[46] For Gellner this means in effect:

the abandonment of any serious attempt to give a reasonably precise, documented and testable account of anything . . . The notions that everything is a 'text', that the basic material of texts, societies and almost anything is meaning, that meanings are there to be decoded or 'deconstructed', that the notion of objective reality is suspect – all this seems to be part of the atmosphere, or mist, in which postmodernism flourishes, or which postmodernism helps to spread.[47]

Gellner characterises it all as 'metatwaddle' which,

in addition to contingent flaws – obscurity, pretentiousness, faddiness, showmanship, cultural name-dropping – commits major errors in the method it recommends: its penchant for relativism and preferential attention to semantic idiosyncrasy blind it to the non-semantic aspect of society, and to the immensely important, absolutely pervasive asymmetry in cognitive and economic power in the world situation.[48]

So Gellner rejects postmodern perspectives because they are based on philosophical relativism. He also has problems with the very opposite – namely, religious fundamentalism – because, in his view, it chooses to depart from Western rationalism and therefore attempts to deny the evident superiority of a system of scientific practice and philosophical principle which underpins the power of advanced industrial societies. But does this mean that, like so many rationalists, he sees no philosophically defensible place for religion in the present-day? It might be thought so.

However, Gellner not only offers a defence of religion but actually advocates a form of religion which would avoid the Scylla of postmodernity and the Charybdis of fundamentalism. He calls it 'constitutional religion' after the model of the UK's constitutional monarchy. This is a system of monarchy which retains the rituals and symbols of genuine monarchy but which leaves the real business of running government and society to technical, secular experts. Ritual, according to Gellner, no longer reflects social reality, but at least it can contribute to social stability by maintaining the fantasy or fiction of past glories. His proposal amounts to a new separation of powers. Accordingly, social arrangements would be legitimated by the old pieties; but, 'when dealing with serious matters, when human lives and welfare are at stake, when major resources are being committed, the only kind of knowledge which may legitimately be used and invoked is that which satisfies the criteria of Enlightenment philosophy'.[49]

This sounds like a twentieth-century version of the Noble Lie. In fact, Gellner admits that his constitutional religion is an 'ironic, non-serious faith, disconnected from genuine conviction about how things truly stand'.[50] He proposes it, however, in the hope that it will help societies to face major crises by giving them the twin advantages of modern technology *and* a pre-modern social liturgy ('treated with limited seriousness').

What is most interesting about Gellner's proposal is that it suggests a future for religion which has little or nothing to do with Bauman's postmodernity, Giddens' high modernity or Beck's new modernity. For, although Gellner's case for religion is also phrased in terms of 'social legitimation' and may therefore seem to have some connection with ethical dilemmas, it is actually a child of Durkheim's argument about the functional need for persuasive symbols of collective identity. It is less to do with the capacity of individuals for solving moral problems than with the apparent need to bolster feelings of collective continuity, solidarity and integrity at a time when the extremes of fundamentalism and postmodern relativism seem philosophically untenable and socially threatening.

Nevertheless, closer inspection of Gellner's ingenious proposal for 'constitutional religion' reveals a striking departure from Durkheim's way of thinking and, as a result, at least one major defect. His categorical distinction between the level of symbolic meaning and the level of 'serious matters' to which only rational knowledge is allegedly relevant flies in the face of the fact that many of the world's most intractable, and therefore 'serious', problems are simultaneously disputes about symbolic meaning or identity and material power. Conflicts in the former Soviet Union, the former Yugoslavia, Central Africa, the Sudan, and the Indian subcontinent, to mention only the most recent sites of major atrocities, are all marked by the inseparability of cultural and material interests. These conflicts show that religion cannot be categorically divorced from material interests. Indeed, it commonly serves as a vehicle for them.[51] Moreover, some differences of religious belief and practice are experienced, and acted upon, by the antagonists in power struggles as no less real than differences of material power. Thus, although an observer may wish to distinguish between cultural and material *factors* for analytical purposes, such a distinction runs the risk of distorting rather than illuminating the complexity of social and cultural life, if it is taken to reflect the ontological priority of one *level* of reality over another. Durkheim would not have approved of the distinction between religion, which he associated with *la vie sérieuse*, and 'serious matters', although he would have accepted that the reality to which religious symbols and rituals point is very different from that in which religious believers have faith. The idea of a 'non-serious faith' might have been attractive and credible to him personally, but it is unlikely that he would have advocated it in such terms as a prescription for societal order and well-being. Nor is there any evidence that religion is heading in the direction of becoming non-serious at present. So, while many of Gellner's frustrations with the concepts of postmodernity and postmodernism are understandable, it does not follow that his proposal for 'constitutional religion' is workable for analytical or practical purposes.

In conclusion, the question arises of whether variants on the notion of postmodernity can usefully shape sociological thinking about religion. Like most of the social sciences and humanities, from time to time, sociology is swept by waves of enthusiasm for novel concepts or theories. The craze for such notions as industrial society, mass society, post-industrial society and so on is a normal feature of attempts to capture the distinctiveness of an era, a mode of production or a type of ideology and then to assess the direction of change. In most cases scattered observations and insights are creatively moulded into a framework of thought which then shapes sociological thinking for a while and with varying degrees of success. Giddens' work on 'high modernity' and Beck's on 'new modernity' have already shown themselves capable of stimulating fresh approaches to empirical research, although their potential for the sociological understanding of religion has not been adequately explored.[52] It may therefore be tempting to consider ideas of postmodernity as if they were also nothing more than the current fashion. This would be a mistake, however, for the following three reasons.

First, it is in the very nature of much thinking about postmodernity and postmodernism to deny even the possibility of subjecting claims to knowledge to any sort of methodical examination. These terms embody a self-denying ordinance which would make it illicit or illogical to ask for evidence in support of their contentions, let alone evidence which might somehow test them. If there really is no possibility of foundational knowledge or of reliable points of anchorage for human reasoning, then it supposedly makes no sense to try to do anything with ideas of postmodernity except perhaps to celebrate their inconsequentiality. If human life is nothing but self-referential text or discourse, then the only thing to do is to keep reading and talking or watching the video replay, not sociologise the process.

Second, postmodernity's self-denying ordinance virtually rules out the point of trying to 'use' its insights in order to explain the world around us. And it certainly does not invite or tolerate offers to 'test' its assertions by empirical means. So, unlike some of the other generative ideas in the social sciences, postmodernity will not be launching a flood of investigations into its applicability or utility. True to itself, it has no instrumental value. It can only express itself. The thing which is most worrying about this intellectual fashion is that it is not, therefore, susceptible to disconfirmation. It cannot be checked or controlled by inconvenient findings. This is closely related to a third difficulty.

Postmodernity's immunity to the antibiotics of empirical evidence implies that it resembles a virus more than a bacterium. It is also like a virus insofar as it needs to reside in a host cell and to distort that cell's development for its own purposes. Postmodernist speculation has therefore run rampant through virtually every field of scholarship, casting doubt on conventional assumptions, procedures and problematics. It has become fashionable to cast everything in postmodernist terms but, more insidiously, to refuse to question the validity of these terms or the utility of what they produce. It cannot be a constructive development because it possesses no resources and no incentive for criticising its own assumptions.

The postmodernist fashion is an intellectual conceit which is reminiscent of the ignorance and snobbishness of Monsieur Jourdain, Molière's *Bourgeois Gentilhomme* of 1670. Significantly, it is a tutor in philosophy to whom Jourdain gives the greatest credit for teaching him that he has been speaking prose for the previous forty years of his life without realising it. Of course, Jourdain is a figure of ridicule for naïvely believing that the world can really be changed by simply re-naming everyday things. What is less often noticed about Molière's plot, however, is that the hired philosopher does nothing to disabuse his pupil of this error. In fact, he promises to return the next day to sell more of his philosophical services.

These three considerations lead to the conclusion that the fashion for postmodern perspectives is not like some other intellectual crazes of the modern era; it is in some respects more diverting because it cuts across so many intellectual fields. But Ernest Gellner has correctly observed that it is also more insidious because it tries to dissolve rationality without offering anything better in its place.[53] This may or may not be fine for the arts and theology but it offers very little to the sociologist who is intent upon making sense of the socio-cultural expressions and vehicles of religion in terms which can be criticised and tested by other scholars.

48. Ibid., p. 70.
49. Ibid., p. 92.
50. Ibid., p. 93.
51. James A. Beckford, 'Religion and power', in Thomas Robbins and Dick Anthony (eds), *In Gods We Trust* (New Brunswick, NJ: Transaction Publishers, 1990), pp. 43–60; and James A. Beckford, *Religion and Advanced Industrial Society* (London: Unwin-Hyman, 1989).
52. But see Phillip Mellor, 'Reflexive traditions: Anthony Giddens, high modernity and the contours of contemporary religiosity', *Religious Studies*, vol. 29, 1993, pp. 111–27; and Phillip Mellor and Chris Shilling, 'Modernity, self-identity and the sequestration of death', *Sociology*, vol. 27, no. 3, 1993, pp. 411–31.
53. Ernest Gellner, *Postmodernism, Reason and Religion, op. cit.*

3 Postmodernity, Architecture, Society and Religion: 'A Heap of Broken Images' or 'A Change of Heart'

Michael York

Postmodernity/postmodernism has become the catchword of the late 1980s/ early 1990s. But the very term 'post-modern' sounds like a contradiction of meanings. If 'modernism' refers to something which is peculiar to or characteristic of modern, contemporary times, anything which is 'after' or 'post' these implies the futuristic. But modernism itself suggests the futur- istic, and therefore by postmodern we tend to comprehend something which is 'after the future'. We might easily ask, 'how is this possible? How can something come *after the future*?' But this type of perplexity seems to be very much what the paradox, parody and playfulness of the postmodern concept centrally entail.

In general, since modernity and futurity have in our century been closely tied to the 'promise of a renewed world', the connotations of postmodern- ity have been largely negative. The end of the millennium is ceasing to be seen as an occasion for optimism but rather as the advent of an era of scepticism and dread. Comparing our culture with that of the *avant-garde* cradle of modernism a century earlier, Robert Hughes suggests that we have lost 'ebullience, idealism, confidence, the belief that there was plenty of territory to explore, and above all the sense that art, in the most disin- terested and noble way, could find the necessary metaphors by which a radically changing culture could be explained to its inhabitants'.[1] Has mod- ernist hope now been replaced by postmodernist despair?

In reviewing Akbar Ahmed's book, *Postmodernism and Islam*,[2] Malise Ruthven comments that 'whatever is meant by postmodernism . . . divers- ity and eclecticism are its most obvious features'. She goes on to add that 'post-modernity is confusing to everyone, not least because to understand it requires familiarity with – if not mastery of – a wide variety of different cultural traditions'. Nevertheless, for her, 'freedom to choose one's religion or lifestyle – to be as "culturally mutant" as one likes – is becoming part of the post-modern condition'.[3] But 'consumer choice' in religion, along with the shifting of what were once 'familiar moral and cultural reference points', threaten traditional religious orientations whether Christian or Islamic. For Ahmed, Western secular materialism has become the dominant ideology or expression of the postmodern world, yet this very materialistic secularism has been associated more with modernism – from which postmodernism supposedly represents a departure.

Postmodernism was at first an aesthetic term, referring originally to an architectural style as defined by the architect and art critic Charles Jencks. It has been subsequently adopted by the disciplines of philosophy, theology and sociology among others. It remains frequently one of those terms one uses but shudders over the possibility that someone may ask what is meant by it. Its very contradictory implications make it difficult to define. But inasmuch as it is grounded on modernity, the modern, we must begin with what is meant by 'modernism'.

The term 'modern' derives from the Late Latin *modernus* which in turn developed from the Latin adverb *modo* with the meaning of 'just now', itself a derivative of the ablative of *modus* or 'measure'. The Indo-European root is given as *med* – 'to take appropriate measures' – suggesting perhaps that 'postmodern' refers to the 'taking of inappropriate measures'. Consequently, in a latent sense, modernism and postmodernism imply the making of value judgements in terms of relevance or utility.

In the broad sense, modernism relates to an affinity or sympathy with modern thoughts, practices or standards. The epitome of architectural modernism consists of straight lines, rational thought and extreme refinement of proportion and detailing: the 'International Style' fostered by Mies von der Rohe. In philosophy and art, modernism has come to refer to a self-conscious and deliberate break with the past and a search for new forms of expression in any of the arts.

Whereas in architecture the modern style became one of functionalism in which, as a philosophy of design, form is to be adapted to use, material and structure, the postmodern has become a movement against an art style and architectural design which is seen as not fulfilling human needs. For example, the house is a home and not merely a functional design project; it is something symbolic of the human need for a cave-like/nest-like shelter.[4]

Consequently, postmodernism moves 'away from the free plan and the abstraction of modernism . . . towards a more catholic architectural approach involving a whole range of revivalist imagery'.[5] If modernism breaks with the past, postmodernism reaffirms it. Things – whether styles or attributes – from earlier times are utilised as being more interesting; they have emotional appeal over the stark, severe forms which have been accepted by modernism as the ideal. Postmodernism becomes a movement against the functional iconoclasm identified with modern times.[6] There are two broad camps within the postmodernist movement: one which represents a fundamental break with the recent past, a negation of modernism; the other a 're-weaving' of modernism with elements of western humanism, a consolidation of 'free-style classicism'.

Postmodernism appears at three junctures. First, for architects, it represents a return to some classical shapes, such as symmetry, use of columns, Beaux Arts architecture; in fact, everything which was thrown out by the Modernists. The turning point between architectural modernism and postmodernism is recognised with Phillip Johnson and John Burgee's AT & T building in New York. Acknowledged postmodern examples in architecture include the Lloyds Insurance building in London and the Beauborg or Centre Pompidou in Paris,[7] on the one hand, and the Transamerican Corporation or Pyramid Building in San Francisco as well as James Fraser Stirling's Stuttgart Neue Staatsgalerie, on the other.

Second, for art more generally, postmodernism is the rejection of modernism which itself represents the conscious questioning and rejection of all accepted values from the past. For the modernist, all has to be new and different from what went before. By contrast, postmodernism is the appropriation of, and impulse shopping from, the entire supermarket of Western civilisation. Its epitome could be said to be found in the works of photographer-artist Sherrie Levine which are the re-photographing of other people's photographs along with an essay justifying her approach as having to do with the contemporary culture of images. The underlying philosophy is that the beginning and end of cultural endeavour is maintaining the circulation of certain pictorial representations; whether original or reproduced makes no difference.

Finally, postmodernism has been joined with the notion of a posthistorical culture. In this sense, modernism represents one of the last movements of cultural change, and we are now supposedly entering a period of stability and unified stasis.[8]

In all cases, postmodernism is defined in counterpoise to modernism. As Rex Ambler affirms in Chapter 8, modernity has probably reached the limit of its sustainability as an expression of self-assertion. Likewise, Grace Davie, in exploring the work of Hervieu-Lèger, contends that modernity depletes the vitality of conventional religiosity for the individual or community but simultaneously demands the creation of new forms of religious life. When we turn to religion, we find that modernism has had several applications. In Christianity, it has tended to be contrasted with both liberalism and fundamentalism. In the wide sense, modernistic movements represent attempts to define Church teachings in terms compatible with modern scientific and philosophical developments – even revolutions – in thought. From a traditional perspective, is this automatically an undermining effort?

Christian modernism has been largely a Protestant movement which first developed in the latter half of the nineteenth century. It endeavours to establish the meaning and validity of the Christian faith in relation to immediate human experience, with the aim of reconciling traditional theological concepts to the empirical bases of modern knowledge. In Anglicanism, it has been accepted that all knowledge which relates to religion must necessarily reaffirm the fundamental truths of the Christian faith, but what is demanded is the Church's restatement of these truths into a language compatible with the intellectual vocabulary of modern times.

Roman Catholic modernism developed concurrently with Protestant modernism until it was condemned by Pope Pius X in 1907. This movement had denied the objective truth of revelation, even that of the entire supernatural world. The Catholic modernist held that religion's only vital element is its power to maintain and communicate religious experience. If we see religious modernism in the light of denying the reality of the transcendent or supernatural, postmodernism in religion may be taken as an affirmation of the otherworldly as real or at least approachable.

One must be careful, however, not to confuse the postmodern with the premodern. This last is something which antedates the present; it is not of the current form or style but is directly located in an earlier moment in time. Postmodernism, on the other hand, may incorporate elements from the past – perhaps even eclectically – but it represents a new synthesis or perhaps even a grafting on to the modern itself.

Postmodernism, in one sense, represents an extension of the new rather than a strict repudiation of it. Looked at this way, fundamentalism is a postmodern reaction which seeks a premodern restitution. It is a premodern literalistic response *to* the modern/postmodern situation. In a sense, the fundamentalist seeks a recapturing of the purity of a past state of being or a former condition of understanding.

The New Age movements, on the other hand, are the more direct legacies of postmodernity. They incorporate various mixtures of the scientific, that is, the modern, as well as the scientistic and the reconstructionistic. They do not seek a return to the past but an incorporation of it (or at least parts of it) into the present. Likewise, they do not so much seek a denial of the modern and scientific as they do an extension of these, or a concurrent

development with them. In this sense, in the understanding of postmodernism from the vantage of its origins as an aesthetic term within the arts,
the broad gamut of the New Age and Human Potential is indicative *of*
postmodernity rather than being, as is fundamentalism, a reaction *to* it.
The contemporary criticism of the postmodern state of affairs in Western societies in which it is argued that 'belief has become fragmented,
consumerism has reduced culture to a commodity, and scepticism or nihilism has become rife' raises several pertinent issues but might equally be
seen as a fair criticism of 'modernism' itself. Against depersonalisation
and utilitarian efficiency, postmodernism is itself a reproach, and postmodernity either a reaction or counterdevelopment. The scepticism or nihilism
of our era is more likely a product of the rationalism or even technical
rationalism which has been exalted as the hallmark of twentieth-century
thought.

In a moment, we turn to look more closely at questions of belief,
fragmentation, the commercialisation of culture and the sceptical/nihil-
istic presupposition, but first it is pertinent to recognise that although fundamentalism may represent the more traditional position concerning the
literal reality of religious truth, the New Age response can also contain word-
for-word belief in the supernatural. True enough, New Age represents a
wide-ranging gamut of differing stances and positions. On one end of the
spectrum, we will find the attitudes embodied in Neo-paganism and psychic
or psychological humanism in which the religious symbol or icon is a metaphor for a non-empirical reality.

Distinct from this interpretative branch of New Age, at the other end of
the mixture's sweep, are to be found the Galactians and Spiritualists who,
though acknowledging the difficulty of empirical demonstrability, affirm
the true reality of unidentified flying objects (UFOs) and discarnate spirits.
This side of New Age, in general more transcendental in orientation, exhibits close affinities with the Evangelical/Pentecostal wing of Christianity
through its pursuit of spiritual guidance, direct experience of the sacred,
unorthodox healing and radical spiritual transformation of the world. But
within the New Age identity itself, an interchange is readily to be found
between the more 'fundamental' wing and the symbolists in that both use
the same basic vocabulary despite differences of interpretation and both
allow the latitude to the other for individual exegesis and personal belief
assessment.

Both fundamentalism *and* New Age represent reactions to postmodernity when the postmodern comprises what Luc Ferry refers to as an emergent 'non-metaphysical humanism'.[9] Here we are dealing with the third
juncture of postmodernism mentioned previously: that of post-historical

culture. But once again, it is difficult to distinguish whether it is modernity or postmodernity which is the catalyst.

What we are concerned with is the current relinquishing of any reference to a subject. For Ferry, this tendency locks up modernism in a desperate flight towards itself. This is perhaps a corollary to Ambler's notion of bankruptcy in the ability to produce new forms of human self-assertion. Both fundamentalism and New Age offer reactions to the illusory quality of relativism and the *avant-gardes* in a return to focus on the self and its salvation and/or development. Where the contrast between the two remains, however, is in what one would label as the premodern certitude of fundamentalism as opposed to the experimental orientation of postmodernity.

Robert Wuthnow has seen the innovative tendency and inclination towards social experimentation as a product of the individual's cultural meaning-system. In 1976, he identified four essential modes: the theistic, the individualistic, the social-scientific and the mystic. The first two together comprise a traditional cultural meaning-system; the social-scientific and mystic together constitute the modern; and any combination of one component of the traditional with one of the modern, Wuthnow terms the transitional.

In a theistic meaning-system, the role of God is stressed as the governing force. In the individualistic, the personal will of the individual assumes this role within a matrix of fixed laws. The mystic mode is similar except that the fixed matrix is denied.

The human role is also emphasised within the social-scientific orientation, but here the individual is socialised, and social influences are the governing forces. For this mode, the social environment assumes primary importance, and the image of transcendence is society itself. As Wuthnow explains, the predominant view of social organisation which this mode conveys is 'libertarian': promoting diversity more than conformity, deviance more than strict obedience to authority, and change and reform more than static order. The social-scientific aspect of the modern meaning-system entertains an evolutionary view of social and cultural history or a radical, apocalyptic view of social change. Rather than characters, souls or psyches, the 'self' becomes the central concept, but this 'self' is neither immutable nor internally consistent but more capable of non-conventional experimentation than the human entity which is central to the individualistic way of thinking.

By contrast, the mystic stresses peak experiences to be as important as the cognitive understandings of the other modes. In other words, ecstatic experiences constitute the primary way of constructing meaning out of reality. Perception for the mystic is one of a larger whole, and ecstatic, personal experience becomes an appeal in a situation in which cognitive belief systems have become too numerous, especially to those who are culturally and socially relative. The mystic mode, Wuthnow explains, allows order to be projected on to an otherwise incoherent reality, which is approached only through analogy. The mystic's theodicy tends to devalue or transvalue the reality of suffering rather than formally explain its existence. This supposedly engenders social and political apathy, antinomianism and anarchy.[10]

If, however, we are to locate a postmodern meaning-system in Wuthnow's terms, it would be post-mystic and post-social-scientific. If it were not also to be premodern, theistic might have to become pantheistic, and individualistic meaning-systems extended to the collective whole of humanity. Postmodernism would replace libertarianism with ecological and holistic conformity, 'Gaiaistic' principles becoming now the governing forces, and Gaia the image of immanent transcendence. This re-sacralisation of the earth, however, and the belief in the collective human response to and responsibility for the planet counters the social and political antinomian apathy characteristic of the mystic mode *per se*. This description is that which applies in general to the New Age and Human Potential phenomena in their multi-facetedness, and this application underscores the holistic movement's very cutting-edge position between the modern and the postmodern.

Turning to consider some of the ramifications and positive responses of the New Age/Human Potential/Neo-pagan development which may extend the idea of postmodernity as merely a reaction to or criticism of modernity, one can contend that the positive contributions inherent in these modern networks and their implicit theologies lie precisely in those areas often cited as criticisms of postmodernity: namely, belief fragmentation, cultural commodity reductionism and nihilistic scepticism.

Religion is an expression of culture. It describes the ways different parts of humanity phrase their relationship to the universe. All human culture conforms to a universal pattern which includes such things as the recognition of a specific language, the use of fire and tools, a food technology, some technical solution to protection from the variations of climate, the family and community, aesthetic elaboration and a system of meaning assignment and value allocation.

Every human culture provides for educating and assimilating those born within it. Intimately connected with any specific culture is its common language system (the pattern or structure of its communication), and like culture in general, all languages change in time as part of the cultural process of realignment and readjustment. It would seem therefore that part of the question of postmodernity and any incipient questioning of it relates to the very problem of cultural and linguistic changes and any inevitable resistance to these. But, as the anthropologist Margaret Mead proclaimed:

> the history of man's ability to change his existing ways of doing things, either by making innovations or by learning from other peoples, is the history of his increasing recognition that the things he himself does are learned – that they are dependent in style on the culture from which they were learned and are in no sense inalienably related to his race, his lineage, his historical antecedents or the particular part of the earth on which he happens to live.[11]

The key idea behind Mead's understanding of culture as a 'system of learned, transmissible, and modifiable behaviour through which the human species has been able to survive, multiply, maintain themselves and elaborate their relationships within groups and between groups, between themselves and their environment'[12] is that cultures change; they are not static or fixed creations. Each new generation 'borrows, invents, modifies, and adapts the system of habits which it receives from its predecessors and the members of neighbouring cultures'. People utilise new customs adapted to different conditions. In their selective use and adaptation, some aspects are emphasised and others de-emphasised to make their institutions workable.[13]

Today, we refer to this process of cultural selectivity and modification as cultural supermarket consumerism. But this very process is in itself indicative of the human being's experience of other ways of life – whether cultural broadly or religious specifically – and his or her ability to value them. Nevertheless, it is facile and erroneous to assess a culture as capable of being or becoming a commodity. Cultural or religious items may be commercial or semi-commercial articles, but a culture or religion itself is a system or pattern or structured social situation – even an organic system – of human inventions and observations which human beings have made and within which they live.

The word 'culture' derives from the Latin *cultus*, the past participle of the verb *colere* which denotes 'tilling', 'cultivating', even 'worshipping'. A culture is something which is cultivated not something which is bought and sold, and the borrowing or incorporation or interchange of meaningful inventions or ideas between different cultures is an inevitable and organic part of genuine directional change. The attribution that postmodern consumerism reduces culture to a commodity is naïve, judgemental and fails to recognise the essential dynamics of social change as well as the different parameters of the contemporary world situation. All culture is in a perpetual process of change, realignment and readjustment, and postmodernity is simply the recognition of the very act of transformation which is occurring at the present within Western society.[14]

The diffusion process of human cultural change, however, has traditionally depended on a degree of separation and isolation between cultures to allow the spontaneous development of significant variations. But now, in our modern/postmodern contemporary world, the striking contrasts between civilisations are ceasing to exist and variation is becoming increasingly dependent on new internal forms. The pluralistic society of postmodernity may provide the basis for spontaneous innovation and invention in anotherwise increasingly homogeneous world.[15] Part of this postmodern pluralism is the variety of religious denominations, cults, sects and new religious movements which make up humanity's religious life.

Though there is the modern recognition that human institutions and cultures are man-made, according to Mead 'new religious cults and sects almost invariably still try to invest the simplest learned procedures of everyday life . . . with some kind of rigid relationship to their own special and recently discovered supernaturally sanctioned way of life'.[16] Mead's observation is equally applicable to the current resurgence of various fundamentalisms. But even so, this condition of religious sectarianism appears to encourage the very emergence of communal distancing necessary to foster a continual ferment of growth, newness and accommodation.

In the postmodern world at large, one increasingly comes to realise that culturally, linguistically and religiously determined forms of behaviour are only 'one of a series' of possible patterns. This awareness allows increase in response and the articulation and development of new social concepts. In a word, postmodernity allows for the very cultivation of culture and not, as its critics contend, its prostitution.

The commodity criticism of postmodernity does not recognise that culture is itself a series of integrated systems based on the structured integration of various basic components and compositions rather than *ad hoc* and random agglomerations. Traditional religion has been formulated in terms of belief, but postmodern religion has increasingly come to assert that belief *per se* is not essential to religious orientation. Where postmodern critics assert that belief has become fragmented, a matter of personal preference and 'a commodity to be packaged for the market-place', much of New Age and Neo-pagan thought contends that belief is optional and of secondary importance. It is perhaps on this point that the new religious networks most challenge the traditional stance of religion.

In a postmodern world in which beliefs, like cultures, are recognised as 'one of a series' of possible options, Wiccan priestess Vivianne Crowley expresses the prevailing attitude when she proclaims that

other than a very simple belief in the life force and the powers of the human psyche, all that is required is that *we accept the framework of ritual and symbolism* in which Wicca operates as containing age-old truths which are not literal but which are hidden and whose truth will unfold over the years as we *integrate* them into our own lives. [my italics][17]

The Neo-pagan writer Margot Adler also stresses that techniques, practice and attitude towards life are the important issues rather than belief which is virtually incidental.

The Neo-pagan consideration that truth is never more than a metaphor and that worship does not necessitate belief is a position which is shared with the Human Potential movement and interpretative branch of New Age. One might say, in fact, that postmodern religion is based on what is *done* rather than on what is *believed*. Prevailing over belief or belief-systems is experience; specifically, what Wuthnow cites as the 'peak experiences' of the mystic mode of orientation which comprise 'altered states of consciousness' as well as intense feelings of ecstasy and joy.[18] Consequently, it is less a question of 'belief-fragmentation' in postmodernity as it is one of 'belief-devaluement'. The loci of the individual and personal exegesis become the determinants of what is to be believed if anything, and it is the shared experience of particular frames of reference which allow the associations and networks which are becoming characteristic of postmodernity.

Postmodern critics tend to translate the abandonment of belief and shared doctrine into a position of scepticism and/or nihilism. True enough, postmodernism in part appears to be a legacy of the existentialism of Sartre and Camus, among others, which stresses the uniqueness of the individual and the isolation of personal experience within a universe which is indifferent, if not hostile, to humanity. But part of this existential inheritance is the consequent emphasis on human freedom, choice and concomitant responsibility for action and meaning.[19] To someone with the perspective of a traditional belief-system which accepts supernatural sanction, the postmodern position is blasphemy. But to the degree that social science presents any particular belief-system as 'one among many' possibilities, it suggests an implicit theology through its relativising of all theologies whether traditional or new.

Through sociology, society and culture themselves become the images of transcendence. This implied theology is what Wuthnow terms the social-scientific meaning system, and its inherent libertarian consequence, promoting diversity over conformity, encourages the very non-conventional experimentation characteristic of postmodernity and challenging to traditional religion.

However, postmodernism, as understood through Human Potential, New Age and Neo-paganism, is in part a sceptical affirmation that absolute knowledge of the supernatural and/or transcendent is not possible and, in this respect, it differs little from the traditional position of Christianity which denies the ability of the finite human mind to comprehend the infinitude of God. Postmodern scepticism – a legacy perhaps from sociology and the sociology of religion in particular – relativises truth as a product of the religio-cultural system to which the individual belongs. In the religious pluralism coming to characterise Western society, the religious choice is no longer pre-set but is a range of different and differently understood options. This situation itself tends to reduce the certitude in any kind of absolute truth but, at the same time, it encourages an unprecedented form of individual and social freedom which allows religion to survive as it is 'consumed' rather than enforced.

Scepticism, of course, is part of the methodology of science – one in which sociology itself partakes. The process of doubting is integral to science's objective of relative or approximate certainty, but where postmodernity differs from scientific modernity is in its acceptance of supernatural and/or metaphorical truth which is nevertheless outside the domain of proper scientific inquiry. The typical, 'trans-sceptical' attitude is expressed by Sig Lonegren, despite his essentialism, in his *Labyrinths: Ancient and Modern Uses*, when he states that 'the point is that we need to find ways of allowing more female, receptive, birth-giving, intuitive energy into our lives today without, at the same time, throwing out all the benefits that the rational scientific mind has brought us'.[20]

The postmodernity of New Age, Human Potential, goddess Spirituality and Neo-paganism does not deny the utility and validity of legitimate scientific inquiry, but it asserts the spiritual reality encoded within the metaphorical world of myth and religion. It has moved beyond the limits of logical positivism and scientific empiricism to explore what it perceives as a magical-mystical reality only fragmentedly retained or perceived in any given traditional religious belief-system.

For the postmodern individual, scepticism frees one from the narrow-minded thinking which comes from too total an immersion within any particular religion to begin the trek toward the spiritual apprehension which unites all religion. Since no two individuals are the same, no two spiritual paths are identical. Each individual must find his or her own particular way. If the individual is confronted with a bewildering array of choice through the spiritual supermarket of our times, perhaps the future of postmodernity is to refine the options and transform this supermarket into what Robert Hughes refers to as the postmodernist delicatessen.[21]

Before the refinement to which Hughes refers becomes a possibility, let alone a reality, any evaluation of the postmodern at present appears to oscillate between assessment in terms of a 'heap of broken images' (pastiche, parody, quotation, self-referentiality, eclecticism and shallowness) or 'shining new styles' (moving beyond the materialist paradigm of modernism, acknowledgement of difference and otherness, the re-enchantment of nature, etc.) *Vis-à-vis* modernity, the postmodern is either critical (i.e., a form of anti-modernism) or it is recognised as the completion of the modernisation process itself. As Frederic Jameson explains, in the process of becoming modern, the old and obsolete are still present; but as the archaic continues to be eliminated, the postmodern is achieved.

A third possibility is that the postmodern surpasses or overtakes the modern. In its monocentric or unitary thought and quest for a monopolistic domination by the rational and technological single paradigm, the modern is perceived as having reached insolvency. The postmodern, then, is that in which the limits of the modern are bypassed. Attempting to graft on to the modern, the postmodern endeavours to extend the new rather than repudiate it. As Jencks expresses this, the postmodern double-codes the modern with something else – whether the classical, the romantic, the nostalgic or the purely innovative – or all these together.

The postmodern itself has been understood as comprising two distinct schools of thought. One is variously labelled as the deconstructionist, deconstructive/eliminative or revisionary branch. The other is known as the *re*constructive branch.

The first has been inspired chiefly by the deconstructionism of Jacques Derrida with its search for meaning behind meaning and the continual dissection of truth as the means toward attaining liberation. In seeing all metaphysics as forms of closure, Derrida aims to discover through a process of intertextual analysis the inherent ontotheological presuppositions in all systems of thought. He denies, of course, that deconstructionism itself is either a system or a methodology.

Also instrumental in the formation of the revisionary perspective is the heterology of Georges Bataille, who understood both the sacred and the erotic in terms of transgression. Bataille denied both the constriction and security of the established boundary. He was seminal to the various philosophers of marginality and alterity – including Adorno, Levinas, Foucault, Kristeva, Iragaray, Derrida, Baudrillard and Lyotard – and their concern with hearing the 'call of the other': the unnamed, disenfranchised and neglected.[22]

Another revisionist is the Marxist critic, Fredric Jameson, who defines the postmodern as the cultural logic of late or consumer capitalism. He sees the emergence of present-day multinational capitalism as integrally connected with the establishment of a global and de-centred communicational network in which the individual subject is lost and alienated. Whilst opposing the post-structuralist rejection of a master narrative, Jameson's 'unheard other' is the dominated labouring class. A unified shared code on the cultural level would allow for him the very possibility of dialogue between dominator and dominated.

In the postmodern shift, Jameson argues, subject fragmentation has replaced subject alienation and resulted in the depthlessness and superficiality that is often cited as characteristic of postmodernity. Another revisionist is Jean Baudrillard, who sees in the vapid and hedonistic mass media culture of our times that simulacrum has displaced metaphor and simulation has eliminated reflection. Baudrillard adds 'hyper-reality' to the traditional categories of the real, the symbolic and the imaginary; he argues that, once inside the artificial environment of simulacra, there no longer is an 'outside'. In this situation, one from which Baudrillard saw no escape, the 'other' is permanently marginalised.

Like Baudrillard, Jean-François Lyotard is a 'televisual' thinker. He argues that the postmodern condition is that in which computerised knowledge has become the principal force of production, and, in the general context of concern for language, knowledge is no longer an end in itself but a commercial commodity. But Lyotard sees postmodern knowledge as a means to refine our sensitivity to difference and encourage our ability to tolerate the incommensurable. In this, Lyotard comes close to the second or reconstructive branch of postmodernism.

In fact, the reconstructionists tend to identify deconstructionism and the deconstructionist school as really manifestations of modernism itself: Margaret Rose terms revisionism 'late modernism'; David Ray Griffin, 'ultramodernism'. Jurgen Habermas, on the other hand, calls the deconstructionist/postmodern critique of Enlightenment values and norms 'neo-conservative', a line of thought he sees running from Bataille through Foucault to Derrida who all leave modernity as an unfinished project. By contrast, the reconstructive form of postmodernism includes the ecological and ecumenical world view of Hans Kung, the eco-feminism of Charlene Spretnak and the double-coding or multi-coding of Charles Jencks. There is here an overriding concern for pluralism and diversity along with the desire to cut across the different 'taste cultures' which currently fracture society.

The reconstructive postmodern enterprise searches for a more integrating and humane cultural articulation which combines the reputed best of all past achievements with an open, all-holds-barred approach toward experimentation, innovation, otherness, world re-enchantment, *jouissance*, and holistic/organic ecology. As with the postmodern of resistance, affirmative postmodernity does not seek a meta-narrative; it, too, is not a totalising discourse. Moreover, both schools of the postmodern are united in their search for identity out of otherness and difference.

Coupling this similarity with the study of Derrida by Bill Martin in which the objective is presented as 'the possibility of a different differential inhabitation on the border lines of language, where community is never finally secure and thus must be carefully attended to, where community must remain awake to the possibility of the non-existence which it already exists within', the two branches of the postmodern are drawn even closer together. Martin's interpretation of Derrida's deconstructive project, which attempts to re-write the Western philosophical canon from the inside out in order to let the other speak, he calls 'intertextual ontological materialism'.[23] The 'new religiosity' understood in New Age, Neo-paganism, goddess Spirituality and Human Potential finds a legitimating dialectic in Martin and other articulations of the postmodern which, after science succeeded in the disenchantment of the pagan and Christian worlds, conceive of re-enchanting the world through a 'postsecular socialism'.

Notes and References

1. Robert Hughes, *The Shock of the New* (New York: Alfred A. Knopf, 1980), p. 9.
2. Akbar S. Ahmed, *Postmodernism and Islam, Predicament and Promise* (London: Routledge, 1992).
3. Malise Ruthven, 'Muhammad for our times', *The Guardian Weekly*, 19 July 1992.
4. Charles Jencks dates the symbolic commencement of the postmodern era with the televised dynamiting of the St Louis Pruitt-Igoe Housing Estate in 1972. For further insights into the link between architecture and postmodernism, see his two books: *The Language of Post-Modern Architecture*, London: Academy Editions, 1977 and *Post-Modernism: The New Classicism in Art and Architecture* (London: Academy Editions, 1987).
5. Deyan Sudjic, 'In the steps of Hawksmoor', *The Guardian Weekly*, 5 July 1992.
6. For Fredric Jameson, however, the negation of modernism through a nostalgic yearning for the past is considered as pastiche – a refusal to engage

with the present. Pastiche is the wish to be recalled to a time less complicated and difficult than our own. The imitation of dead styles replaces stylistic innovation. It becomes, in fact, a masking for the contemporary 'inability' to think historically, one which Jameson regards as symptomatic of living in a perpetual present: the schizophrenia of consumer society. The resultant series of perpetual presents yields a fragmentation of time, a timelessness, which Jameson sees as characteristic of postmodern society. For the pessimistic celebration of the depthless icon, the simulacrum, the flat 'screen' image, see the work of Jean Baudrillard.

7. This ascription to postmodernism is not shared by all, however. Hughes refers to the 'relentless kitsch-modernism of *le style Pompidou*'. See Robert Hughes, *The Shock of the New, op. cit.*, p. 34.

8. Of course, Jameson, would view the loss of history as a loss of a necessary epistemological category. He rejects Lyotard's rejection of history and all meta-narratives. But for Lyotard, the postmodern condition is one in which the master narratives of modernity have lost their credibility. History is seen as the narrative of human mastery over nature. The postmodern 'end of history' is the disillusion of the legitimating function of the *grand recit* to compel an established consensus. See Fredric Jameson, *Postmodernism: Or, The Cultural Logic of Late Capitalism* (London: Verso, 1991). From the pluralistic postmodern perspective, the 'end of history' might signify the beginning of many, simultaneous, histories. See Bill Martin, *Matrix and Line: Derrida and the Possibilities of Postmodern Social Theory* (Albany: State University of New York Press, 1992).

9. Luc Ferry, *Homo Aestheticus: L'Invention du Goût l'Âge Démocratique* (Paris: Grasset, 1990), *passim*.

10. Robert Wuthnow, *The Consciousness Reformation* (Berkeley: University of California Press, 1976).

11. Margaret Mead, 'The modern study of mankind', in Lyman Bryson (ed.), *An Outline of Man's Knowledge of the Modern World* (Garden City, New York: Nelson Doubleday, 1960), p. 329.

12. *Ibid.*, p. 328.

13. *Ibid.*, pp. 330ff.

14. This represents a different interpretation of the postmodern from that of James Beckford who rejects the notion on the basis of its refusal to accept reality as the one sole means to truth. During the Bristol conference on *Postmodernity and Religion*, Beckford proclaimed the consequent inconsequentiality of postmodernism. See also his contribution in this volume (Chapter 2). The hermeneutics of postmodernity, however, is still at the point where the postmodern struggles to define itself.

    The post-structural deconstructive project of Jacques Derrida on which much of the theoretical framework of the postmodern is founded does not so much deny truth as see it as contextual and forever receding the closer one approaches it. In fact, for Derrida, like Nietzsche and Davidson, 'truth' is a 'mobile army of metaphors'. See Bill Martin, *Matrix and Line, op. cit.*, p. 107.

15. For comment on Foucault and Lyotard's emphasis on the local, the particular, the 'micro-revolt' of new social movements and the *petit récit* as 'the quintessential form of imaginative invention', see Jean-François Lyotard,

The Postmodern Condition: A Report on Knowledge, trans. Geoff Bennington and Brian Massumi (Manchester: Manchester University Press, 1984), p. 37 forward and p. 60. See also Madan Sarup, *An Introductory Guide to Post-Structuralism and Postmodernism* (Athens, Georgia: University of Georgia Press, 1989).

16. Margaret Mead, 'The modern study of mankind', *op. cit.*, p. 331.
17. Vivianne Crowley, *Wicca: The Old Religion in the New Age* (Wellingborough: Aquarian Press, 1989).
18. Margot Adler, *Drawing Down the Moon: Witches, Druids, Goddess-Worshippers, and Other Pagans in America Today* (Boston, MA: Beacon Press, 1986), p. 154.
19. For comments on the insecurity of modern social life and the inherent liberating consequences of its form of realisation and condition, see Peter L. Berger, *The Precarious Vision: A Sociologist Looks at Social Fictions and Christian Faith* (Garden City, New York: Nelson Doubleday, 1961). Berger also stresses the role the social sciences have played in producing this sense of precariousness as well as the freedom of alternation which can develop from it. Thus, Berger suggests that for some people 'we are now living at the beginning of the "post-Christian era"': ibid., p. 19.
20. Sig Lonegren, *Labyrinths: Ancient and Modern Uses* (Glastonbury: Gothic Image Publications, 1991).
21. Robert Hughes, *The Shock of the New, op. cit.*, p. 412.
22. See Georges Bataille, *Erotism, Death and Sensuality*, trans. Mary Dalwood (San Francisco: City Lights Books, 1986); *Theory of Religion*, trans. Robert Hurley (New York: Zone Books, 1989); *On Nietzsche*, trans. Bruce Boone (New York: Paragon House, 1992).
23. Bill Martin, *Matrix and Line, op. cit.*, p. 124.

4 De-traditionalisation of Religion and Self: The New Age and Postmodernity

Paul Heelas

This chapter considers a number of claims concerning the de-traditionalisation of the cultural realm. This process reflects the movement from the externally organised to the vagus (the 'wandering' or 'straying' as the SOED puts it). The context is thus set for exploring a particular instance of the internalising shift to the apparently de-traditionalised and thus postmodern, that known as the New Age movement. It can be argued that this form of spirituality is *not* postmodern, one reason being that, in practice, it could well be more traditionalised than first appearances might indicate; another being that New Age sacralisation of the self aims to provide an essentialised foundationalism of identity and authority. The central purpose of this chapter is to challenge the link between New Age beliefs and postmodernism.

Organised culture with its sustained voices of moral authority serves to differentiate values, to distinguish between what is important and what is not, and to facilitate coherent, purposeful identities, life-plans or habits of the heart. But all these elements attached to organised culture have disintegrated – or so it is claimed. The shift is variously conceived as being: from 'fate' to 'choice' (and associated 'hyper-reflexivity'); from communalism to individualism; from the other-directed to the inner-directed; from authoritative 'basics' to an utilitarian or 'emotivist' culture; from the 'auratic' to the 'anti-auratic'; from exclusivistic truth-commitment to relativistic abnegation of judgement; from certainty to uncertainty and risk; from the traditional and the modern to the postmodern. Thus, Lash and Urry suggest that:

> the introduction of post-modernism within popular culture – in advertisements, television, video, pop music, and everyday experience of the social in which representations multiply and telescope to the point at which they intermix and become largely indistinguishable from the

64

real – breaks for a final time the mould of organized capitalist certainty centred around a set of more stable cultural forms. Contemporary culture, operating through a combination of often figural, anti-auratic, electronic and spectacular symbols has had the effect of disintegrating older modes of individual and collective identity . . . All that is solid about organized capitalism, class, industry, cities, collectivity, nation-state, even the word, melts into air.[1]

The overall argument, then, is that 'the cultural', the framework of modernity, has collapsed: it no longer serves as an established and directive realm or meta-narrative providing value, discrimination, discernment, judgement and order. Looking at the situation more analytically, and with an eye on several interrelated, albeit not necessarily mutually coherent, usages of the term 'postmodernity', theorists have drawn attention to the following characteristics of our (supposedly) de-traditionalised world.

First, and most fundamentally, it is *de-differentiated*. Distinctions, between 'representations' and 'the real', and between 'high' and 'low' culture, have been eroded. As Crook *et al.* suggest, 'a differentiated cultural modernity reaches its limit when "hyperdifferentiation" leads to a proliferation of divisions which effectively erodes the significance of distinctions between autonomous [cultural] spheres'.[2]

Second, and very much bound up with this kind of claim, our world is dominated by a *postmodern consumer culture*. De-differentiation of the cultural realm means that people do not have to worry about contradictory commitments to particular cultural formations. Instead, they can draw on the cultural 'reservoir' at will. Thus, Savage *et al.* suggest that people 'remain far less awestruck with certain lifestyles and cultural forms than previous generations. They can as easily engage in ballet, opera, rock music and "Californian sports", treating none of these as *the* culture, each being an activity to be sampled – albeit in an apparently "depthless", pastiche, manner.'[3] Writing in a similar vein, Crook *et al.* speak of 'the modulation of hierarchical cultural tradition into a postcultural emporium of styles'.[4]

Third, and also very much bound up with the theme of de-differentiation, our world is one in which the collapse of the subject–object distinction, combined with the collapse of judgement-informing cultural foundationalisms, leaves us unable to treat 'difference' in any other way than signifying the 'differently "true"' or, most minimally, the simply 'different'. In the words of Ernest Gellner, who is among those who emphasise considerations of this variety, 'postmodernism would seem to be rather clearly in favour of *relativism* . . . and hostile to the idea of unique, exclusive, objective, external or transcendent truth' (my italics).[5]

The next two characteristics of the (postulated) postmodern condition have to do with the disembedded, de-situated selves of the de-traditionalised world. Some theorists have noticed the extremes of *utilitarian selfhood*, arguing that it generates a more forceful version of postmodern consumer culture than that which has just been introduced. An important aspect of 'the cultural logic of late capitalism', it is claimed, is that producers are ever-increasingly effective in ensuring that subjects – namely consumers – are 'captured' by what is on offer. The aim is to ensure, as Ogilvy puts it, that 'people look at products as if they were mood-altering drugs'.[6] In this setting, the person fragments into all those different desires belonging to the utilitarian mode of being, becoming absorbed by whatever drug-like consumer 'intensity' their wishes have prompted them to select. Kellner suggests that 'in postmodern culture, the subject has disintegrated into a flux of euphoric intensities, fragmented and disconnected'.[7] For Kroker and Cook, 'the TV self is the electronic individual *par excellence* who gets everything there is to get from the simulacrum of the media: a market-identity as a consumer in the society of the spectacle; a galaxy of hyperfib-rillated moods . . . traumatized serial being'.[8] Then there are those theorists who attend to the *expressivist* form of being, a mode which, historically, belongs to the Romantic movement. Coming into greater prominence with what might be thought of as the 'countercultural logic' inspired by capital-ism during the 1960s, Parsons has referred to this period as 'the expressive revolution'[9] and Inglehart to the 'silent' version.[10] Dismissing the utilitarian mode as involving a crude, vulgar, debasing enthusiasm for the externals of life, the expressivist turns to the depths of the self to seek what is really important about being human. 'Post-materialists', to use Inglehart's term, value 'authenticity'; 'love'; 'being centred'; sensitivity; freedom; self-creativity, authenticity; and 'an experiential sense of self-fulfillment' as Anthony *et al.* express it.[11] Although Bauman does not use the term 'expressivism' in his *Postmodern Ethics* it is clear that his postmodern 'moral self' belongs to this mode of being.[12] Indeed, Turner, among others, also equates expressivism with postmodernity.[13]

The final and sixth characteristic treats the postmodern condition in terms of a *periodised* view of history. Jameson is among those who are prepared 'to grant some historic originality to a postmodernist culture', emphasising 'the enormous social and psychological transformations of the 1960s, which swept so much of tradition away on the level of *mentalités*'.[14]

Before attempting to ascertain whether this sixfold characterisation applies to the New Age, it is necessary to spend a little time introducing this – as yet relatively ill-explored – form of utopianism. New Agers themselves like to refer to 'inner spirituality'. In somewhat more detail, this is all about a highly optimistic, celebratory and radically expressivistic (being couched in terms of 'spiritual' rather than 'psychological') humanism, more holistic renderings emphasising the spirituality of the natural order *in toto*. Ultimacy – god, the goddess, the higher self – lies within. It serves as the source of vitality, creativity, love, tranquillity, wisdom, responsibility, power and all those other qualities which are held to comprise the perfect life, and which, when applied in daily practice, are held to ensure that all will become utopian.

In more detail still, New Agers think in terms of a basic *lingua franca*, what can be called the discourse of self-spirituality. A primary assumption, to use a favoured expression, is that 'your lives are not working'. This (supposedly) means that the (unenlightened) mass of society are victims of any number of negative habits and beliefs. For example, as formulated by the Breakthrough Centre in London, it refers to 'when you feel angry or depressed, in a self-defeating way, this is the result of negative or irrational inner-speech that you may not even be aware of . . . These evaluations are linked to earlier times, when they were instilled by force of painful experience.'[15]

Another assumption is that life can only work – and thereby enable the New Age to dawn – when contact is made with what lies within. Thus, Californian Jane Hundley provides an illustration of the experience after such contact has been made. She claims that 'beauty in the New Age is a reality of self-love emanating harmony, grace, and light in the world'.[16]

A third great assumption is that the adoption of a variety of practices can effect the transformational 'shift' from the contaminated mode of being to true selfhood. So Master Charles provides 'High-Tech Meditation' for 'the contemporary experience of human growth and transformation'.[17]

Other characteristics of the New Age relate to an *internalised* form of spirituality, *de-traditionalised* in discourse if not in practice. Authority lies with the *self*, or more broadly, the *natural*. This is seen in the fact that New Agers attach great importance to an inner-directed *self-ethic* which entails the exercise of *self-responsibility* and which, more generally, serves as a *'meta-"narrative"'* operating at the *experiential* level. Finally, de-traditionalisation is also associated with the movement's *perennialised* outlook.[18]

There is ample evidence that the New Age – if only in discourse – claims to be quite radically de-traditionalised and anti-authoritarian, even the voices of individual spiritual experts sometimes being regarded with suspicion. An excellent illustration of comprehensive rejection of external 'others' is provided by Adams and Haaken. Discussing 'the anticultural aspect of LIFESPRING' (an est-like movement) they write:

> *anticultural culture* refers to any meaning system or set of values that deny the legitimacy of meaning systems or values having their origin outside of the individual . . . those participating in an anticultural culture do not believe that legitimate values exist outside of themselves. Thus the prescriptions of others, of tradition, of experts, of religious texts, and all such external sources are not considered legitimate.[19]

Est is considered 'beyond "belief"' in its rejection of external – to 'experience' – formulations of authority. As an est graduate, Adelaide Bry, puts it:

> belief: a nonexperiential way of knowing, which often prevents you from experiencing and thereby accepting what's so; a preconception, usually a misconception, that you once learned and which keeps you from seeing what's going on right now; used in the expression 'belief system', which is a whole bunch of beliefs on a particular subject, such as 'love', 'success', 'Mother'.[20]

Finally, it may be noted how leading British New Ager, Sir George Trevelyan, does not expect others to heed his wisdom as though it were authoritative. Perry summarises how Trevelyan thinks people should respond to his views: 'this is what things look like to me. If it doesn't seem like that to you, you don't have to accept what I say. Only accept what rings true to your own Inner Self.'[21]

Certainly, it appears that the New Age is quite radically de-traditionalised. It rejects established traditions (Christian commandments, for example) but also those 'mini-traditions' known as 'beliefs'. It claims that even those who appear to speak with wisdom should not be heeded: unless, that is, their utterances have been tested by way of personal experience. As authority has to come from somewhere, de-traditionalisation goes hand-in-glove with the deployment of the inner-directed Self-ethic. As Ma Satya Bharti, citing Bhagwan Shree Rajneesh, states, 'Seeker of truth, follow no path . . . The truth is here.' She adds, 'within you. Within your desires and your motivations. Within the dark, undiscovered jungle of your unconscious. Out of the mud, the lotus grows. A spontaneous flowering. A benediction.'[22] The rejection of external voices of authority entails reliance on what is taken to be the only reliably authentic 'voice', that provided by the inner spiritual realm. The following are offered as examples. Thus, Vivianne Crowley commenting on 'the [Wiccan] truth of the Great Mother Charge', claims that 'if that which thou seekest thou findest not within thee thou will never find it without thee'.[23] Californian Sheila states, 'I believe in God . . . My faith has carried me a long way. It's Sheilaism. Just my own little voice.'[24] An est trainer, discussing Werner Erhard, makes the point that he 'is coming from a place beyond Mind, from Self, and from a conviction that the Self is able to act appropriately without benefit of patterns and programs'.[25] A brochure of 'The Life Training' affirms, 'a "Kairos" moment [is one] in which you will make your choice, out of your own sense of what is right for you at this time in your life'.[26] Finally, a leading Theosophist Radha Burnier has stated, 'action is not made right by the rules of society or the codes of behaviour approved by convention. Right action issues from a mind which has discarded the notion of "I", the false personality, and shed the fetters forged by self-seeking.'[27]

A central question emerges at this point: is the New Age postmodern? Six ways of characterising postmodernity were introduced earlier, with claims concerning de-differentiation, relativism, milder and stronger versions of postmodern consumer culture, utilitarian selfhood, expressivism and a periodised view of history. On the surface *all* of these would appear to apply to the New Age, rendering it postmodern. First, de-differentiation is a major theme of the movement. In most versions of New Age thought, inner spirituality does not acknowledge difference. All people are held to share the same inner spirituality, together with the spirituality of the natural order as a whole. It is not a matter of having the same in the sense of serial identity, but of belonging to 'oneness'.[28] Furthermore, differences between various religions are dismissed on the grounds that they are tradition-informed. The de-traditionalisation of the tradition-informed, with associated de-differentation, ensures that all religions are held, in perennialist fashion, to be about the same experiential wisdom.

Second, relativism appears to be another closely related major theme. New Agers draw on an extraordinarily diverse range of apparently contradictory religions (theistic as well as monistic). As Harris suggests, this can lead commentators to conclude that participants 'swim in a sea of muddy relativism where every religion is equal and every ideology worthy of respect'.[29]

Third, it can be argued that the New Age enters into the relatively mild kind of postmodern consumer culture charted by Savage *et al.*[30] De-traditionalisation and associated de-differentiation of New Age practices enable people to participate in 'shamanic' weekends, followed by some 'Zen' or 'yoga', and then a visit to some 'Christian'-inspired centre. Because the New Age lacks tradition-informed 'depth' and is devoid of tradition-informed demands for exclusivistic commitment, its components can be drawn upon or utilised in ways which are incoherent from the point of view of traditionalists.

A certain amount of evidence suggests that some combine New Age(y) pursuits with other, apparently contradictory, consumer activities. Thus, Savage *et al.* draw attention to those private sector professionals and specialists who adopt a 'health-with-champagne' lifestyle, the 'health' component including 'yoga'.[31] It can be claimed that 'Champneys "spirituality"' – as it might be called after the pre-eminent health resort where yoga and Tai Chi Chuan, etc., are combined with champagne possibilities – is postmodern. This is not simply because it is disorganised but because what is on offer is treated (to recall Savage *et al.*) in a '"depthless", pastiche, manner'. It is 'depthless' precisely because it is also incoherent. One cannot take one's yoga very seriously if one also indulges in alcoholic drinks; for this suggests that yoga has now become a way of pleasuring the self, an entertainment.[32]

Fourth, and turning to that more extreme rendering of consumer culture – namely, that which is held to be able to 'disintegrate the subject into a flux of euphoric intensities' – it could well be argued that certain New Age provisions are akin to 'mood-altering drugs'. Participants might indeed experience 'euphoric intensities' whilst engaged in rituals or seminars; they might experience disintegration, as many New Age practices involve quite savage assaults on the everyday or socialised identities of those involved.[33]

Fifth, if indeed the expressivist mode of being is postmodern, the New Age – as a radical form of expressivism – clearly belongs to this register. This relates to the sixth point, which echoes David Lyon's suggestion that the 'New Age is a religious expression of postmodernity' because (among additional considerations) 'both postmodernity and New Age are all about a new era'.[34]

The basic thesis of this chapter is that the New Age is not, in any significant or useful sense, 'postmodern'. Although the New Age involves, indeed positively encourages, the collapse of *cultural* meta-narratives, it also very much involves the amplification of an experiential meta-'narrative'. An inner 'tradition', that of timeless 'wisdom', is seen as having a common voice; as facilitating the same cross-personal promptings, intuitions, alignments, indeed words, which are, so to speak, inscribed 'within' it.

The operation of an experiential meta-'narrative' does a great deal to ensure that the New Age is not de-traditionalised in postmodern fashion. Thinking of this in terms of the criterion of de-differentiation, New Age holism must be balanced against the fact that it is also profoundly differentiating. Inner wisdom teaches that there is a world of difference between the realm of contaminated or false consciousness and the realm of the auratically authentic, natural and spiritual. Accordingly – and unlike the postmodern condition – the New Age has a relatively stable, uniform and prioritised set of values and experiences: inner tranquility *versus* outer distress; authenticity *versus* inauthenticity; creativity *versus* living life as a victim; and so on. There is little that is relativistic about these elements. Regarding issues to do with the postmodern consumer culture, we have seen that one of the reasons why Savage *et al.* apply the expression 'postmodern' to the culture which they have identified is that it shows signs of being disorganised if not contradictory ('health-with-champagne'). Another reason is its 'depthless' quality. Thinking of such claims in connection with the New Age, there is surely nothing disorganised about engaging in Eastern, Christian and Pagan practices and the experiential meta-'narrative' teaching that all these apparently different practices are actually serving the same goal. Viewed in a perennialised light, they are all serving one inner wisdom. Even supposing that some use the New Age as a consumers' delight, for pleasuring the self in depthless fashion, 'serious' New Agers would not be at all happy at being dismissed as hedonists. Their self-understanding would claim that the practices in which they are engaged take them far beyond the realm of utilitarian gratification. Finally, and thinking of the stronger 'disintegration-of-the-self' thesis, those who are imbued with the experiential meta-'tradition' of the movement typically appear to have obtained a strong sense of coherent identity, for example as a spiritual being or as a goddess.

The expressivist nature of the experiential meta-'narrative' also counts against the idea that New Age is postmodern. The reader will recall that Turner is one of those who equates postmodernity with expressivism. He is able to do this because he defines modernity in a particular way, namely 'as a process of rationalisation and secularisation within the context of an urban industrial civilisation'.[35] He suggests that 'oppositional movements', including the expressivist 'romantic movement', are postmodern.[36] This logic is defective in that it commences with much too narrow a view of what counts as modernity. Modernity is surely best portrayed in the fashion of Emile Durkheim, Robert Bellah or Charles Taylor: that is, as a complex of different modes of ethicality, clusters of values, or 'moral sources'.[37] It is not merely that modernity is much too complicated to be captured by definitions of the kind provided by Turner. More fundamentally, modernity has taken the forms that it has because it has involved the dynamic interplay of traditionalist, utilitarian and expressivist trajectories (to name but three). It follows that expressivism is as much a part of modernity as are the values of urban industrial civilisation. *Ipso facto* the New Age, as a form of expressivism, is not postmodern.

This leads on to the closely related point, made earlier by Lyon, that the New Age could well be postmodern by virtue of the fact that both 'are all about a new era'. Leaving to one side, for the moment, objections which might be raised against the very existence of a 'new' postmodern condition, my main worry is that very little is significantly 'new' about the New Age. As has just been observed, it is a version of the long-standing expressivist trajectory. Thus, Mircea Eliade wrote of those eighteenth-century *theosophes* who aimed to 'reintegrate man with his lost "Adamic privileges", i.e., to recover the primeval condition of "men-gods" ';[38] Huysmans' *fin de siècle* Paris had a distinctly New Age flavour to it;[39] E.P. Thompson discussed such tendencies during the last two centuries and before[40] and Norman Cohn takes us further back, to certain medieval millennarian movements.[41] This evidence – and much more – shows quite conclusively that the New Age belongs to modernity, and before. If this is correct, it can be noted and if the New Age is 'a religious expression of postmodernity' as Lyon claims, it follows that postmodernity belongs to modernity, and is not about a new era at all.

Two main objections have been raised in connection with the thesis that the New Age is postmodern. One hinges on the fact that the New Age is not de-traditionalised in the kind of way which supposedly results in the postmodern condition. The experiential meta-'narrative' of the movement, it has been argued, is held to provide verities, essentialised (and therefore secure) identities, a basis for making differentiating judgements, and foundational provisions for life-planning. As for the second objection, it has been argued that the New Age is quite clearly an aspect of modernity (and the pre-modern), it not being therefore necessary to conceptualise it as belonging to some 'post' condition.

It still might be claimed, however, that the postmodern condition has dawned, and that the New Age should be *theorised* accordingly. The objection to this move is that the postmodern condition – seen as a shift into a new era – has not arrived. For reasons which are too complicated to explore here, it is much more profitable to think in terms of a dynamic interplay between de-traditionalisation, re-traditionalisation, tradition-maintenance and tradition-construction than it is to think in terms of (nineteenth-century-like) periodisations.[42] One advantage of this point of view – that is, treating the (ill-conceived) term 'postmodernity' as merely signifying de-traditionalised aspects of the times in which we live – is that it is no longer problematic to find 'postmodern' characteristics, including its consumer culture, in the past.[43] Another advantage is that full recognition can be given to the fact that our times have witnessed the development of new(ish) traditions, not least (because of its direct relevance to the development of the New Age) Durkheim's 'religion of humanity'.[44]

There are yet more reasons for supposing that the New Age is far from being postmodern. These basically involve the claim that the New Age is more traditionalised and authoritative than might appear on first sight. As has already been noted, New Agers generally suppose that their lives are informed by what can be thought of as a de-traditionalised, inner-wisdom, 'tradition'. However, it can also be argued that the New Age tends to be associated with, indeed even encourages externally-informed or traditional voices of authority, together with those of a more individualised nature. This is seen in the role played by belief systems and belief-adherence; established codes of conduct; systems of guidance and duty; the exercise of individual leadership: all of a kind, it should be emphasised, which run counter to the basic expressivist and 'epistemologically individualist' thrust of the New Age.[45]

Rachel Kohn's observation that 'where radical subjectivism is encouraged among followers, radical authority will be exerted by their leader' would seem to be supported by a considerable amount of evidence.[46] Looking briefly at Findhorn, radical subjectivism – the self as authority – is well in evidence. In the words of Carol Riddel, 'the experience of the nature of the Divine is sought through contemplation, or through practices which turn one inward. What is discovered becomes the source of the morality of action.'[47] Talk is of 'spiritual management', of seeking to find ' "what wants to happen" by inner attunement'. Reference is made to 'focalisers', those who 'have responsibility without authority over others in their working groups'. They are seen as playing key roles. The language is 'of the heart' and the aspiration is to develop 'spiritual democracy'. There are 'few dogmas'.[48]

At the same time, however, Riddel draws attention to the fact that Peter Caddy's 'authority was virtually absolute', at least during the early 'patriarchal' days of the community. During the 1970s, 'authority' was increasingly exercised by the Core Group.[49] Without going into further details, one is left with the clear impression of a community torn between the ideal that it should be run by way of collectively shared but individually validated experience and the reality of hierarchically organised authority structures, often traditionalised around charismatic leaders. Much of the same tension, crudely between discourse and practice, can be found in many New Age communities, including, for example, the Programmes group of companies (London), Auroville (South-East India) and, with very much the emphasis on the authoritarian hierarchical, Rajneeshpuram in Oregon, during the earlier 1980s.[50]

More generally than community-focused evidence of this variety, it can well be the case that New Agers in general heed the supra-self 'outside'. As a whole, the New Age movement is routinised in the sense that it involves the operation of a relatively fixed, established order of things or 'timeless truths'. It could be the case that this is due to participants coming to 'attune' to the same spirituality, thereby facilitating the operation of a shared monistic ethicality. Although academics cannot pass judgement on such possibly ultimate matters, we have to bear in mind another probability, namely that the New Age is 'routine' because those involved have been appropriately socialised, thereby acquiring (relatively) similar substantive values, 'experiential' discourses and accounts of what has been wrong with their lives. From this point of view, the experiential meta-'narrative' of self-spirituality involves an internalised *culture*.

Many New Age groups and practices incorporate voices of authority external to the individual disciple that draw from tradition. For example, leaders like Peter Caddy, legitimating themselves by reference to their heightened spirituality, issue orders or sanction regulations.[51] Sometimes New Agers turn to channelling and astrology of a kind which enables them to receive wisdom and instructions from external spiritual agencies.[52] Another related instance is when the spiritual realm is seen as operating to regulate or guide human affairs.[53] There is also the question as to whether 'context setting' – the notion that certain conditions or rules can enable participants to discover their own autonomous spirituality – is actually an exercise in substantive supra-self directionality, a context serving to instil new beliefs, values and duties.[54] Finally, it could well be the case that New Agers decide what to value and how to act not by way of inner-informed truth-acquisition but because they are actually heeding the voices of all those who have become enshrined in what amounts to a traditional canon: one largely comprised of all those volumes written by, and about, the acknowledged spiritual masters.

Fredric Jameson writes of 'the unceasing overthrow of the objective forms that shape the life of man'.[55] S. Radhakrishnan, summarising the teaching of Ramana Maharshi, states that 'we are given here a religion of the spirit which enables us to liberate ourselves from dogmas and superstitions, rituals and ceremonies and live as free spirits'.[56] We seem to be in the same world in that both authors are writing of radical de-traditionalisation. But the first is making a claim about postmodernity; and the second was written – in language which would be called New Age if used in the West – by the Vice-President of India in the early 1950s. Assuming, as we surely can, that Radhakrishnan (or Ramana Maharshi) cannot usefully be thought of as postmodern, it can be claimed that radical de-traditionalisation need not result in the postmodern condition.

As should be apparent, little or no evidence has been found to suggest that the New Age should be conceptualised or theorised as postmodern. James Beckford's formulation of postmodernity, with his emphasis on disorganised de-differentiation, leads him to conclude that 'putatively post-modern forms of religion would embrace diversity of discourse and the abandonment of unitary meaning systems; cross-references between, and pastiches of, different religious traditions; collapse of the boundary between high and popular forms of religion; and an accent on playfulness or cynicism'. But the New Age differs in that it shows a considerable degree of unity in its basic discourse of self-spirituality; 'different' religious traditions are treated in perennialised fashion and so become (more or less) the same; 'serious' New Agers would insist that all their spirituality was 'high'; and they would deny that they were spiritually playful or cynical.[57]

It has been argued that the (putative) experiential meta-'narrative' or inner 'tradition', together with evidence suggesting the operation of external voices of authority, ensures that New Age beliefs possess a 'shape' with values, discriminations, discernments, judgements and order which do not accord with the criteria used in this chapter to characterise the collapsed 'culture' of postmodernity. It should be added, however, that other ways of characterising postmodernity can serve to designate the New Age in terms of this category.[58] Furthermore, to raise a final objection, the New Age has developed a prosperity wing, inner spirituality being put to use to improve the operation of the capitalistic system of production.[59] This development, it should be apparent, serves to locate the activities of a fair number of New Agers within that trajectory of 'utilitarian religiosity' which is a long-standing feature of modernity.[60]

Rather than concluding on a negative note, that the New Age might sometimes be used in 'postmodern' fashion, but, essentially, does not belong to this (supposed) register, it might be useful to turn to the other side of the coin, briefly indicating one or two of the ways in which the movement can be theorised in terms of modernity.[61] More exactly, the New Age can be profitably explored by thinking in terms of a number of well-established and pervasive cultural trajectories and processes.

Perhaps the most significant concern relates to 'the turn to the self'. There is little doubt that what Charles Taylor calls 'a form of individualism' has become an important aspect of Western culture.[62] This expressivistically-inclined version hinges on the notion that 'everyone has a right to develop their own form of life, grounded on their own sense of what is really important or of value'. Taylor adds, 'people are called upon to be true to themselves and to seek their own self-fulfilment'.[63] 'Self-determining freedom' is an important value.[64] To give another formulation of this mode of being, Edward Shils writes of a

metaphysical dread of being encumbered by something alien to oneself. There is a belief, corresponding to a feeling, that within each human being there is an individuality, lying in potentiality, which seeks an occasion for realization but is held in the toils of the rules, beliefs, roles which society imposes. In a more popular, or vulgar, recent form, the concern to 'establish one's identity', to 'discover oneself', or to 'find out who one really is' has come to be regarded as a first obligation of the individual.[65]

This kind of individualism, then, involves the ascription of value and truth to the self. Being de-traditionalised, the self has a 'metaphysical dread' of whatever might be imposed from without. The ideology of this entity is but a 'milder' (as more psychological or humanistic) rendering of the self-spirituality of the New Age. It can then be argued that the development of the New Age movement in the West owes a great deal to the cultural climate of the expressivistic self. Relatively de-traditionalised selves – if spiritually-inclined – quite naturally gravitate to de-traditionalised religiosity: to versions of spirituality-cum-ethicality which are internalised (the god/goddess within suiting those who attach high value to themselves or what they could be); and, conversely, to versions which de-value or promise to disregard external voices of commandment.

Another process has to do with that central feature of modernity, the liberal ethic. Premised, crucially, on the injunction 'respect the other', it is but a short step from 'we have our ways which we believe in, you have yours and we respect (most of) them' to 'at heart, all our ways are equally worthy of respect'. Then it is but another short step to 'at heart, all our ways are equally true'. For present purposes, ignoring what fuels this process, the point is that an historically demonstrable development, in collaboration with the shift to the self, has generated an ethic of humanity. Underneath cultural divergences, of a kind which cannot be 'respected' (the reason offered being that they belong to misguided or erroneous authoritative traditions) lies the 'truly human'. The perennialisation of what it is to be human – the shift from exclusivistic ideas such as those embodied in nineteenth-century evolutionary progressivism to the inclusivistic United Nations climate of 'all humans have rights, duties and obligations by virtue of *being* human' – has consequences for the development of the New Age. Its teachings, concerning the idea that there is a core truth – to do with being authentically human – at the heart of apparently different religions, reflect, as well as being directly bound up with, cultural assumptions concerning the idea of a highly valued 'humanity': a de-differentiated human-kindness beyond socio-cultural divisions. In short, the New Age, promising that it is possible to experience this spiritually-informed sense of humanity, is associated with a major, perennialising, shift within modernity.[66]

Having indicated some of the ways in which the New Age can be studied in terms of long-standing cultural trajectories and associated processes, it remains to make a final point. The interrelated processes under consideration, dealing with de-traditionalisation, the turn to the self, the internalisation and perennialisation of the sacred and of what it is to be human, as well as other processes, the consumerisation of sacred provisions, the shift from 'fate to choice', the apparent fragmentation of previously exclusivistic and institutionalised religious formations, are also widespread in the religious sphere as a whole.[67] Thus, James Hunter finds evidence of a turn to a Pelagian-like self within conservative American Christianity.[68] Reginald Bibby writes of 'fragmented Gods', the dispersion and consumerisation of unitary religious systems which had once elicited more exclusivistic commitment.[69] In a related fashion, Robert Wuthnow argues that 'religious expression is becoming increasingly the product of individual biographies'.[70] Alan Race nicely pins down aspects of de-traditionalisation, when he writes:

> the 'radicals' have inflicted a considerable dent on received tradition. Since the 1960s, numerous orthodox assumptions seem to have been undermined: the image of God as transcendent Substance . . . , realism in language about God . . . , the interventionist activity of God in the world . . . , the incarnation of God in Christ . . . , assured historical knowledge about Jesus . . . , normative Scripture untroubled by cultural relativity . . . , and the uniqueness of Christianity among the world's religions.[71]

If it is conceded both that the New Age is not postmodern and that it exemplifies most of those processes widespread within religion in the West, it becomes difficult to see what could be postmodern about religion *as a whole.*[72]

Notes and References

1. Scott Lash and John Urry, *The End of Organised Capitalism* (Cambridge: Polity Press, 1987), pp. 312–13.
2. Stephen Crook, Jan Pakulski and Malcolm Waters, *Postmodernization: Change in Advanced Society*, London: Sage, 1992, p. 57 and pp. 36 and 69; see also Scott Lash, *Sociology of Postmodernism* (London: Routledge, 1990).
3. Mike Savage, James Barlow, Peter Dickens and Tony Fielding, *Property, Bureaucracy and Culture* (London: Routledge, 1992), p. 129.
4. Stephen Crook *et al., Postmodernization, op. cit.* pp. 37, 55 and 221.

5. Ernest Gellner, *Postmodernism, Reason and Religion* (London: Routledge, 1992), p. 24.
6. James Ogilvy, cited by Christopher Lasch, *The True and Only Heaven* (London: W.W. Norton, 1991), p. 522.
7. Douglas Kellner, 'Popular Culture and the Construction of Postmodern Identities', in Scott Lash and Jonathan Friedman (eds), *Modernity and Identity* (Oxford: Blackwell, 1992), p. 144.
8. Arthur Kroker and David Cook, *The Postmodern Scene* (New York: St Martin's Press, 1986), p. 274.
9. Talcott Parsons, *Action Theory and the Human Condition* (London: The Free Press, 1978), pp. 320–2.
10. Ronald Inglehart, *The Silent Revolution* (Princeton, NJ: Princeton University Press, 1977). Meredith Veldman provides an innovative account of 'romantic protest', dwelling on the 1945–80 period. See *Fantasy, the Bomb and the Greening of Britain* (Cambridge: Cambridge University Press, 1994).
11. Dick Anthony, Bruce Ecker and Ken Wilber, *Spiritual Choices* (New York: Paragon House, 1987), p. 7.
12. Zygmunt Bauman, *Postmodern Ethics* (Oxford: Blackwell, 1993).
13. Bryan Turner, *Religion and Social Theory* (London: Sage, 1991), p. xviii.
14. Fredric Jameson, *Postmodernism: Or, the Cultural Logic of Late Capitalism* (London: Verso, 1991), p. xx.
15. Brochure, The Breakthrough Centre, 1993.
16. Jane Hundley, 'Beauty in the New Age or the Power of Personal Presence', in Sondrad Ray (ed.), *How to be Chic, Fabulous and Live Forever* (Berkeley, CA: Celestial Arts, 1990), p. 207.
17. Brochure, The Breakthrough Centre, 1993.
18. Useful additional material on the New Age is provided by James Lewis and J. Gordon Melton (eds), *Perspectives on the New Age* (Albany: State University of New York, 1992). Those of my publications which bear most directly on themes explored in this chapter include: 'Californian Self-Religions and Socialising the Subjective' in Eileen Barker (ed.), *New Religious Movements: A Perspective for Understanding Society* (New York: Edwin Mellen Press, 1982), pp. 69–85; 'Cults for Capitalism. Self Religions, Magic and the Empowerment of Business', in Peter Gee and John Fulton (eds), *Religion and Power, Decline and Growth* (London: British Sociological Association, Sociology of Religion Study Group, 1991), pp. 28–42; 'The Sacralization of the Self and New Age Capitalism', in Nicholas Abercrombie and Alan Warde (eds), *Social Change in Contemporary Britain* (Cambridge: Polity Press, 1992), pp. 139–66; 'The New Age in Cultural Context: the Premodern, the Modern and the Postmodern', *Religion* (special issue on 'Aspects of the New Age', ed. P. Heelas), vol. 23, no. 2, 1993, pp. 103–16; 'The Limits of Consumption and the Post-modern "Religion" of the New Age', in Russell Keat, Nigel Whiteley and Nicholas Abercrombie (eds), *The Authority of the Consumer* (London: Routledge, 1994), pp. 102–15; 'On Things not Being Worse: the Ethic of Humanity', in Paul Heelas, Scott Lash and Paul Morris (eds), *Detraditionalization: Critical Reflections on Authority and Identity* (Oxford: Blackwell, 1995), pp. 200–22; *Celebrating the Self. The New Age Movement and the Sacralization of Modernity* (Oxford: Blackwell, 1996).

19. Richard Adams and Janice Haaken, 'Anticultural Culture: Lifespring's Ideology and Its Roots in Humanistic Psychology', *Journal of Humanistic Psychology*, vol. 27, no. 4, autumn 1987, pp. 502–3.
20. Adelaide Bry, *est* (London: Turnstone Books, 1976), p. 175.
21. Michael Perry, *Gods Within* (London: SPCK, 1992), p. 147.
22. Ma Satya Bharti, *Death Comes Dancing* (London: Routledge & Kegan Paul, 1981), p. 118.
23. Vivianne Crowley, *Wicca: The Old Religion in the New Age* (Wellingborough: Aquarian Press, 1989), p. 219.
24. Robert Bellah, Richard Madsen, William Sullivan, Ann Swidler and Steven Tipton, *Habits of the Heart* (London: University of California Press, 1985), p. 221.
25. William Bartley, *Werner Erhard* (New York: Clarkson N. Potter, 1978), p. 174.
26. Brochure, 'About the Life Training', p. 1.
27. Brochure, the Theosophical Society, Adyar, Madras.
28. See Stephen Crook *et al., Postmodernization, op. cit.*, p. 49 on the dedifferentiated nature of the Romantic movement which, so to speak, lies behind the New Age.
29. Martyn Harris, 'A Meeting of Mind and Body', *The Daily Telegraph*, 24 May 1993, p. 19.
30. Mike Savage *et al., Property, Bureaucracy and Culture, op. cit.*
31. Ibid., pp. 116 and 120.
32. A good illustration of how the New Age can be used as a consumer good is provided by Marla Trump: 'I was in labour for 10 hours. I created a beautiful environment in the hospital. I had candles, a picture of me and Donald, I had my New Age music playing; aromatherapy, which is supposed to be very calming' (*The Sunday Times*, 13 February 1994). For more on New Age and 'postmodern' consumer culture, see James A. Beckford, 'Religion, Modernity and Postmodernity', in Bryan Wilson (ed.), *Religion: Contemporary Issues* (London: Bellew, 1992), pp. 19–21; see also Paul Heelas, 'The Limits of Consumption and the Post-modern "Religion" of the New Age', *op. cit.*, on 'spiritual Disneylands'.
33. See Paul Heelas, 'The Sacralization of the Self and New Age Capitalism', *op. cit.*, and 'The New Age in Cultural Context: The Premodern, the Modern and the Postmodern', *op. cit.*
34. David Lyon, 'A bit of a circus: notes on postmodernity and the New Age', *op. cit.*, p. 121.
35. Bryan Turner, *Religion and Social Theory, op, cit.*, p. xviii.
36. Ibid., p. xviii.
37. Emile Durkheim, 'Individualism and the Intellectuals', in Robert Bellah (ed.), *Emile Durkheim. On Morality and Society* (London: University of Chicago Press, 1973), pp. 43–57; Robert Bellah, *et al., Habits of the Heart, op. cit.*; and Charles Taylor, *Sources of the Self* (Cambridge: Cambridge University Press, 1989).
38. Mircea Eliade, *Occultism, Witchcraft, and Cultural Fashions* (Chicago: University of Chicago Press, 1976), p. 50.
39. See, for example, Marie-France James, *Esoterisme, Occultisme, Franc-Maçonnerie et Christianisme* (Paris: Nouvelles Editions Latines, 1981).

40. E.P. Thompson, *Witness against the Beast* (Cambridge: Cambridge University Press, 1993).

41. Norman Cohn, *The Pursuit of the Millennium* (London: Granada, 1970), especially ch. 9.

42. Matters are pursued by a number of contributors to Paul Heelas, Scott Lash and Paul Morris (eds), *Detraditionalization, op. cit.*

43. Concerning the past and claims to do with postmodern consumer culture, Rosalind Williams provides useful material in *Dream Worlds. Mass Consumption in Late Nineteenth-Century France* (London: University of California Press, 1982). Jacques Le Rider offers an explicit analysis, dwelling on turn-of-the-century Vienna: *Modernity and Crises of Identity* (Cambridge: Polity, 1993).

44. Emile Durkheim, 'Individualism and the Intellectuals', *op. cit.*, p. 48. See also Paul Heelas, 'On Things not Being Worse: The Ethic of Humanity' *op. cit.*, pp. 200–22.

45. The term 'epistemological individualism' is taken from Roy Wallis, *The Elementary Forms of the New Religious Life* (London: Routledge & Kegan Paul, 1984), p. 100.

46. Rachel Kohn, 'Radical Subjectivity in "Self Religions" and the Problem of Authority', in Alan Black (ed.), *Religion in Australia* (London: Allen & Unwin, 1991), p. 136.

47. Carol Riddel, *The Findhorn Community* (Findhorn: Findhorn Press, 1991), p. 25.

48. Ibid., pp. 93, 98, 60, 90, 32.

49. Ibid. pp. 77 and 83.

50. On the last, see Judith Thompson and Paul Heelas, *The Way of the Heart, The Rajneesh Movement* (Wellingborough: Thorsons, 1986); see also Lewis Carter, *Charisma and Control in Rajneeshpuram* (Cambridge: Cambridge University Press, 1990).

51. See Elizabeth Clare, Prophet of the Church Universal and Triumphant, spelling out how to live: 'Get down to the basics in life', and so on in this vein. See also Anon., 'Love, Marriage, and Beyond', *Heart* (Autumn 1983), pp. 29–33; 100–3.

52. It should be noted, however, that channelling is often understood to involve making contact with one's 'higher' or inner self and thus operates in a de-traditionalised fashion.

53. The School of Esoteric Studies provides an illustration, with an advertisment which states that:

> behind all constructive human effort stand the guidance and inspiration of the inner subjective government of the planet. Given different names by people in the East and West, such as the spiritual Hierarchy, the Masters of the Wisdom, and Christ and His disciples, or the Company of Illumined Minds, its members function as custodians of the Divine plan. They are watching over our evolution and guiding the destinies of mankind.

See *New Humanity*, February/March, no. 91, 1990, p. 10.

54. See, for example, Steven Tipton's discussion of what he calls est's 'rule-egoism'. Thus, 'acts of rule compliance and agreement are right, because they produce such ["experiences of well-being and satisfaction"] . . . in the

agent'. See *Getting Saved from the Sixties* (London: University of California Press, 1982), p. 185. For a similar point, together with a more general discussion of issues here under consideration, see Paul Heelas, 'Californian Self-Religions and Socialising the Subjective' *op. cit.* especially p. 77.

55. Fredric Jameson, *Postmodernism, op. cit.,* p. 173.

56. S. Radhakrishnan, 'Foreword' to Arthur Osborne, *Ramana Maharshi and the Path of Self-Knowledge* (Bombay: Jaico Publishing House, 1954), p. xi.

57. James A. Beckford, 'Religion, Modernity and Post-modernity', *op. cit.* p. 20.

58. For example, if the postmodern is simply regarded as that which comes after modernity, the New Age, as the name implies, is indeed that which aspires to bring about the 'post'. See for example, Houston Smith's usage in his *Beyond the Post-modern Mind* (London: The Theosophical Publishing House, 1989). Again, the New Age is postmodern in terms of some of the senses accorded the term by Charles Jencks, who includes 'the re-enchantment of nature' among his criteria. See his *The Post-modern Reader* (London: Academy Editions, 1992), p. 7. David Lyon, in an excellent discussion, also introduces criteria which would appear to render the New Age 'postmodern'. See his essay 'A bit of a circus: notes on postmodernity and the New Age' *op. cit.*

59. See, for example, Paul Heelas, 'Cults for Capitalism. Self Religions, Magic and the Empowerment of Business', and 'The Sacralization of the Self and New Age Capitalism', *op. cit.*

60. This is a point well-made by Louis Schneider and Sanford Dornbusch, *Popular Religion. Inspirational Books in America* (London: The University of Chicago Press, 1958).

61. Although, in previous publications, especially in 'The Sacralization of the Self and New Age Capitalism' and 'The New Age in Cultural Context: The Premodern, the Modern and Postmodern', *op. cit.,* I have explored the New Age in terms of the postmodern consumer culture, I am now much less happy with this move. As suggested earlier, matters are best seen in terms of relatively long-standing aspects of modernity.

62. Charles Taylor, *The Ethics of Authenticity* (London: Harvard University Press, 1991), p. 14.

63. Ibid.

64. Ibid., p. 27.

65. Edward Shils, *Tradition* (London: Faber & Faber, 1981), pp. 10–11.

66. An indication of the extent to which this viewpoint has become (relatively) mainstream is that Prince Charles has felt able to give it public voice. Reflecting on his future position as head of the Church of England, he recently said, 'I personally would much rather see it as Defender of Faith, not "the" Faith, because it means just one particular interpretation of the Faith which, I think, is sometimes something that causes a great deal of a problem'. See Anon., 'Charles: The Private Man, the Public Role', Granada TV, 29 June 1994.

67. De-traditionalisation, it might be noted, also involves the process of 'de-institutionalisation'. See Arnold Gehlen, *Man in the Age of Technology* (New York: Columbia University Press, 1980). The expression 'from fate to choice' is taken from Peter L. Berger, *The Heretical Imperative* (New York: Anchor/Doubleday Press, 1979).

68.   James Hunter, 'Subjectivization and the New Evangelical Theodicy', *Journal for the Scientific Study of Religion*, vol. 21, no. 1, 1982, pp. 39–47.

69.   Reginald Bibby, *Fragmented Gods* (Toronto: Stoddart, 1987).

70.   Robert Wuthnow, *The Struggle for America's Soul* (Grand Rapids: William B. Eeerdmans, 1989), p. 116.

71.   Alan Race, 'Orthodox Ripostes', *The Times Literary Supplement* (15 September 1992).

72.   Of course, there are a number of strategies for arguing against conceptualising and theorising contemporary Western religion as postmodern. An obvious one is to draw attention to the fact that apparently large numbers of people continue to be involved in much the same way as in the traditional past. For example, the longitudinal Middletown studies with Howard Bahr reported that 'there is no evidence of a decline in participation in *organized* religion': see 'Shifts in the Denominational Demography of Middletown, 1924–1977', *Journal for the Scientific Study of Religion*, vol. 21, no. 2, 1982, pp. 99–114. A second is to argue that, for example, there is nothing 'postmodern' about people exercising choice to put together their own religious '*bricolage*': see Karel Dobbelaere and Liliane Voyé, 'From Pillar to Postmodernity: The Changing Situation of Religion in Belgium', *Sociological Analysis* (51(S), 1990), pp. 1–13. Among other factors, it is highly likely that this is a long-standing feature of modernity (and before); Durkheim, for example, claims that 'there are no religious societies where, as well as the gods whom everybody is compelled to worship, there are not also others which anyone can freely create for his own personal use', and he goes on to refer to 'a free, private optional religion, fashioned according to one's needs and understanding': see W.S.F. Pickering, *Durkheim on Religion* (London: Routledge & Kegan Paul, 1975), p. 96. A third factor is that such '*bricolage*' activity is, in all likelihood, often less disorganised than it might appear, inclusivising-cum-perennialising tendencies ensuring that selected components can be taken to have much the same meaning. See Robert Wuthnow, *The Struggle for America's Soul, op. cit.*, for example p. 15.

5 The Goddess/God Within: The Construction of Self-Identity through Alternative Health Practices

Maxine Birch

The issue of the self and postmodernity generates questions of its social construction in an era of risk and anxiety. The fragility of the self in the context of postmodernity has meant recourse to therapy groups that enable narratives to be established and constructed. These self-help groups have become a feature of debate on postmodernity. Yet little attention has been given to understanding this process of the construction of the self and the holistic assumptions made in these therapy groups which partly belong to the alternative health field, but which also can be understood as alternative forms of religion. The belief systems embodied in these groups relate to the growth of an inner self, the goddess/god within. These involve facilitators and practitioners who construct a meta-narrative that challenges some of the domain assumptions of postmodernity. This chapter examines the practices of these groups and the facilitators who work with them in relation to debates on postmodernity. These alternative forms of therapy develop legitimation procedures that seek to challenge the assumptions of postmodernity.

The narratives explored in this chapter arise from written and spoken accounts of the facilitators who have devised and led the groups described. These facilitators fulfil particular roles discussed below. Four examples illustrate the structures of these groups.

First, Martha runs an introductory group on Re-evaluation Co-counselling (RC), which is a closed group that meets one night a week for 12 weeks. Access to the group is through advertisments and recommendations. The group is open to everyone, although an informal selection procedure operates at the initial interview with the facilitator. Once the introductory course is completed, the participant is then a member of the RC community and receives contact numbers of counsellors and a local news-letter. Re-evaluation Co-counselling is an international organisation and Martha is an accredited facilitator of this organisation. The information and structure of the group are set centrally by its founder, Harvey Jenkins, in North America. The group structure and formation of the RC community has formalised rules and regulations governing membership. The objective of this organisation is to bring everyone to a process of counselling so that all members are all equally able to be both the counsellor and the counselled. Payment to the group is based on a sliding scale. After the introductory course, co-counselling is then based on a reciprocal exchange. The RC local organisation continues to arrange workshops on specific issues open to any member.

The second example relates to Jill, an American trained facilitator of workshops, who follows Louise Hay's doctrine of 'Heal Yourself'. This handbook is published as a self-help therapy originally from North America but is now available in many high street book shops. The purpose of workshops is to provide help and guidance in using Louise Hay's methods. This takes place as a weekend workshop and is open to both sexes. Response is primarily through advertisement.

Third, Claudia is a trained practitioner in Chinese medicine and has been involved in Jungian therapy for many years. Through her own interest, she has developed a closed women's support group that uses the rhythms of nature and seasonal celebrations to explore what is happening in the lives of the participants. Membership is primarily through recommendation and new members are sought when old members leave. It is a continuous ongoing group that meets at the festival times of Michaelmas, Samhain, Candlemas, Mayday and Midsummer.

The final example is the partnership of Tony and Hy who have developed their own form of working from Jungian therapy called self-regulation. They run weekend workshops, called 'seed groups', every month. This group is open to everyone without prior selection on a come-along basis. Membership is flexible and predominantly through recommendations by friends.

These four groups form the main part of the wider ethnographic style of research that uses observer participation. These narratives are used in relation to a sample drawn from other facilitators who also promote self-discovery work. Allan runs a men's group and promotes nature and ecology as understanding the self in conjunction with Reichian therapy. This is a closed group for a fixed period or weekend workshop. Paul is the partner of Jill (a Louise Hay facilitator) and, although they do not run groups together, there is a vast overlap in their work and courses are often planned together. Jen works in California and is trained in Neuro Linguistic Programming (NLP), a formalised system of counselling to promote self-change and empowerment. Michael and Pat are a partnership and run groups together and weekend workshops combining a wide variety of approaches such as crystals, yoga, myths and legends.

The facilitators come from a wide variety of backgrounds before their work in the field of alternative therapy. Three of the facilitators have completed formal education to degree level. One facilitator has formal psychoanalytic credentials. Previous employment includes work in business, building and child care. The credentials of the alternative facilitators are based on their experience of discovering themselves through their own work and attending other therapies and in-service training when available. Three facilitators work together with their partners. Two of the other facilitators also have personal partnerships with people involved with similar work but do not work with them. The two remaining women facilitators are at present single. All facilitators use their homes as a venue from which to work and, in the case of the four partnerships, have developed their home to become a therapeutic venue. All facilitators can also be on tour, as they are invited by specific centres that host these groups. All facilitators work with individuals as well as groups. House ownership applies to two couples while the remainder live in rented accommodation. They are all self-employed and their ages range from 38 to 60.

From this diversity of backgrounds, their work exhibits a fundamental characteristic: the objective of self-knowing. Exploration of the self is deemed to offer the chance of individual change and this is promised to be an improvement. Excerpts from advertisements for these groups illustrate the point.

What we attempt to do in the group is to acknowledge and work with the internal process of self-regulation that keeps our mind and body in balance. (Tony and Hy, written introduction to the Seed Group)

This may enable us to gain deeper understanding both into and beyond our individual lives, in particular as women of today. (Claudia, written introduction in advertisement to the Women and Seasons group)

Explore any limitations or difficulties in this area and begin to attract more satisfaction and fulfilment. (Jill, written introduction in advertisement to the Louise Hay's Workshop)

The aim is to become better informed, a calmer and more steady human to deal with stress and perhaps shine with a light when all around is dark. (Michael and Pat, written in advertisement for group 'Weaving Your Spiritual Path')

The groups are advertised mainly in the following outlets: alternative directories, book shops, fairs and exhibitions and alternative Health and

Healing centres. An informal network of recommendations by both participants and practitioners in this field appears to outnumber the response to advertisments for many of the groups.

It is argued that this link between self-discovery and improved individual change suggests the location of these groups within the alternative health field. All facilitators share the alternative concept of health of the balance of mind, body and spirit in understanding the relationship between self-identity and the experience of well-being.

The primary focus of this essay is on the facilitators. Self-understandings of the role are illustrated, for instance, by Claudia. She says:

> I see myself as a facilitator, as a thinker about it and the one who lays the framework, who points to the awareness of the seasonal festivals. I have gone through a conscious journey of the seasons. So I bring a framework and I hopefully give impulses to people to explore this for themselves to understand. I always say to people I am not a therapist, as people must take their own responsibility for their reactions. It is a learning self-development support group. I hold it, but it is not in my control. I send impulses through the structure and people can use it for their own journey.

This quotation illustrates a consensus in the facilitators' approach to their work. First, self-discovery is seen as a journey that each individual makes. The facilitator can guide and teach ways and routes of this journey but each individual is responsible for the particular way they choose. Self-responsibility is central to this form of work. Second, all the facilitators develop their own particular framework or way of working. Even the facilitators that work along an already prescribed format such as in RC, Louise Hay and NLP, stress the importance of developing their own style. The framework of Michael and Pat's work and Tony and Hy's work demonstrates the freedom to develop and to select any knowledge and reference points that may be helpful to discover the self of the participants in the group. All facilitators have created specific terms with particular meanings. Thus, 'interface' refers to the meeting between the unconscious and the ego; 'inner directed movement'; the 'inner child, inner voice'; 'discharge, re-emergence' to the expression of emotions, and the resulting change from that expression; and 'dis-ease' to being uneasy with oneself.

The 'journey' and 'framework' show two vital aspects of this work: first, the selection and appropriation of knowledge and the emphasis upon experiential knowledge; and second, the self as something to be discovered which is fundamental to Western psychological therapies. Self-exploration and self-analysis are developed from Freud's initial concept of analysis.

A crucial component of Freud's work was the exploration of his own life.[1] Psychoanalysis depends upon the individual's responsibility to reveal hidden aspects of the self. The therapist's responsibility is to provide the analytical framework to understand the emotions and feelings uncovered. This position presumes that there is a hidden self waiting to be discovered and that this can be discovered by bringing the unconscious forward through language.

All the facilitators acknowledge an awareness of Freud's initial conception of discovering the unconscious in order to understand the self. While these alternative therapies acknowledge self-exploration as a means to reveal a hidden self, they also challenge the role of interpretation that the formal psychotherapies continue to portray. Jung is credited with this key change in the way of understanding the unconscious. Three groups in particular described their way of working as Jungian. The work of Reich and Adler was also mentioned. Jung, Reich and Adler are described as unorthodox: that is, as being located out of the more formalised accepted forms of practising psychotherapies.[2] In particular, Jung's system of knowledge is described as a metaphysical system that permits the inclusion of many forms of knowledge as well as the emphasis upon the individual's own understanding. This psychological understanding is combined with the concept of self from Eastern philosophies and spiritual traditions.

Central to the Eastern philosophy of Buddhism is the tenet that the self has a spiritual essence and that this is realised through various regimes and disciplines. The self, the internal, the subjective is paramount and less attention is paid to the world outside. This is highlighted by the Upanishad belief that influenced Buddhist and Hindu thought that 'the self is as great as the world and the world is in the self'.[3] Hence knowledge of this self is deemed to promise freedom through an altered state of consciousness referred to as enlightenment. In contrast to the conscious/unconscious division of the psychotherapies, the Eastern body of knowledge posits the existence of a hierarchy of consciousness levels. The ultimate objective is to achieve the highest level of consciousness that removes this self-understanding from the everyday practical level to a spiritual sense. For the Buddhist, unity is achieved by the state of cohesion between the Brahman and the Atman, the god and the human self. It is this spiritual sense of the god within the self that captures the message 'I am god'.

All the facilitators acknowledged Buddhism as an important influence. Four of the facilitators came to their groups from Eastern beliefs through the practice of yoga. Two of the facilitators had studied with an Indian guru. At present, four facilitators are in contact with what they term a spiritual teacher from an Eastern tradition. Two facilitators on this spiritual path now say they have achieved a certain state of consciousness where they are able to let go of the mind, the intellect. This enables them to be open to receive information from outside sources, such as spirit guides and life beyond earth. This is referred to as channelled information.

From these two major bodies of knowledge, Jung and Buddhism, the narratives of the facilitators describe a different sense of self and connection. The experience of the self is described in terms of phrases such as: the 'bigger I and little I' (Hy); 'the Me in everyone' (Jill); 'True self' (Allan); 'Inner self' (Martha); 'Core self' and the 'self is not limited to the body' (Tony). This understanding of self can only be felt and not taught, though the methods to reveal this inner feeling state can be conveyed. This process of self-understanding is described as a natural inherent ability to reclaim authentic feelings. The process may uncover the unconscious and different levels of consciousness. The facilitators' narratives include descriptions of realisations where an important understanding of this process has been reached and accepted.

These realisations portray this experience of self with connections to the universe, the cosmos and the environment. An important justification for touching this inner self is explained by the inhibiting restrictive nature of everyday social life. Society is described as: 'squashing everything down into a horizontal mode' (Pat); 'too many unspoken social taboos and restraints' (Tony); 'living in a world that makes no sense' (Claudia); and 'social life is characterised by fear, defence and boundaries' (Martha).

The metaphors of connection with life beyond the everyday social milieu accentuate experiential knowledge as opposed to socially constructed knowledge. These metaphors are described as: 'pure knowledge' (Jen); 'inner guide, inner wisdom' (Claudia); and 'information from within' (Tony). The term 'trust the process' used in all the groups describes the techniques of recovering this pure knowledge and inner guidance away from the social construction of the mind. It is described as coming to a 'true' essential state.

This selection and appropriation of knowledge from Western psychology and Eastern philosophy is seen in the practice of groups that explicitly link themselves to the objective of releasing unrealised potential. The psychologist Maslow is accredited with this sentiment of the Human Potential movement 'whereby people can find new ways to identify themselves and live a fuller life'.[4] This theme is linked to the Eastern promise of liberation. The mixture of self-discovery and self-empowerment reconstructs the self as an area of unrealised potential. The aim is to help individuals explore and realise a different state of consciousness away from the everyday practicalities of life. This process of realising this potential through therapeutic practice is referred to as personal growth.

In this study, self-discovery becomes the link between the personal growth and healing promises made by the facilitators and the groups they run. This is nothing new and a recent historical focus traces the link between personal growth and therapy which blossomed in certain alternative or fringe groups during the 1960s. The Esalen Centre in California pioneered the objective of 'a meeting place for different spiritual traditions and for the exploration of consciousness'.[5] This centre included a wide range of therapies from the humanistic psychology and psychoanalytical schools with Eastern disciplines such as yoga and meditation. At various points in its history, social practices that develop this objective of knowing the self as an improved state of well-being have received attention. One such example is Foucault's work on *The Care of the Self* that discussed self-examination and awareness practices in classical Greek and Roman culture.[6]

The present day groups and facilitators described in this study present the contemporary combination of such practices. The elements of realising a true potential through discovery of this inner self draws upon Eastern and Western associations. The facilitators seek to reclaim a spiritual identity of self described as 'true' in contrast to a social self that is perceived as 'false', 'constructed' and 'manufactured'. The emphasis on the spiritual notion of the self seeks to tap an inner power and wisdom that is referred to as the god or goddess within. In the selection of knowledge, this intention can use any belief from around the world, from indigenous cultures such as the North America Indian, to the resurgence and reclamation of Celtic mythology. Universal symbolism from Jung's psychology and the awareness of the environment and ecology is used to attach these beliefs to nature and in turn to the natural or the essence of being human.

It is from this broad sweep and selection that the facilitators lay a framework that enables the participant in the group to reconstruct narratives of identity. The analysis of the facilitators' narratives reveal how this reconceptualisation of a spiritual identity enables their discussion of gender and politics to be reformed.

The experience of spirituality is described by the facilitators in terms such as: 'touching god'; 'sense of peace'; 'the process of life'; and 'the core self in relation to the spirit, the void'. Even the practitioners whose framework is set by a more rigid centralised source and who adhere to a more formal psychotherapeutic discipline, as in the case of RC and NLP, share this belief system. The narratives portray a dissatisfaction with the experience of spirituality in the social world through organised religious systems. Thus some in the groups stated that: 'my religion was ripped away from me by the church'; and that 'we need to shed the frameworks given to us to live and believe, to regain the rootedness of what it means to be alive'. These comments express a belief that the experience of spirituality is something to be discovered within and is something in all. This spirituality continues to reconstruct gender and political identity. The experience of being a man or woman is therefore felt inside through this inner wisdom in contrast to the social roles of gender. It is fundamental to Jungian theory that each individual contains masculine and feminine aspects. The prime objective of these groups is to balance these parts and appreciate what it is to feel an authentic woman or man. Again legend, myths, and cultural beliefs are brought forward to aid the experience of this inner-directed gender identification. Political identity also becomes intermingled with this notion of spirituality. All facilitators directly link individual change with certain forms of social change. For example, the acceptance of Buddhist beliefs concerning interdependence and connection is linked with the ecological spirituality of healing the planet. It is felt that the world will only change with each individual change and any change in the individual will affect another.

From these descriptions, it is suggested that this continuous emphasis upon the inner self develops a particular belief system that brings forward many questions in the debate on modernity and postmodernity. A study of these therapy groups suggests that there is a distinct change of focus within the alternative health field. The analysis of the way that the stories are told and of their content suggests how these stories are being reconstructed. It also points to an understanding of why the format of reconstruction through therapy groups is increasing in popularity.

The reconstruction of the life stories depends upon the function of experiential knowledge in representing the quest of the inner self for guidance and wisdom. The facilitators attempt to promote the revelation of this inner self through the expression of emotions. This expression is encouraged through the various techniques of counselling, using movement, meditation, visualisations, guided imagery, dream analysis and exploration through creative activities such as drawing, and music. Whatever techniques are used, the revelation of the emotion involved occurs in the format of the confessional.

Each person revealed how they felt to another. This expression of emotions here relates to a sociological concept developed by Elias that combines two distinct ideas. First, the private expression, the feeling part, the intimate, is believed to represent the real person hidden inside.[7] In this context, the belief of the group is confirmed. Second, this expression of emotion goes beyond this private feeling through this shared belief by forming a whole relational component. Thus, it is suggested that 'emotions and the related movements or expressions are, in short, one of the indications that human beings are by nature constituted to a life in the company of others, for life in society'.[8] In this setting, this practice of the groups to encourage the expression of emotions shows how this format consolidates belonging and membership to the group. The group framework provides a very distinct set of guidelines where identity claims can be tested and reflected upon with a conducive audience. This set of social relations provides a different 'generative structure' or 'figuration' to reconstruct a sense of identity.[9] It reflects an overall belief in the inner self that guidance can be obtained from within, as opposed to without, from external voices.

Therefore, as with any system of beliefs, a social practice is organised around the sharing and consolidation of these beliefs. Initiation into the belief system is observed through the guidance of new members to the groups' structure. New members are encouraged to work with participants who are already well versed in the practice. The facilitators, in their endeavour to counteract the professional/client boundary, while acting as leaders, also take on the role as a group member where their intimate expression of emotions is also revealed.

Another aspect of developing this belief system is that the reconstruction of narratives enters the arena of transformation. The metaphors that guide the story change, hence the meanings can be transformed. This use of the term metaphor draws upon Rom Harré's proposition that there is something particular and unique to our personal being that permits us to express this individuality. Thus, Harré argues that 'personal being arises only by a transformation of the social inheritance of individuals. It is essentially a semantic transformation and arises through the use of cognitive processes typified by metaphor to transform social inheritance.'[10]

The facilitators provide many different and imaginative metaphors to reconstruct narrative identity. For example, the intention to tap this god/goddess within is a metaphor that imaginatively implies one's own power to create and to change one's identity, thus balancing the masculine and feminine aspects of a reconstructed life story. Reconstruction of life events transforms meanings previously attached to the phenomena experienced. The metaphor changes, so that the meanings are transformed and are reconstructed. The participants in the role of the confession re-tell past, present, and even realisable future life stories that bring together this possible revelation of a truer, a more authentic self. Identity is changed in relation to biography and its potential. These changing metaphors can be understood by exploring some of the characteristics associated with theoretical propositions of contemporary society perceived as high or late modernity or postmodernity.

One of the main characteristics of modernity concerns the proposition that this historical period has progressed in such a way as to constitute increased risks to our sense of security. From the recognition of global problems to local everyday experience, from increased economic freedom and choice of life-style, the problems of choice and responsibility are increasingly individualised. With increased risks, a sense of belonging appears more complex and unstable. The identity relations of work, personal and social relationships and environment appear more transient and in flux.[11] Thus it may be more difficult to gain a secure sense of identity. This is apparent in Giddens' definition of modernity where our social construction of time and space is constantly challenged by technological innovations, which correspond to the disembodied features of social activities and our increased self-awareness of identity and response.[12] Such characteristics of modernity suggest that it may be increasingly more difficult to gain a secure sense of self-identity.

The alternative therapy groups provide practices that transform the risks of these characteristics. The different beliefs engage a sense of connection that transcends the social milieu, using the fragmentation of time and space to support the belief in something beyond everyday life. The group provides an alternative setting for the experience of identity claims such as belonging, intimacy and trust. If modernity has created unstable reference points for this identity to be sought from friends, family and locality, the group narratives serve to transcend these identifications by providing the ability to connect these feelings within the group. Therefore the identity references become fixed in the group through the emphasis upon experiential knowledge. This experiential knowledge is the expression of emotions. This is then reconstructed into the revelation of what this experience means so new meanings are attached through the selection of knowledge that the group beliefs have shared and taught.

The facilitators account for the need for a sense of belonging and connection. Their own personal life events frequently refer to stories from the experience of work and relationships that bring unhappiness and confusion. Their values are questioned and the search for resolution from personal growth begins. By looking within the frame of an essential inner self the spiritual can perhaps reconstruct these paradoxes. As in the case of religious healing, the pain of the risks (such as divorce, redundancy and growing older) is transformed by the reconstruction of these life events as growth experiences that link knowing to the realisation of potential. One facilitator noted the development of an 'in house' joke shared by facilitators. The phrase 'Not another PGO' (personal growth opportunity), described someone coming to them in an emotional crisis.

So can the increased popularity in social practices that promote this inner search be explained as a direct result of the harshness of modern social life? The characteristics of modernity, as well as being transient and fragmented, present a culture without faith.[13] In the search for certainty in a culture without faith, the only route possible may be the one of privatised well-being.[14] The understanding of well-being incorporates every emotion and component of social life that is individualised. Removed from the confusion and risks of modern life and corresponding to the demise of public and communal life, alternative therapy groups offer an attractive promise through the promotion of well-being.

Secularisation theories denote modernity as a culture without faith. Within this secularisation debate it is argued that the decline of religious institutions permitted medicine and the practice of therapy to play an increasing role in the rational and scientific response to understanding everyday life, thus providing a new moral code of behaviour.[15] Thus theorists have proposed that the role of therapy from this development of medicine and its corresponding practice of therapy has become extended in our everyday lives. This is illustrated by the title of Reiff's work, *The Triumph of the Therapeutic*.[16] It is described by Illich as a situation where 'social life becomes a giving and receiving of therapy'.[17]

Perhaps these explanations exceed the impact of medicine in our everyday life because our conception of health is far removed from the absence of disease. The notion of well-being is explained further by locating this concept in the ideology of healthism. Healthism can be seen as the self-awareness of trying to maintain and improve the quality of one's life by taking on the messages of keeping fit and well from the holistic perspective of mind and body.[18] This permits the inclusion and development of psychological therapies that promote personal growth. These have an ideological property, serving to capture the meaning of how a set of beliefs is incorporated into everyday lives and indicating the part they play in the reproduction and transformation of ideas and cultural practices.[19] Well-being, as a belief and value, therefore is central in the delivery of healthism which plays an important role in the structuration of the social world. Alternative therapies enhance an understanding of cultural practices.

Two theoretical explanations are offered for the growth of these therapies in modernity. First, Christopher Lasch describes this growth as a retreat in a culture without faith, a route of withdrawal and conversion to a never-ending search for well-being. He suggests that:

as the world takes on a more and more menacing appearance, life becomes a never-ending search for health and well-being through exercise, dieting drugs, spiritual regimes of various kinds, psychic self help and psychiatry. From those who have withdrawn interest from the outside world except in so far as it remains a source of gratification and frustration, the state of their own health becomes an all absorbing concern.[20]

This is indicated in the growth of political and sociological comment on the decline in quality of our public and communal lives.

The increase of privatisation and individualisation amidst the globalisation of patterns of mass consumption and mass media presents the self-discovery groups as an attractive option where the promise of an authentic self alleviates the confusion of modern life. This option of life-style choice becomes another aspect of consumption. Thus, alternative therapies are described as the new supermarket of the self, the cult of the Californian self. Within these consumption patterns, the lure of a space to escape from the everyday routine and commonplace activities represents an area of individuality and of difference. Nevertheless, it represents a product just as much for sale as any other leisure pursuit.[21]

Second, while accepting the uncertainty of self-identity in modernity and the globalisation and privatisation of consumption, Giddens presents a counterargument to suggest that this is not a route for withdrawal from the social but a means of individual empowerment through the accessibility and reception of knowledge outside professional bodies. He asks:

is the search for self identity a form of somewhat pathetic narcissism, or is it, in some part at least, a subversive force in respect of modern institutions? The benefits of exercise and dieting are not personal discoveries but come from the lay reception of expert knowledge, as does the appeal of therapy or psychiatry. The spiritual regimens in question may be an eclectic assemblage, but include religions and cults from all round the world vastly more extensive in character than anyone would have contact with in the pre-modern era.[22]

This lay reception of knowledge can be seen by the development of the facilitators outside formalised health care. But it also needs to be related to the discussion about the collapse of cultural meta-narratives. Alternative therapy groups operate in the context of Heelas' argument on the move from other-directed to inner-directed notions of the self, from an authoritative to an emotivist culture, from truth commitment to relativistic judgement.[23] Lay reception of knowledge permits infinite interpretations that may well illustrate the postmodern concept of self through the difference of interpretation.[24] The facilitators who select and appropriate experiential forms of knowledge permit new ways of seeing the world. A plurality of realities and multiple meanings can be advanced in their framework of this reception of knowledge.

The postmodern condition embodies a contradiction of highlighting the homogenisation of identity through mass consumption and culture while also recognising the growth of specific minority groups that reclaim knowledge in the attempt to make sense of something special and unique.[25] Meanwhile, the deconstructionalist perspective demonstrates it may not be a collapse of the meta-narrative culture but just another narrative that seeks to gain legitimation in a new format. The analysis of power and knowledge formations provided by this analytical method of deconstruction permits the role of the facilitator to be considered. Could Giddens' optimistic account of the lay acceptance of expert knowledge deal with the role of the facilitators?

The fields of alternative health abound with new experts and different knowledge. Apparently, anyone can become their own therapist and counsellor. The question of individual relativity falls into abeyance when the power and knowledge formations of cultural relativism are the significant component of the analysis. As suggested above, the beliefs that surround the discovery of this inner self and wisdom structure a social practice which constitutes a cultural system. Understanding can only occur through the discursive practices taught to represent meanings. Terms like 'trust the process' become commonplace within these settings. The shared intersubjectivity of trusting this process now structures a whole set of meanings and relations possible. Each facilitator sets his or her own agenda and designs a style of practice even within the therapies that have a framework established by a recognised leader elsewhere, such as RC and Louise Hay's work.

The shaping of subjectivity can be described by the practice of becoming a group member and sharing the characteristics of membership. Each group has an initiation stage to inform new members of the practice expected of them. The experiential 'pure knowledge' also has its own hierarchical status. Participants who have been on this path or journey of self-discovery for a longer time are considered wiser and more informed. The knowledge bases of these alternative therapies do not require a passive lay reception but an active engagement where the ideas become integral to a proposed way of life. Hence all who experience this route of self-discovery can become appointed helpers and eventually facilitators themselves.

This is an explicit practice of RC where individuals who have done the training course before are requested to assist with the group. The RC facilitator uses these members to discuss and to plan the group. Louise Hay's work has a wealth of published material to initiate new members. The social setting of this intersubjectivity is placed in the framework of the responses expected in which the participant receives an informal training. Informality of training can lead to indeterminacies and confusion. It raises questions about how free is the discretion permitted in these groups in the exercise of guidance. Some explanations of the self might not be accepted by those who felt they knew more. The confessional style of the group and the demand for the reciprocal sharing of intimacy to reveal this inner self are also the means to judge, which governs the responses of the individuals. This leads the individual to a potentially vulnerable position of acceptance or rejection from the person listening. The listener's judgement is based on the encouragement of experiential knowledge. But this contains an unclear and diffuse property that provides a subtle formation of power which can be at the heart of the therapeutic relationship. Thus Rose notes that:

> in confessing, one is subjectified by another, for one confesses in the actual or imagined presence of a figure who prescribes the form of the confession, the words, the rituals through which it should be made, who appreciates, judges, consoles, or understands. But in confessing, one also constitutes oneself. In the act of speaking, through the obligation to produce words that are true to an inner reality, through the self examination that precedes and accompanies speech, one becomes a subject for oneself. Confession then is the diagram of a certain form of subjectification that binds us to the other at the very moment we affirm our identity.[26]

The concepts of 'technologies of the self', 'technologies of autonomy' and 'the therapies of freedom' that appear in Nikolas Rose's work are developed from Foucault's perspective of the private self, that experience of subjectivity is shaped and governed by power and knowledge formations.[27] The groups described here develop such a practice of shaping subjectivity by the role of facilitators and other members judged to be more experienced and aware of the responses expected by the framework of the specific group.

Whether Foucault and Rose would regard themselves as part of the postmodern tale is a further matter for debate. Their emphasis upon power and knowledge, however, reinforces the point that the construction of self-identity is dependent upon the social setting in which this self arises.

Therefore this inner self only receives its validity through the social practices of the therapy groups. The prominence of power and knowledge governing the experience of the subjective in postmodern theories suggests that no self exists and that the conscious and unconscious experience of subjectivity is the effect of power inscribed upon the surface. Therefore if no self exists we need to look for other terminology which Nicholas Fox informs us is a surface, a 'body without organs'.[28] The deconstruction of this governing and shaping of our subjective experiences exposes the tale of self-discovery in modernity as a fictional text, one of romanticism, where the self is not discovered or raised from its hidden depths because to discover the self is only to uncover the inscription.

Another key component of the postmodern debate is the self-awareness and monitoring activity of the individual.[29] This is linked to the central notion that the legitimation procedures of knowledge have changed.[30] We are now far more aware not only of extensive knowledge but of the ways it is produced and received. The frameworks generated by the facilitators are indeed another power knowledge matrix, but its change in openness and accessibility shows many possibilities. Whereas the priest in modernity was replaced by the professional, we now face the breakdown of the professional by the facilitator. The credentials of a facilitator on the experiential path of self-discovery cannot be judged by the same criteria employed in professional accreditation. This is a cause of much concern for professional bodies that wish the issues of responsibility and accountability to be governed on a formal basis. The EEC is at present bringing forward policies which control the use of the word therapist.[31]

The alternative health field setting provides many examples of heterogeneous claims to knowledge where no one claim has a privileged place. We may reached a state where anything goes and where Smart's comment is apt that 'heresy has become virtually a universal condition and that plausibility structures have become increasingly particularistic and open to challenge'.[32]

Study of the narratives explored by the facilitators reveals a strong cohesion in the belief of an inner authentic essential self. As the title of Michael York's Chapter 3 suggests, the alternative therapy groups are not 'a heap of broken images' but represent 'a change of heart'.[33] The challenge to the meta-narratives of Western medicine, and its corresponding associations with the definition of health and psychology, is made by the alternative conception of mind, body and spirit that underpins the understanding of holistic health. It also seeks a change in the legitimating procedures that permit the lay reception of knowledge. This leads to paradox as these procedures reform and reconstruct a very distinct and shared narrative.

The particularistic character of the combined experiential and selected knowledge remains continuously open to challenge. Nevertheless, underlying this point is the strong cohesion of the belief in the inner, authentic, essential self that reveals this inner wisdom and guidance of the god/goddess within. This strange companionship of cohesion and separation is perhaps the pivotal paradox upon which the postmodernty debate depends: the constant assembly of different ways of knowing within a clearly defined framework.

Notes and References

1. David Stafford-Clark, *What Freud Really Said* (Harmondsworth: Penguin, 1985). See ch. 10, 'The Profession of Psychoanalysis: Creation and Legacy', especially pp. 170–3.

2. J.A.C. Brown, *Freud and the Post-Freudians* (Harmondsworth: Penguin, 1985). Brown reviews the theories of Jung, Adler and Reich in comparison with the orthodox development of Freudian analysis. In particular, he draws attention to the critique of Jung's work as a metaphysical system: see p. 43. Brown highlights the argument that Jung's deductive reasoning lacks the logic and discipline necessary for the demands of a scientific discourse thus giving rise to the critique of metaphysics.

3. See James K. Feibleman, *Understanding Oriental Philosophy,* revised edition (New York: Meridian Books, 1984), Part One on the Philosophy of India, especially pp. 14–16 where he argues that the Upanishad system of thoughts, written between the fourth and eighth centuries BC, influenced all subsequent beliefs, the key influence being the identification of the Godhead as the self.

4. Stanley Cohen and Laurie Taylor, *Escape Attempts: The Theory and Practice of Resistance to Everyday Life,* 2nd edn (London: Routledge, 1992), p. 150.

5. Nevill Dury, *Elements of Human Potential* (Dorset: Element Books, 1989). This study examines the growth of the Human Potential movement and mentions the development of the Esalen Centre in California.

6. Michel Foucault, *The History Of Sexuality, The Care of the Self,* trans. Robert Hurley (Harmondsworth: Penguin, 1990) Vol. 3, pp. 51–9.

7. Norbert Elias, 'On Human Beings and their Emotions: A Process-Sociological Essay' in Mike Featherstone, Mike Hepworth and Bryan S. Turner (eds) *The Body* (London: Sage Publications, 1981), p. 120.

8. Ibid., p. 125.

9. For a discussion of the terms 'generative structure' and 'figuration' see Ian Burkitt *Social Selves. Theories of the Social Formation of Personality* (London: Sage Publications, 1991), pp. 185–7 and pp. 205–8.

10. The use of metaphor is developed from Rom Harré's work, discussed in Ian Burkitt, *Social Selves, op. cit.*, p. 67.

11. Scott Lash and Jonathan Freidman (eds), *Modernity and Identity* (Oxford: Blackwell, 1992). See especially introduction and ch. 1 'Why modernism still matters'. Marshall Berman has pursued this theme that modern society is uncertain and full of risk, although this has enabled people to be freer which creates a tension with the identification of the self. See pp. 33–58.

12. Anthony Giddens, *The Consequences of Modernity* (Cambridge: Polity Press, 1991), p. 53.

13. The term 'culture without faith' is drawn from Christopher Lasch's works, *The Culture of Narcissism* (New York: W.W. Norton, 1979) and *The Minimal Self: Psychic Survival in Troubled Times* (London: Pan, 1985). The term arises from Lasch's description of a narcissistic culture that promotes a self without faith. The self is placed against uncertain foundations which present fleeting images that are separate and specialised. He suggests that the ideology of personal growth is superficially optimistic as it is based on an insecurity of not knowing what the future holds for the next generation. Lasch terms New Age faith as 'the faith of those without faith' (see *The Culture of Narcissism, op. cit.*, p. 51.) This notion of lack of faith results in Lasch's description of a minimal self in his following publication that is preoccupied with the strategies of survival.

14. Christopher Lasch, *The Culture of Narcissism, op. cit.*, p. 140.

15. Malcolm Bull, 'Secularisation and Medicalisation', *The British Journal of Sociology*, vol. 41, no. 2, June 1990, pp. 245–61.

16. Philip Reiff, *The Triumph of the Therapeutic: Uses of Faith after Freud* (London: Chatto & Windus, 1966).

17. Ivan Illich, *Limits to Medicine. Medical Nemesis: The Expropriation of Health* (London: Marion Boyars, 1975), p. 123.

18. Robert Crawford, 'Healthism and the Medicalization of Everyday Life', *International Journal of Health Services*, vol. 10, no. 3, 1980, pp. 365–88.

19. Diana Adlam, Julian Henriques, Nikolas Rose *et al.*, 'Psychology, Ideology and the Human Subject', *Ideology and Consciousness*, no. 2, October 1977, pp. 4–56.

20. Christopher Lasch, *The Culture of Narcissism, op. cit.*, p. 140.

21. Stanley Cohen and Laurie Taylor, *Escape Attempts: the Theory and Practice of Resistance to Everyday Life, op. cit.* The notion of Foucault's Californian self (p. 21) and the supermarket of the self (p. 232) describes a new area of consumption.

22. Anthony Giddens, *The Consequences of Modernity, op. cit.* p. 123.

23. Paul Heelas, 'De-traditionalisation of religion and self: The New Age and Postmodernity' in this volume, pp. 64–82.

24. Ian Burkitt, *Social Selves, op. cit.*, pp. 103–5 where he discusses the Derridian theory of difference.

25. Barry Smart, *Postmodernity* (London: Routledge, 1993).

26. Nikolas Rose, *Governing the Soul: The Shaping of the Private Self* (London: Routledge, 1991), p. 240.

27. Ibid., pp. 240–58.

28. Nicholas J. Fox, *Postmodernism, Sociology and Health* (Buckingham: Open University Press, 1993), pp. 35–42. See also discussion of the term 'body

without organs' in Scott Lash, 'Genealogy and the Body: Foucault/Deleuze/ Nietzsche', in Mike Featherstone, Mike Heptworth and Bryan S. Turner (eds), *The Body. Social Process and Cultural Theory* (London: Sage Publications, 1991), pp. 268–70.

29. Zygmunt Bauman, *Modernity and Ambivalence* (Cambridge: Polity Press, 1991), p. 272.
30. Barry Smart, *Postmodernity, op. cit.*, p. 119.
31. Tom Huggson and Alan Trench, 'Brussels Post-1992: Protector or Persecutor?', in Mike Saks (ed.), *Alternative Medicine in Britain* (Oxford: Clarendon Press, 1992), pp. 241–9.
32. Barry Smart, *Postmodernity, op. cit.*, p. 126.
33. Michael York, Chapter 3 in this volume, pp. 48–63.

6 Religion and Modernity: The Work of Danièle Hervieu-Léger

Grace Davie

Danièle Hervieu-Léger has made an original and important contribution to the debate about religion and modernity. Drawing extensively from theoretical and empirical texts in the sociology of religion as it is practised in France, she provides many fresh insights into the major debates of the sociology of religion. The multiple strands in her work – most of which remains untranslated – are diverse but interrelated.[1] This chapter will refer briefly to Hervieu-Léger's early work; her two most recent publications will be discussed in more detail.

One aspect of her early publications, frequently in conjunction with Bertrand Hervieu (a rural sociologist), was concerned with the neo-rural communities of postwar France. This work can be divided into two phases. In the first, the inquiry focused on the attraction of rural life for young people from urban backgrounds, within which Hervieu-Léger explored the idea of a utopian community as a form of social protest.[2] A second phase of this collaboration, from 1979 on, was more explicitly concerned with religion. These neo-rural utopias, moving through radical forms of ecology to more distinct links with a range of apocalyptic groups, sought common genealogies to legitimate their experiences. One source of inspiration was the monastic tradition of Western Europe. A number of themes elaborated in Hervieu-Léger's later work were already opening up: the kinds of religiosity that are nurtured by and flourish in modern societies (the importance of a small community) and the forms of legitimation that such groups will use to justify their existence (the seeking of an appropriate tradition).

The emphasis on community can be seen again in a later series of case studies edited, this time, with Françoise Champion under the title *De l'emotion en religion: renouveaux et traditions* in which the authors looked at the role of emotional communities in the very diverse religious traditions that can be discovered in contemporary society.[3] These case-studies are wide ranging: they cover an assortment of mystical and esoteric communities (including some manifestations of the New Age), the emergence of Soka Gakkai in France, examples of renewal movements in both the Catholic and the Jewish tradition, an Action Catholique movement – the *Jeunesse étudiante chrétienne féminine* – and the Confrérie des Issawa, an Islamic group in Algeria. The very considerable variety within this collection is recognised, for not all such movements fit easily into a single theoretical framework. Common themes emerge, nonetheless, not least the problem of defining or limiting the field of study, which forms a recurring motif in Hervieu-Léger's work. In this particular volume, the question of limitation or definition presents itself as follows: how is it possible to distinguish religious emotion from any other kind of emotion? A whole range of answers emerges for there is no universally agreed definition. The authors recognise, however, that all emotion, including that experienced within the religious field, must be related to questions of socialisation. In other words, it contains a communal element.

The analysis of common elements in these case studies leads to an even more basic issue: the place of emotion itself in the contemporary religious scene. This raises some distinctive dilemmas. On the one hand, individuals, caught up by the emotional qualities of contemporary religious movements, are escaping from the dominant traditions which have shaped the religious parameters of Western society. In this way the emotional community represents a release. But, on the other hand, the experiences described in the collected case-studies demonstrate the extreme fragility of this type of experience. It is, essentially, a transitional phase and one that reflects above all the nature of the surrounding society. Very often the intensity of the emotion diminishes as the individual becomes reintegrated into an alternative community, religious or otherwise. Or, to put the paradox in a slightly different way, 'in every case, the emotional experience reveals itself to be both provisional and unstable; it may, first of all, mark a transition from the edge to the centre of a community, it may also indicate movement from the centre to the edge of a religion'.[4]

How should such evidence be assessed? There are, as ever, multiple points of view. There is one school of thought for whom emotional communities provide indisputable evidence of an active and vibrant religiosity, embracing individuals who are looking for meaning and identity in an increasingly fragmented world. They stand, therefore, as a counterargument to secularisation. But, Hervieu-Léger maintains, communitarian tendencies should also be seen as evidence *for* or *of* secularisation, since emotional or communitarian movements demonstrate, amongst other things, the breakdown of traditional religious controls. The result can be seen as a dialectic: just as one form of religious tradition shows signs of collapse, other forms of religious identity emerge to take its place.

These paragraphs, based upon the introductory chapter of Champion and Hervieu-Léger's series of case-studies, introduce in essence many of the theoretical questions present in Hervieu-Léger's single-authored works. The two most recent, *Vers un nouveau christianisme?* (with the collaboration of Françoise Champion) and *La religion pour mémoire* explore the emergent issues in considerable detail.[5] Together they form a major contribution to the debate concerning religion and modernity.

Vers un nouveau christianisme?, published in 1986 is a long book and, like all Hervieu-Léger's work, it is demanding, especially for the non-French reader. It is doubly so in this case, for not only does the mode of thinking reveal trains of thought unfamiliar to those formed in the Anglo-Saxon tradition, the book also draws heavily on French examples. Some background reading of the history and development of religion in France may well be necessary in order to appreciate fully the particularly sharp encounter between religion and modernity that has taken place on the other side of the English Channel.[6]

Like so much else in Hervieu-Léger's sociological reflection, the central thesis of the book revolves around a paradox that can be summarised relatively simply. Indeed it reflects the ambivalence already outlined with respect to religious emotion. By their very nature, modern societies sap the strength of traditional religions. Thus the notion that there exists a structural incompatibility between the demands of modern societies and the prosperity of traditional forms of religion is correct to a considerable extent. On the other hand, modern societies cannot exist without some form of religiosity. They require, and so generate, innovative expressions of religious life without which they could not continue in their present form. This paradox is easy to outline, but rather more difficult to expand, for it rests on particular understandings not only of religion, but of the notion of modernity itself. Each stage of the argument requires both elaboration and clarification.

Hervieu-Léger's work begins with the contradictory data concerning the religious life of Western societies.[7] First there exists abundant evidence to support the view that modern societies are destructive of conventional forms of religion, and particularly so in Western Europe. The marked fall in religious practice, the slower but nonetheless perceptible decrease in the numbers of people seeking the Church's blessing at the turning points of life and the collapse in vocations, both for the priesthood and for the religious life (a dramatic collapse in the French case), provide the obvious and quantifiable evidence.[8] With statistics such as these there can be little doubt that the Church (and in France this means the Catholic Church) has lost and is continuing to lose its control over the daily lives of most French citizens.

The counterevidence of religious activity is equally pervasive, however. It is to be found first of all in the wide range of religious communities, sects and cults more than adequately documented by the sociology of religion. A second, rather different source of supporting data can be found in the persistence of *religion populaire* especially in Southern Europe (it is largely a Catholic phenomenon), alongside the growing attraction of sacred places, both old and new, which are emerging (or re-emerging) as the *hauts lieux* of religious experience.[9] Once again the French can provide some impressive examples. On the traditional side the significance of Lourdes as a place of Catholic pilgrimage shows no sign at all of diminishing (the numbers of pilgrims increase every year). More innovatively, the establishment of Taizé as an internationally known religious community, drawing individuals and groups from every Christian denomination, is widely recognised. It is especially popular amongst young people.

A third source of information, the nature of contemporary religious belief, is more ambivalent and can be claimed by either side. Those rooting for the persistence of the sacred note the variables concerned with feelings, experience and the more numinous aspects of religious belief. These show remarkable resilience in most parts of Western Europe.[10] In contrast, those in favour of the secularisation thesis underline the indices which measure religious orthodoxy; these reveal a decline rather similar to that displayed in religious practice. In short, there is an abundance of data, much of which is contradictory and capable of many different interpretations. Conflicting data make heavy demands on sociological theory, especially in its search to understand the nature of contemporary religion.

What has emerged on the whole is a rather black and white pattern of reactions: on the one side the partisans of secularisation; on the other those convinced by the return of the sacred. Both views are held with equal tenacity and, very frequently, with heavy ideological overtones. Hence the following question emerges over

> the collapse of Christianity *or* the return of religion; the collapse of religion *and* the return of the sacred? The debate concerning the situation of Christianity in our supposedly 'secular' and modern societies – a debate which includes a strong undercurrent of polemic – focuses on these alternatives. For some, the religious impulse, if it exists at all, can only be a backward and irrational step, one that emerges in times of trouble or uncertainty. For others, the same step demonstrates the religious nature of man, a nature which has outlasted the triumphalism and illusions of positivism.[11]

Thinking clearly within such an atmosphere is not easy. Not all will agree with Hervieu-Léger's approach to the problem posed by secularisation, but many will feel she is asking the right questions.

How then does she begin to formulate an answer? Hervieu-Léger asserts strongly that there is no incompatibility between the vigorous and growing forms of religious life – whether in traditional or non-traditional contexts – and the nature of modern societies. In other words, she argues cogently *against* the school of thought which maintains that the upturn in certain forms of religious life in recent decades is a sign of modernity's disintegration or failure. Instead, she claims that such developments should be seen as the *products of modernity itself.* They are part and parcel of the process of modernity which is ongoing and open-ended. The argument becomes thereafter progressively more positive. Not only is modernity deemed compatible with an ongoing religious presence; as a form of society it is inevitably and intimately related to religious sensibility for it embodies, as part of itself, a sense of utopia and of utopian space. So long as the latter is present, the requirement for a religious dimension will be there. It follows that it is the nature of modernity itself, and more specifically its in-built and unavoidable contradictions, that form the crux of the whole presentation.[12]

To understand these contradictions, it is essential to grasp two aspects of modernity that represent its essence: the historical and the utopian. It is the historical dimension of modernity which is corrosive of traditional forms of religion, indeed of religion itself. Gradually, religious discourse is rendered redundant as answers are found elsewhere. On the other hand, the utopian dimension works in a different direction. It creates a permanent space or gap between experiences in everyday life and the expectations that lie on or beyond the horizon. Modern individuals are encouraged to seek answers, to find solutions and to make progress, to move forwards. As modern societies evolve, such aspirations become an increasingly normal part of the human experience. But their realisation is, and must remain, infinitely problematic, for the horizon will always recede. The image of utopia must always exceed reality and the more successful the projects of modernity, the greater the mismatch becomes. Hervieu-Léger offers 'the hypothesis that this ever increasing utopian space – ever increasing in view of the constant speeding up of knowledge and technology – becomes the space within which religious representations are constantly reorganised. Such representations are, however, subject to an equally permanent destruction by the forces of rationalism.'[13] Hence the paradox of modernity which in its historical forms removes the need for and sense of religion, but in its utopian forms cannot but stay in touch with the religious, for it is permanently creating the space which religion – structurally – is called upon to fill. It is, therefore, modernity itself that nourishes new forms of religiosity, just as it is modernity that is destructive of what already exists in this respect and what will exist in the future. The sense of movement and dialectic dominates the theory.

It follows, surely, in contradiction to other approaches outlined in this book, that contemporary expressions of religion should be seen in terms of the modern rather than the postmodern. Indeed, in a certain sense, an open-ended and mobile understanding of modernity as a process rather than a particular societal form renders the concept of postmodern very nearly, if not completely, redundant. It is true that the postmodern might, perhaps, maintain at least some significance in terms of the types and forms of religious life that are most likely to flourish at the end of the twentieth century, for their character will reflect a particular and identifiable form of society. The last few pages of *Vers un nouveau christianisme?* introduce this possibility. But Hervieu-Léger is cautious. She concludes by rejecting the notion of a *christianisme post-moderne*, arguing instead for a modified view of modernity. The sense of crisis following the collapse in oil prices is described as a 'modernité désutopisée' in which the religious (and here she is concentrating on Christianity), partially deprived of the space that it would normally occupy, must discover innovative ways of surviving. The emotional community appears to be one of the most successful in accomplishing this task.

One further aspect of *Vers un nouveau christianisme?* requires examination before moving on to its sequel. This relates to the discussion of how different branches of Christianity relate to the pressures and demands of modern society. Three chapters of the book take up this theme, the first of which is primarily historical. In all three the French example predominates. First of all, the contrast is drawn between the Protestant and Catholic churches of nineteenth-century France. Protestants exemplify the capacity not only to adapt to the emergence of modern France but to contribute wholeheartedly to the changes taking place, most notably in the field of education. Catholicism, on the other hand, displays a much more negative stance, a degree of intransigence to the point of non-cooperation. It is important, however, to avoid oversimplified divisions into political left or right. The underlying contrast requires a rather different formulation, in that 'the real line of demarcation lies between a protestantism, which thinks and speaks from the inside of modernity, of which it is a component part, and a catholicism which opposes modernity in all its forms – both liberal and socialist – and transcends whatever they have to offer'.[14]

How far does this pattern continue to hold in the contemporary period? For French Protestants, their very success in contributing to the emergence of modern France and identifying with its values raises a corresponding challenge: how are they to maintain their own theological, spiritual and political identity? The dilemma remains, very largely, unresolved. For French Catholics, the issues are qualitatively different. The transformations wrought by the Second Vatican Council affirmed those who welcomed moves towards greater cooperation with the secular world. It offered new ways of thinking and relating to society. More recent events have, however, re-opened this debate. The reassertions of conservatism, associated in particular with the papacy of John Paul II, have led some commentators to question the degree of transformation that had taken place in the post-conciliar period. Hervieu-Léger articulates the underlying question: 'might it not be the case that the theme of openness to the world – so essential to post-conciliar discourse – was, in the last analysis, only an ideological symbol? Underneath, the deep structures of the Catholic body – implacable in its opposition to modernity – remain intact?'[15] The discussion remains inconclusive for the time being. Without further analyses of Catholicism in general and French Catholicism in particular, the future is difficult to predict. An essential feature of this work must, however, involve a greater understanding of the person and influence of John Paul II, a truly charismatic figure.[16]

What conclusions can the Anglo-Saxon reader, either British or American, draw from *Vers un nouveau christianisme?* about the nature of modernity and its effect upon religion? A British sociologist nurtured in a noticeably different religious and intellectual atmosphere can learn a great deal from Hervieu-Léger's conceptualisation of modernity and its in-built contradictions, for nothing comparable exists in the English-speaking literature. In England, however, compromise and accommodation with modernity are more likely strategies than the choice between unequivocal support or open confrontation, a situation accounted for by a very different ecclesiastical history. In Britain, as a whole, a noticeably more developed pluralism at an earlier stage of historical development led to a greater sense of accommodation, not only between Church and society but also between Church and Church.[17] An Established Church, moreover, has conditioned the framework in which such negotiations take place. There is no British equivalent to the notion of *laïcité* (of neutral space) so central to French reflections about the role of the state. The catalogue of differences between France and Britain could, but need not, be elaborated. Indeed they should not be exaggerated for, despite such contrasts, the British case remains a European variant. It remains, more specifically, a variant to which Hervieu-Léger's analysis can be applied but in a necessarily modified form.

The American situation is altogether different, for the secularising process so evident in Europe has not occurred on the other side of the Atlantic. Alternatively, it has indeed occurred but in ways so different that the two cases cease to be comparable. Either way, it is hardly surprising that an increasing number of sociologists on both sides of the Atlantic are beginning to revise their understandings of European religion.[18]

Such revisions take the following form. The moderately developed secularisation of Europe, and of Northern Europe in particular, should not be seen as a prototype of global religiosity or as the necessary adjunct of modernisation. It is, rather, a special case, responding to a specific combination of economic, social and historical conditions peculiar to Europe. It follows, perhaps, that Hervieu-Léger's analysis is a particularly appropriate tool for the better understanding of the European case. It is less easy to discern its application to American society, where there has been no comparable drop in religious practice and where modernity interacts with religious life to form combinations almost unknown on this side of the Atlantic.

One of the ironies of modern religious life is that those institutions which resist, and indeed oppose, the developments of modernity most effectively appear to be those that flourish in the contemporary world. Conservative, uncompromising religions, both Christian and non-Christian, prosper in the late twentieth century; not only do they hold on to the members that they have already, but they succeed in attracting newcomers. The adapters, on the other hand, have increasing difficulty in remaining distinct from the surrounding society (a feature nicely illustrated by the French Protestant community). They become progressively compromised. There is, however, an alternative way of looking at this situation. The successful churches of contemporary society must, surely, both accept *and* resist modernity. It is the particular combination of variables which becomes the decisive factor. Hervieu-Léger's analysis of the historical and utopian aspects of rationalisation seems especially helpful in discerning what this particular combination might be. Those religious groups that edge too close to modernity itself must, inevitably, compromise their own utopian space. On the other hand, those that disregard modernity altogether maintain their utopian space; what they lose is their capacity to operate effectively within it.

Hervieu-Léger's second volume develops logically out of the first. The earlier book took as its central theme the reformulation of the process of secularisation. Religion was not so much disappearing from contemporary Western society as undergoing a more or less permanent process of reconstruction as it responded to an ongoing series of changes. The next stage, then, is to probe the logic of this reconstruction. What exactly is going on? It is at this point, however, that the sociologist falters for how, precisely, is he or she to proceed with this extremely difficult task without the conceptual tools appropriate (indeed, necessary) for the job? It is this conceptual challenge that *La religion pour mémoire* seeks both to elucidate and to answer. In so doing Hervieu-Léger opens up the second side of the religion and modernity debate. If her first book analysed in considerable detail the nature of modernity, the second concentrates on the concept of religion. More specifically it tackles one of the oldest questions in the sub-discipline of the sociology of religion, and that is the definition of religion itself.

Sociologists of religion have grappled with definitional issues from the outset and rightly so, for the answers that emerge from their debates depend very largely on the precise conceptualisation of the subject that they have chosen to adopt. There are two possible approaches to definitions of religion. The first one opts for an inclusive approach to religion. It encompasses within itself all systems of meaning by which individuals, groups or societies attempt to make sense of their experience. The second is much more restrictive and includes only those meaning systems which invoke the symbols, references and beliefs (and especially supernatural beliefs) which belong to the historic religious traditions. The first definition is broadly synonymous with a functional view of religion (what religion does); the second pays far greater attention to substantive issues (what religion is). Both views have advantages and disadvantages but the debate between them has become sterile and repetitive. In many ways it echoes the debate about secularisation itself. Those who define religion according to the content of belief and the ritual practices connected to this tend to view society as becoming increasingly secular. There is a good chance, however, that they will miss the possibly religious character of a set of phenomena which would at the very least fit the Durkheimian description of the sacred. On the other hand there are those who consider all responses given by men or women to the ultimate questions concerning life, death and suffering as religious, in which case they are most unlikely to perceive growing trends towards secularisation. It becomes, however, ever more difficult within such a framework to distinguish the specifically religious from any other meaning system, of which there are – potentially – an enormous number.

The key chapters within *La religion pour mémoire* endeavour to escape from this circle, to find a new and creative definition of religion which will, amongst other things, initiate innovative lines of research. An answer gradually emerges in the form of a specific mode of believing; it is this which characterises the truly religious. It is, in other words, possible to specify a particular way of organising meanings and practices – a feature shared by the traditional religions – which can be identified as religious, but need not be confused with every type of meaning system. In coming to such a conclusion, Hervieu-Léger's approach is essentially ideal-typical. The ideal type she evolves takes as its organising axis some sort of reference to the legitimating authority of a tradition or a shared system of belief. From this point of view a religion implies, and calls into existence, a believing community. This can take the form either of a concrete social group (formal or informal) or of an imaginary genealogy, which maps out the generation of believers both in the past and in the future. The crucial point to grasp is the *chain* which makes the individual believer a member of the community – a community which gathers past, present and future members – and the tradition which becomes the basis of legitimation for this religious belief. From this point of view, religion is the ideological, symbolic and social device by which both individual and collective awareness of belonging to a particular lineage of believers is created, maintained, developed and controlled.

Having established this theoretical framework, the book turns back to the debate about secularisation, but from a rather different point of view. It confronts the following question: are modern societies less capable than the societies of the past of generating meaning systems characterised by this chain of believing, or – to use Hervieu-Léger's own word – of memory? And if so, why? It follows that modern societies may be less and less familiar with religion, not because they are more rational (quite clearly they are not), but because they suffer from collective amnesia. In other words they are less and less capable of maintaining a living, collective memory as a source of meaning both for the present and for the future. It is here that decline in religious practice becomes crucial. Episodic attendance at the turning points in life cannot replace the week by week repetition of liturgy which involves physical presence at a particular place and regular contact with religious personnel. Memory, however, does not disappear overnight and it is at this point that careful sociological analysis can clarify what is or is not happening in Western society as the twentieth century draws to a close.

However, Hervieu-Léger maintains that this is not the whole story, for it is equally necessary to take into account the very varied compensatory processes which emerge to fill the symbolic space which is, bit by bit, vacated by the major religious traditions. Or, to put this a different way, a range of small surrogate memories appears – multiple, fragmented and separated from each other – but which permit the construction of collective identities. Indeed the dynamic of rapid social and cultural change, which renders both individual and collective experiences ephemeral, paradoxically generates a proliferation in both calls for and establishment of 'small memories'. These are formed from bits and pieces; they can at times be invented. The later chapters of *La religion pour mémoire* document the restructuring of these 'pieces of memory'. It takes two particular examples: the upsurge of small emotional communities and the affirmation of ethno-religions. In the former, the argument rejoins a theme already outlined. In the latter, it reflects the changing nature of religion in the contemporary world, for the affirmation of ethno-religions both within Europe and outside this continent is an undeniable trend. It can, however, be extraordinarily varied in content. The illustrations from Europe, for example, range from the bitterest of conflicts in the Balkans to the understated sense of belonging within the Swedish Church.[19]

Two short extracts from Hervieu-Léger's other publications can be used to exemplify the major ideas of *La religion pour mémoire*. The first, already available in English, concerns the conscious efforts on the part of the Catholic Church to perpetuate the memory that it knows to be under threat.[20] Hervieu-Léger's study involves a close examination of the 're-evangelisation of Europe' campaign initiated through the course of the 1980s by John Paul II. The campaign has many facets. One of these, the emotional mobilisation of memory, is discussed in particular detail. Such mobilisation takes place primarily in the huge gatherings held in the presence of the Pope himself, in which he employs all the resources of his personal charisma. Such gatherings are, however, carefully staged. They take place, more often than not, in established Catholic sites, *lieux de mémoire* which embody the Catholic past. They are designed with a specific purpose to 'bounce' into the present, in an immediate and accessible form, the collective memory that used to be, but is no longer, part of a common culture. Young people in particular are targeted and respond in huge numbers whether in Rome (1985), in Santiago (1989) or in Czestochowa (1991).

Hervieu-Léger's empirical work on these young pilgrims is necessarily limited.[21] It reveals, nonetheless, the mismatch between the intentions of the organisers and the 'take-up' by the young people themselves. Not necessarily in conflict, the two points of view are interestingly different. To be more precise, the young people respond in an immediate and emotional way with little regard for history. It is the subjective experience that counts, not the authority of an institution or that of a cultural tradition. Part of this response relates to the nature of youth culture itself; it is not only in the religious – let alone Catholic – sphere that such experiential learning and reactions occur. Such responses must, nonetheless, colour the religious experience of young people. The memory inevitably mutates.

Papal visits draw together impressive numbers of pilgrims, including the young. But young Catholics form a tiny minority among the youth of France, most of whom have little or no contact with the discourse of religion, whether this be Catholic or anything else. Indeed, French young people will have even less knowledge of religion than their British equivalents, for the latter, at the very least, will have been exposed to some sort of religious education (inadequate though this may be) through most of their school lives. By contrast, the French system of public education has been rigorously secular since the separation of Church and State in 1905.

To suggest a series of classes or lectures on religious themes within a Paris *lycée* caused, therefore, something of a stir. Such classes were nonetheless well received by all those involved, for they filled an inevitable void in the French education system. Indeed, there were two voids: the first cultural, and the second more related to the changes in contemporary society. Both can be exemplified by extended quotations from the headteacher's introduction to the published version of these lectures. The first supplies ample evidence that the chain of memory in terms of traditional religion is perilously close to breaking among even the most educated of young people in France. The idea of a series of lectures on religion at the Lycée Buffon originated with the headteacher, whose observations can be found in the introduction to *La religion au lycée*. She stated that:

> in the course of conversations with students wishing to specialise in the plastic arts, I began to grasp their almost total ignorance of certain fundamentals of European culture. These students possessed some vague notions about Greek mythology, but had almost no knowledge of the Bible. How could they possibly appreciate either literary texts or works of art from the past without minimum reference either to scripture or to the Christian religion?[22]

The headteacher also expressed the need for a better understanding of alternative – even competing – memories; an ever more likely feature in an increasingly mobile and unstable world. She asked:

> how can young people today be expected to understand the events so widely reported by the media, without a better knowledge of the various cultures, very frequently religious cultures, that divide the populations of the world? How can they possibly comprehend the sometimes violent manifestations of fundamentalism in some Muslim countries, the passions and actions observed in various European countries – passions and actions directed against Islam or against Islamic communities – or, finally, the displays of antisemitism that have occurred in both Western and Eastern Europe in recent years?[23]

Either way there is work to be done, inadequately provided for by an educational system that eliminates discussion of religious or spiritual material. The place of religion in schools – both in France and elsewhere – becomes in fact a crucial area of investigation in terms of religious memory. It remains a sharply contested area in many European societies.

Inevitably, *La religion pour mémoire* is an exacting book to read for it struggles with conceptual issues that have proved intractable from the outset. It will be equally inevitable that Hervieu-Léger's reformulation of the definitional problem of religion and memory pleases some scholars more than others, for difficulties are bound to arise in the application of her new formulations.

The proposed ideal type, for example, takes as its organising axis some sort of reference to the legitimating authority of a tradition; a point of view which postulates the existence of a believing community, either concrete or imaginary, linking the individual believer to something beyond him or herself. Such links become a chain of belief, the crucial focus of interest. But precisely which chains are to be included or excluded in the definition of religion will depend once again on the judgements of the observer. There are bound to be differences of opinion as disputed and marginal cases catch the attention of sociologists.

There can be no doubt, however, that Hervieu-Léger's analysis offers a major step forward in the sociology of religion. The concept of memory as a way of looking at religion opens up new and creative formulae. For instance, one set of possibilities could include systematic and empirical work on the classic sociological variables of class, gender and race in order to discover which are the crucial groups in society who take responsibility for the creation, maintenance, development and control of a memory. In some ways, this kind of approach represents a new look at an old debate. It relates to Weber's preoccupation with the decisive social strata that were bearers of a particular religion.[24] More recent lines of sociological inquiry might pick up the themes of age and gender rather than those of class or status, for men and women quite clearly behave differently with respect to a wide range of religious variables. In addition, men and women have different responsibilities for the handing on of a tradition from one generation to another, a crucial task in the perpetuation of a memory.

Inevitably, this kind of thinking introduces the concept of generation, a critical unit of time in the understanding of religious change and one that both draws from and contributes to an analysis based on the concept of memory. For over and above the idea of time, a generation involves the sense of passing something on. A failure in this respect is noted; in other words it breaks a chain that should, it seems, be continued. But generation should also be seen collectively, for some generations appear to be more believing than others. Why should this be the case? What are the contingent factors that determine a greater or lesser sense of believing? The way is immediately open for a whole range of empirical studies that relate generational factors to wider sociological debate.

A second set of questions follows on; these concern larger memories, regional, national or international in scale. The analysis in this case can proceed in any number of ways: historically, empirically, quantitatively, qualitatively and so on. Two short illustrations will suffice to indicate the potential in this approach. One of these is quintessentially English; it concerns the reconsiderations of memory now taking place with respect to the English Reformation.[25] Prompted at least in part by the debate surrounding the ordination of women within the Church of England and by the associated uncertainties about the nature of Anglicanism, a whole clutch of books have emerged with a common theme. They look again at a pivotal moment in English history, Henry VIII's break from Rome and the establishment of an English Church. The author of one such publication, Christopher Haigh, encapsulates the underlying argument when he suggests that 'it was the break with Rome which was to cause the decline in Catholicism, not the decline of Catholicism which led to the break with Rome'.[26] This new orthodoxy, as it has become known, arises from a series of ethnographic studies which have sought to rediscover the essence of British religiosity in the early sixteenth century. And if we conclude – as many of these authors do – that Britain was indeed a Catholic country at this time, how then was the Catholic memory lost so completely and for so long? And why now, at the end of the twentieth century, should a different version of the memory begin to assert itself so powerfully? The answer depends on contemporary and sociological factors just as much as historical ones.

A second example refers to the question of Europe and its emergence as a global region in the post war period.[27] Once again the long-term historical view turns out to be crucial, for the religious factor has played a whole variety of roles in the creation and recreation of the entity that we have come to recognise as European. There have been times when a common memory was one factor which moulded the continent into a unity in which secular and temporal power were barely distinguishable. Later centuries saw this common memory disintegrate into a whole variety of national and regional variations in which competing religious memories became a crucial variable in emphasising difference. In the 1990s, as the Single European Act becomes, however tentatively, a reality; the situation alters once again and all sorts of possibilities might present themselves.

Examining these possibilities within the framework elaborated by Hervieu-Léger seems a fruitful approach to the some of the most crucial questions facing the European continent. The concept of *religion pour mémoire* has in this case an immediate and very practical application.

Notes and References

1. Danièle Hervieu-Léger is the Director of Studies at the Centre d'Etudes Interdisciplinaires des Faits Religieux at the Ecole des Hautes Etudes en Sciences Sociales in Paris. She is the author of some hundred articles in the sociology of religion, has written four single-authored books and has collaborated on a number of others. All translations in this chapter are by Grace Davie.
2. The idea of a utopia had already formed a theme within Hervieu-Léger's thesis (*thèse de troisième cycle*) on the Catholic student groups of the late 1960s and within a subsequent study of 'base communities' in French Catholicism. See: *De la mission à la protestation. L'évolution des étudiants chrétiens en France (1965–1970)* (Paris: Cerf, 1972) and 'Le développement des communautés de base et leur contexte religieux en France', *Archives Internationales de Sociologie de la Coopération et du Développement*, no. 31, Jan.–June 1972, pp. 2–48.
3. Françoise Champion and Danièle Hervieu-Léger, *De l'emotion en religion: renouveaux et traditions* (Paris: Centurion, 1990). The principal ideas from the introduction to this book can also be found in Danièle Hervieu-Léger, 'Present-day emotional renewals: the end of secularization or the end of religion?', in William H. Swatos (ed.), *A Future for Religion? New Paradigms for Social Analysis* (London: Sage, 1993), pp. 129–48.
4. Françoise Champion and Danièle Hervieu-Léger, *De l'emotion en religion, op. cit.*, pp. 14–15.
5. Danièle Hervieu-Léger (with Françoise Champion), *Vers un nouveau christianisme?* (Paris: Cerf, 1986), and Danièle Hervieu-Léger, *La religion pour mémoire* (Paris: Cerf, 1993).
6. Grace Davie, 'God and Caesar: religion in a rapidly changing Europe', in Joe Bailey (ed.), *Social Europe* (London: Longman, 1992), pp. 216–38. This essay provides a brief introduction to the French context. See also David Martin, *A General Theory of Secularization* (Oxford: Blackwell, 1978).
7. The most obvious source of data in this respect is the growing number of publications emanating from the European Values Study. An up-to-date list of these can be found in David Barker, Loek Halman and Astrid Vloet, *The European Values Study 1990–1991. Summary Report* (London/The Netherlands: The European Values Group, 1993). The American comparisons are included.
8. Hervieu-Léger's own statistics for this type of statement are taken from

French data, which offer a particularly striking example of her argument. See *Vers un nouveau christianisme?*, ch. 1, 'La fin des pratiquants' *op. cit.*, pp. 19–60.

9. Stephen Sharot, 'Traditional, modern or postmodern? Recent religious developments among Jews in Israel' in this volume, pp. 118–33.

10. The most notable exception to this phenomenon is beginning to emerge in the case of former East Germany. Here an articulate and destructive form of secularisation has resulted in a sharp line between the active participants of religious organisations and the non-believing majority. The middle ground – normally made up of moderately large numbers of nominal Christians – has in this particular case moved towards unbelief. See Allan McCutcheon, 'Generations, religion and the state: a cohort analysis of the newly unified Germany'; paper given at the International Sociological Association Conference, Bielefeld, Germay 1994.

11. Danièle Hervieu-Léger, *Vers un nouveau christianisme?* *op. cit.*, p. 9.

12. Ibid., pp. 223–7.

13. Ibid., p. 225.

14. Ibid., p. 259.

15. Ibid., p. 290.

16. It is interesting to note in this respect the detailed analyses of the Pope's visit to France carried out by a number of French sociologists of religion. See Danièle Hervieu-Léger *et al.*, *Voyage de Jean-Paul II en France* (Paris: Cerf, 1988) and Jean-Paul Willaime (ed.), *Strasbourg, Jean-Paul II et l'Europe* (Paris: Cerf, 1991).

17. For a full discussion of this point, see Grace Davie, *Religion in Britain since 1945. Believing without Belonging* (Oxford: Blackwell, 1994), pp. 14–18 and 93–100. See also Alan Gilbert, *Religion and Society in Industrial England* (London: Longmans, 1976).

18. For example Peter L. Berger and David Martin. For the latter, see especially 'The secularization issue: prospect and retrospect', *The British Journal of Sociology*, vol. 41, no. 3, 1991, pp. 465–74. The traditional dispute is well summarised in Steve Bruce (ed.), *Religion and Modernisation* (Oxford: Oxford University Press, 1992).

19. See Danièle Hervieu-Léger, *La religion pour mémoire, op. cit.*, pp. 228–37 for a discussion of post-1989 Europe in these terms.

20. Danièle Hervieu-Léger, 'Religion, Memory and Catholic identity: Young people in France and the "new evangelisation of Europe" theme', in John Fulton and Peter Gee (eds), *Religion in Contemporary Europe* (Lewiston/ Lampeter/Queenston: Edwin Mellen Press, 1994), pp. 125–38.

21. The empirical investigation involved a relatively small group of French pilgrims visiting Czestochowa in 1991. See ibid., p. 131.

22. Danièle Hervieu-Léger (ed.), *La religion au lycée. Conférences au Lycée Buffon 1989–1990* (Paris: Cerf, 1990), p. 7.

23. Ibid., pp. 7–8.

24. Max Weber, 'The social psychology of the world religions', in Hans H. Gerth and C. Wright Mills (eds), *From Max Weber: Essays in Sociology* (London: Routledge & Kegan Paul, 1961), pp. 267–301.

25. See Eamon Duffy, *The Stripping of the Altars. Traditional Religion in*

England 1400–1580 (New Haven and London: Yale University Press, 1992). For an excellent summary article of the scholarship in this area of revisionism, see Patrick Collinson, 'Reformation or Deformation', *The Tablet* (22 January 1994).

26. Quoted in *The Tablet, op. cit.*, p. 74.
27. For a fuller discussion of this question, see Grace Davie, 'The religious factor in the emergence of Europe as a global region', *Social Compass*, vol. 44, no. 1, 1994, pp. 95–112.

7 Traditional, Modern or Postmodern? Recent Religious Developments among Jews in Israel

Stephen Sharot

Many social scientists believe that the nature and magnitude of the economic, political and cultural changes that Western societies have undergone over the last two to three decades justify the use of the term 'postmodern society'. Although the depictions of the characteristics of postmodern society are by no means uniform, there does appear to be a fair consensus that the characteristics of postmodern society began to display themselves during the late 1960s and early 1970s. David Harvey pinpoints 1973 as a benchmark year: it was the year when the long postwar boom came to an end, and since then there has been a transition in capitalism ('from Fordism to flexible accumulation'), an intense phase of time-space compression, and considerable changes involving uncertainty and disruption in political and cultural life.[1] For Israel, 1973 was the year of the October or Yom Kippur War, a war that ended the feelings of confidence and optimism that characterised the Israeli-Jewish population after the Six Day War in 1967.

Israel's military victory in 1967 was followed by massive foreign investment, a considerable rise in the standard of living of large sectors of the population, and rapid changes in consumption patterns in imitation of the West. These economic changes may have been moving the society in the direction of postmodernity, but, although some religious Zionists had interpreted the Six Day War as a God-given victory that was part of the process of messianic redemption, for most Israelis the war had served to confirm the image of a society that had undergone successful modernisation and whose efficiency and rationality, at both the technological and social levels, had defeated the tradition-bound Arabs. The new riches and consumerism were making the socialist Zionist values of pioneering and egalitarianism appear increasingly outmoded, but the effects of economic changes on national symbols and ideology were contained within the triumphalism and renewed feelings of national identity and community that followed the 1967 war.

If part of the postmodern condition is a questioning of meta-narratives and a fragmentation of beliefs, then this condition was greatly accelerated in Israel by the Yom Kippur War in 1973. The questioning and criticism that followed the war went beyond the loss of authority and credibility of the Labour establishment and extended to new appraisals of the meanings of Zionism and the Israeli state. The relatively high level of consensus that had been reflected in the continuing rule of the Labour Party was shattered, and in the years following the war the society appeared increasingly fragmented along ethnic, economic, political, cultural and religious lines. Consumerism continued apace and a significant development in the compression of space and time took place with the introduction of cable television in 1991 with more than thirty, mostly foreign, channels instead of a single Israeli channel. These changes were no longer contained by consensus over national objectives.

Some explanations of recent religious developments among Israeli Jews have focused almost entirely on the Yom Kippur War and its effects. Beit-Hallahmi interprets such phenomena as the conversion of secular Jews to ultra-Orthodox Judaism, the widespread appeal of the occult, and the growth of new religious movements outside the boundaries of Judaism as 'roads to salvation' of those Israelis who reacted most acutely to the general crisis of the society that followed the Yom Kippur War.[2] However, his portrayal of Israeli society as changing over a short period from integration and consensus to disintegration, anomie, pessimism and feelings of hopelessness is overdrawn and overdeterministic. Life in Israel is often presented as being in a state of hypertension and chronic anxiety, but such exaggerated portrayals provide too-easy explanations of too many phenomena, ranging from the high rate of road accidents to conversions to ultra-Orthodoxy. The religious developments during the last two decades are radically different from each other with respect to their religious features and their social carriers, and it would be an oversimplification to present them as alternative solutions to a single cause. The strategy taken here is to compare the developments by asking whether they represent traditional, modern or postmodern phenomena. This can be seen as an initial step toward sociological explanations.

Four developments are considered: the revival of pilgrimages to the graves or shrines of saints on their anniversaries; the increased strength of ultra-Orthodoxy; the religious Zionist movement Gush Emunim (Bloc of the Faithful); and the new religious movements.

The *hillula* or pilgrimage to a saint's burial place was central to the religion of many Jewish communities in North Africa, especially in Morocco and Tunisia, but during their first years in Israel, following their migration in the 1950s and 1960s, Jews from North Africa appeared to be abandoning the custom. Cut off from the tombs in North Africa, the anniversaries were celebrated by small numbers in homes and neighbourhood synagogues. However, in the 1970s and 1980s participation in the *hillulot* (plural of *hillula*) grew enormously, and what began as small family gatherings became grand, massive events. Certain *hillulot* draw thousands who come to pray, to light candles, to eat, drink, dance, and to seek help from the saints to cure illnesses and overcome infertility.[3]

The saints that have become popular in Israel may be divided into three categories. First, there are the saints from the Talmudic era whose reputed graves have been pilgrimage centres from the early Middle Ages, but which have drawn greatly increased numbers in recent years. Second are the saints whose graves are in North Africa but whose souls are believed to have been relocated to new shrines in Israel. The most successful of these, which draws some 15 000 to 20 000 pilgrims on the day of the anniversary, began in 1973 when a forest worker dedicated a small room in his modest apartment in Safed to a saint buried in the Atlas Mountains. The worker related that the saint had appeared to him in a number of dreams and had indicated a wish to reside in his house.[4] Third, saints who emigrated to and died in Israel. The two largest *hillulot* of this type, drawing thousands of participants, are located in Beersheba, at the tomb of a rabbi from Tunisia who died in 1957, and in the small town of Netivot, at the shrine of a rabbi who died in 1984.[5]

The second religious development is the increased strength of the *haredi* ('God-fearing') or ultra-Orthodox community who are characterised by their traditional clothes and appearance, their use of the Yiddish language, and their comprehensive and strict observance of the religious law. They are concentrated in particular neighbourhoods, largely segregated from neighbourhoods of other Israelis, and conduct much of their lives within the confines of their own autonomous and semi-autonomous institutions. It is estimated that the *haredi* population in Jerusalem, which is their major centre in Israel, grew from 52 000 in 1978 to over 80 000 in the middle 1980s, constituting 27 per cent of the Jewish population of Jerusalem.[6] Part of this growth was a consequence of immigration, of natural growth (families are very large), and a small part can be attributed to the phenomenon of *baalei teshuvah*, Jews from secular or only partially religious backgrounds who are spoken of as 'returnees' to (ultra-Orthodox) Judaism. Of those returnees who were born in Israel, the majority converted after 1973 and their number was estimated in 1983 as 8200.[7]

In contrast with the *haredim* (plural of *haredi*), who tend to be either non-Zionist or vehemently anti-Zionist, the third religious development, the Gush Emunim movement, is Zionist in an ultra-nationalist sense. Its spokesmen and leaders have proclaimed that the Zionist movement, the establishment of the state of Israel, and the conquest and settlement of the whole of the Land of Israel are part of the messianic redemption of the Jewish people. Although the seeds of the movement can be traced back at least as far as the 1950s,[8] the movement was formally established in 1974 and its support from among the Jewish population has been impressive. The movement has not had a formal membership; it has had a core of two or three thousand families, from which its activitists, mostly students from the *yeshivot*, have been drawn, and a wide periphery of sympathisers and supporters.[9] Although support has come principally from the religious-Zionist population, it has also come from secular Zionist groups, political parties, and the Likud governments. Its settlements in the West Bank during the Labour government from 1974 to 1977 usually started as illegal activities which drew public support and succeeded in obtaining concessions from the Labour government. The movement's settlement activities were legalised when the Likud came to power in 1977. During the first Likud government, it continued to be the major force behind the settlement process when it established many small settlements thinly distributed over an extensive territory. The second Likud government changed the settlement pattern by building large urban settlements or suburbs which provided inexpensive housing near to the high density central zone, but Gush Emunim continued to be a significant force in the growth and expansion of settlements.[10] There has been some dispute over the impact of Gush Emunim on Israeli society. Claims that the movement has 'been responsible for a renewed debate concerning the nature of Zionism, Judaism and the state',[11] and that it 'has fundamentally influenced the fabric of Israeli society'[12] may be exaggerated. The movement can be viewed as an extreme formulation of wider changes that occurred in Israeli society.[13]

The fourth religious phenomenon, new religious movements of both the world-rejecting and world-affirming types, was a post-1973 development in Israel. A study published in 1972 listed ten new religious movements with a total membership of no more that 250. The movements attracted more members and became more prominent after that date, but they remained small and marginal to the major religious patterns: in the early and middle 1980s, when the new religious movements in Israel were at their peak, there were about twenty movements with a membership that probably never rose above 3000. However, Human Potential and psychotherapeutic movements, some of a quasi-religious character, have attracted large clienteles. It has been calculated that Israel has had the highest rate of Transcendental Meditation practitioners in the world.

A branch of est (Erhard Seminar Training), one of the best known of the Human Potential movements in the United States, was established in Israel in 1980, and by 1987 the number of Israelis who had attended its workshops had reached about 7500. Even more successful was the I Am organisation which started in South Africa and was transferred by its founder to Israel where, in the late 1980s, the movement attracted thousands to its encounter group psychotherapeutic sessions. The largest of the new movements, with a highly involved and committed membership rather than just a clientele, was the Emin, an esoteric group that grew in England during the 1970s and founded an Israeli branch in 1977 with a membership that was reported to be over 550 in 1983. The members of Emin are provided with various esoteric meanings of its name, pronounced EE-men, but it may simply be an abbreviation of a name by which the movement was first known, the Eminent Way. The movement draws its beliefs from occult traditions and combines them with concern over electrical pollution and emphases on hard work, frugality, and loyalty to the nation-state.[14]

A clarification of terms is a preliminary to a discussion of whether these developments may be characterised as traditional, modern, or postmodern. Traditional religion refers here to forms of belief that are legitimised by perceived identification or continuity with the past. Change or innovation occurs, but it has to be justified in terms of its replication of past practice. It is taken for granted in traditional societies that the religion of previous generations is being perpetuated. Conformity with the past is a relatively unselfconscious endeavour, and the very notion of the past, as a discrete phenomenon from the present and the future, may lack clear contours.

Reflexivity is particularly limited in those traditional societies where members have no conception of the tradition as something apart from themselves. Where reflexivity is more extensive, it is likely to be associated with literacy and to be focused on the clarification and reinterpretation of tradition. In the traditional Jewish community the less reflexive forms of traditional religious practice took the form of generational continuity within familial and community contexts. The more reflexive forms legitimised practice by reference to the sacred texts, collectively known as the Torah or *Halakha*. The rabbinate, the major conveyer of the written tradition, accommodated to change by producing additional or new formulations that were justified as inherent in the texts.

In place of the inheritance of the past, modern religion refers to the future as its major justification. Orientation to the future implies far more reflexivity than was the case in traditional society. There is a self-conscious selectivity of beliefs and practices informed by positively perceived trends that are believed to be underway in the present and to stretch into the future. Reliance on the past is understood as confining, but only in extreme cases does this take the form of a desire to abandon totally the religious tradition. Those parts of the tradition that can be accommodated to the new circumstances or justified in the light of present knowledge and expected trends are retained in a partial or modified form. Modern religions have endeavoured to be part of, or accommodate to, the grand narratives of the Enlightenment with its notions of progress and the application of rationally received knowledge.[15]

The development of Reform Judaism in the nineteenth century was the clearest expression of modernity in Judaism. It rejected the absoluteness of both the tradition of codes and the tradition anchored in the daily life of a traditional community. It was presented as a religion that expressed the universal ethical principles of the Enlightenment, fully in accord with the scientific laws of modern society, and suitable for Jews as equal citizens in a rational society. The move away from the legal and ritual dimensions of Judaism was represented as a break from the confinements of tradition, and its emphasis on a universal message, which was believed to have been expressed in an early form by the Jewish prophets of the Bible, conveyed a development toward an enlightened future. The Jews were 'chosen' in the sense that they had a mission to bring higher moral ideals to the wider society, and the realisation of the 'messianic hope' meant the establishment of truth, justice, and peace for all humankind. As individuals, Reform Jews could select freely those practices from the tradition that were found to serve their purposes or could be accommodated to their circumstances.[16]

Postmodern religion makes no attempt to justify itself in terms of either the past or the future. Although the past is ransacked for elements that provide nostalgia, it does not provide a coherent frame of reference, and no progress or comprehensive resolutions of problems are anticipated in the future. Postmodern religion abandons all meta-narratives or attempts to produce a coherent system of meaning and knowledge, and it brings together (in a consciously eclectic fashion) symbols, beliefs and practices from diverse sources, disembedding them from their original contexts of time and place. It rejects the possibility of arriving at an ultimate, immutable truth, and it embraces and celebrates what it regards as the segmented, ephemeral and chaotic nature of contemporary life. Cultural syntheses and social order are no longer considered plausible; conflicting values have to be entertained; and it is necessary to live the paradoxes and ambiguities produced by multiple worlds.[17]

Postmodern forms of religion, such as New Age movements, have remained small and marginal in Israel. The most successful forms of what is sometimes called postmodern religion are rejections of modern or postmodern society. The designation of 'fundamentalist' and other religious movements that attempt to regenerate or reconstitute traditional forms of religion as postmodern is confusing, and other terms, such as neo-traditional, are more appropriate. The choice of tradition by neo-traditionalists clearly involves reflexivity, but obliviousness to the radical nature of their strategies in reappropriating tradition enables them to present themselves as the conservers of traditional religion.

In the Christian context, the emergence of fundamentalist Protestantism in the late nineteenth and early twentieth centuries represented a reaction to modern religious trends, especially critical biblical studies, liberal Protestantism and the Social Gospel. At a later date, Protestant fundamentalism developed a broader critique of modernity in ideological and mass cultural areas and, although it directs attacks against what has been called 'secular humanism',[18] it may also be seen as a reaction to the relativism of a postmodern society, a society that legitimates diverse life-styles which are seen as an affront to Christianity. It is significant that it is the fundamentalist or neo-traditional religious movements, rather than modernist religious movements, that are the most vehement opponents of postmodernism.

In discussing anti-modernist religious movements in the Jewish context, it is important to distinguish between 'neo-Orthodoxy', which emerged in Germany as a rejection of Reform Judaism, and 'ultra-Orthodoxy', which emerged in Eastern Europe and directed its attacks against secular ideologies, especially socialism and Zionism, which began to gain support among Eastern European Jews in the later part of the nineteenth century. Whereas neo-Orthodoxy combined an adherence to the tradition of codes with an accommodation to what were now considered the non-religious aspects of the wider culture, ultra-Orthodoxy sought to continue the non-differentiated form of the traditional way of life. The ultra-Orthodox despised the neo-Orthodox for their adoption of secular education, linguistic acculturation, and accommodation to modern life-styles. The rallying cry of the ultra-Orthodox was 'all innovation is prohibited by the Torah', but in order to serve their cause of traditionalism they engaged in a considerable shaping, filtering and recasting of the tradition.[19]

It was ultra-Orthodox Jews from Eastern Europe who established in the nineteenth century the basic patterns of Judaism in what came to be known as the Old *Yishuv*, the pre-state Jewish society, in Palestine. They sought to establish a community devoted to religious prayer and study that was free of worldly matters because it was dependent financially on the contributions of diaspora communities. However, in the early decades of the twentieth century they came to be outnumbered by secular Zionists from

Eastern Europe who were in rebellion against the traditional way of life. These new settlers, who established what became known as the New *Yishuv*, believed that the Jewish people could only achieve 'normalisation' by a collective reconstruction of Jewish society within a national territory in accordance with scientific principles and universal values. The major institutions and dominant cultural forms of the new state were established by secular Jews, but the 15–20 per cent of the Israeli Jewish population who define themselves as 'religious' (roughly equivalent to the Orthodox and ultra-Orthodox) have often been prominent in the politics and culture of the society.

The Jewish religious population in the Yishuv and the state of Israel came to be divided between the anti-Zionist or non-Zionist ultra-Orthodox and the Zionist religious sector, but the vast majority of the latter remained Orthodox Jews and Orthodoxy (including ultra-Orthodoxy) is the only Judaism that is officially recognised and financially supported by the state. Jews from North Africa and Asia, who were unfamiliar with modernist forms of Judaism, were able to establish their ethnic congregations in conformity with the requirements of the Orthodox establishment.[20] As long as religious differentiation was in accord with the basic patterns of Orthodoxy, particular ethnic religious customs have been acceptable.[21] The Reform and Conservative movements have had little success in Israel. Their major support comes from the small numbers of Jewish immigrants from English-speaking countries. Thus, religious pluralism among Israeli Jews had tended to be confined within Orthodoxy and ultra-Orthodoxy. It should be remembered that prior to 1973 there had been very little religious experimentation in Israel.

Against this background of the unimportance of modernist forms of religion and the division between secular and religious sectors, we can now return to a consideration of the religious developments of the last two decades in Israel. How should these be characterised in terms of tradition, modernity, and postmodernity?

The first development, the revival of the *hillulot*, has been portrayed by the folklorist Ben Ami as the persistence of a tradition among Jews from North Africa despite their experiences of the modernisation of Israeli society. The initial influence of modern society had been to diminish the importance of the *hillulot* in the years after immigration, but this has now been reversed. The worship of saints had been so central in the religion of North African Jews that it is natural that it should be revived after the disruptive effects of migration had been overcome.[22]

The popularity of the *hillulot*, however, is not part of a comprehensive revival of the traditional culture of Jews from North Africa. In addition to the older first generation who remember the custom in North Africa, the *hillulot* have drawn younger Israelis of North African Jewish extraction, many of whom were born in Israel. Deshen took these points into consideration when he argued that the *hillula* compensates for the feelings of loss that accompanied diminishing levels of religious observance and the disappearance of the traditional way of life.[23] Weingrod suggests that the *hillula* is not so much a reaction to modernisation as a consequence of it. After a rise in living standards, and having undergone considerable acculturation to the dominant secular values and patterns of behaviour of Israeli society, Jews from North Africa now feel secure enough to assert their specific ethnic identities as Moroccan or Tunisian Jews. As an occasion for the gathering together of considerable numbers in celebration of part of their cultural heritage, the *hillula* allows North African Jews to express their ethnic identity, solidarity and power.[24]

In relating the *hillula* to tradition and modernity, these interpretations differ in their emphases and can be viewed as complementary rather than as alternative explanations. The *hillula* encompasses cultural themes which are continuous with customs in North Africa as well as practices acquired in Israel; it is a revival of a traditional custom which expresses a new form of ethnicity that emerged through participation in modernity. Its meanings with respect to tradition and modernity no doubt differ among its participants. For some, it is part of a traditional way of life which they seek to follow in many other ways; for others, it is just one of a very few customs with traditional meanings which they practise within a life-style that is otherwise modernised and secular. It provides a vehicle for many Jews from North Africa, who have abandoned a large part of the religious ritual, to express their respect for the tradition of their ancestors and community. Although it is not a postmodern form of religion in the sense that its participants are embracing a fragmented culture, for some it may be part of what has become a fragmented cultural landscape in which nostalgia for a past, which was never experienced, is conveyed as part of an assertion of an emergent ethnic identity.

In contrast with most participants of the *hillulot*, the *haredim* seek to conform to a comprehensive system of religious law which they believe was the way of life of the vast majority of European Jews prior to the incursions of modernity. The term 'neo-traditional' is an appropriate one for the *haredim* because they self-consciously represent and reassert what they regard as the authentic Jewish tradition against what they perceive as the threats of modernity. Ultra-Orthodoxy has spread to Jews of North African and Asian origins in recent years, but most *haredim* stem from Eastern Europe and it is the Eastern European communities of the past that provide the model for emulation. Secular defections from the Jewish tradition in Eastern Europe began in the last decades of the nineteenth century and most of the communities were destroyed in the Holocaust. In the post-1945 period the survivors have succeeded in establishing or considerably strengthening ultra-Orthodox communities in the West and in Israel.[25]

Menachem Friedman writes that it is inadequate to describe the *haredi* communities as remnants of traditional society. Ultra-Orthodoxy in the post-1945 world had to be constructed on the basis of voluntary communities in which there was a more overt commitment to a strict religious way of life than had been the case in the past when the traditional way of life was largely taken for granted. The improved economic circumstances made possible the support of *yeshivot* (educational institutions for advanced religious studies) in which a large proportion of male youth and young adults could focus on religious studies for a number of years. Removed from the concerns of earning a living and often sheltered from the pressures of families and local communities, the *yeshivah* students have stressed the most stringent interpretations of the religious law. The tradition of written codes has gained in strength at the expense of folk traditions anchored in the families and local communities, and younger *haredim* often supersede their fathers in their religious knowledge and strict conformity to the *Halakha*.[26]

Like other neo-traditionalist movements, the ultra-Orthodox are postmodern in their rejection of modernist ideologies and of the social and cultural features of modern and postmodern societies. The most radical *haredim* are vehemently anti-Zionist. They regard Zionism in all its forms, religious as well as secular, as a betrayal of the Jewish people's destiny and covenant with God. Zionism is viewed as a satanic force which is held responsible for the disasters that have befallen the Jewish people in recent times. The establishment of a Jewish state before the coming of the messiah is seen as a blasphemy which holds up messianic redemption. These groups believe that God placed the Jews outside the natural laws of causality, and that the attempt by the Zionists to integrate the Jewish people into the history of nations and to pretend that they are subject to the same socio-historical factors as other peoples represents a revolt against the Divine.[27]

Although anti-Zionist *haredi* groups try to avoid contact with the agencies of the Zionist state, most members have accommodated to the state. They attempt to defend and to increase religious regulations under the auspices of the state. Through their own political parties, they seek to attain preferential allocation of resources to their communities and institutions. But whether their stance toward the state is ideologically anti-Zionist or pragmatically non-Zionist, all *haredim* condemn the secular life-styles of most Israelis and seek to distance themselves from these. The message of the ultra-Orthodox that is emphasised by those Jews from secular or partially religious backgrounds who have become *haredim* is that the secular ideology of Zionism has failed and that secular Jews lead meaningless and directionless lives.[28] Thus, from the point of view of the ultra-Orthodox, it may be said that a modernist ideology has only led to a postmodern condition of meaninglessness, a condition from which the only escape is a return to tradition.

The third religious development, the Gush Emunim movement, is not a neo-traditional movement. Like the ultra-Orthodox its members condemn the penetration of what they see as Western materialism into Israeli society, but their solution is not to reconstruct or to emulate a past society. For Gush Emunim the First and Second Jewish Commonwealths (13th to 6th centuries B.C.E. and 2nd century B.C.E. to 2nd century C.E.) are positive historical references, but these do no more than foreshadow the messianic Third Commonwealth which they believe is at an important stage of emergence. Gush Emunim puts less emphasis than the ultra-Orthodox on the need for secular Jews to conform like themselves to the *Halakha* and emphasises instead the sacred meanings of recent and current historical events and processes.

Gush Emunim believe that secular agencies, and particularly the secular Zionists who settled the land, who established the Israeli state and who built up its army, have been instrumental in bringing closer the messianic kingdom. A crucial event in the process of redemption was the conquest of Judea and Samaria (the West Bank) in the Six Day War. The most important messianic task became the Jewish settlement of the historic Land of Israel. The secular Zionists failed to take up this task. It is now the turn of the religious Zionists to hasten the messianic process. Gush Emunim believe that the secular Zionists have fallen into a state of confusion, but they had been essential in the earlier stages of the realisation of the messianic vision. They were manifestations of a hidden divine process which they did not understand. They were 'saints despite themselves', consciously secular but essentially sacred.[29]

The appropriation by sacralisation rather than rejection of a modernism by Gush Emunim makes it difficult to characterise this movement in terms of tradition, modernity and postmodernity. The movement's ideologists have made reference to certain traditional messianic texts in order to justify their 'rational' form of messianism, but they have broken with the more traditional passive messianism of *haredi* groups who believe that the coming of the messiah is unrelated to worldly activities and political endeavours. Rather than seeing messianism as an antithesis of reality, Gush Emunim believe that the messianic process is rooted in reality which, moreover, is a modern one.[30] The movement is certainly modern in its means. In order to obtain the maximum possible resource allocation for its settlements, Gush Emunim has adopted a pragmatic and technocratic approach to political and planning systems.[31] But the movement's meta-narrative, in which both religious and secular Jews are placed, is hardly a modern one. The historical actors are seen as part of a cosmic, supra-historical necessity. They may be able to accelerate or delay the process, but the final outcome has been preordained by the divine. Gush Emunim is not an example of a postmodern form of religion, but it may characterised as postmodern in the sense that its meta-narrative goes beyond both tradition and modernity.

The most activist supporters of Gush Emunim were drawn from the sub-culture of religious Zionism. The membership of the new religious movements and the participants in the quasi-religious psychotherapeutic movements come principally from a secular background, from families who observe a few Jewish religious practices in secularised forms. The modernist ideology of socialist Zionism that provided an important focus of identity for many of the older generation has lost its hold among secularised Jews and appears outmoded in the postmodern world. Some of those who have searched for meaning and commitment in a fragmented culture have ended their search in the neo-traditionalism of the ultra-Orthodox. Others have joined new religious movements which draw upon religious traditions remote from Judaism.

The religious eclecticism of the Emin can be interpreted as a product of a postmodern culture. Its beliefs and practices draw upon several occult traditions and include a recognition of gods from several religions, reincarnation, alchemy, numerology, astrology, palm reading, aura reading and cleansing, animal magnetism and electromagnetic healing. The values of the movement include an emphasis on hard work, respect for the law, opposition to the use of drugs, sexual conformity and a strong patriotism toward the Jewish nation and state.

The disparate origins and eclectic combinations of the movement's beliefs and practices appear to make the Emin a contender for the category of postmodern religion in Israel, but the movement is best interpreted as a defence against, rather than an acceptance of, the postmodern condition. Although the movement's teachings may appear to the outsider as an incoherent pastiche of occult sources and the Protestant ethic, they are presented by the movement as a comprehensive counter-science that covers natural science, psychology and physiology. A concern with the defence of the self is expressed in the movement's fears of pollution and its emphasis on cleanliness, punctuality, and good manners. The formal dress adopted by its members, including suits and ties for men, indicate the English origins of the movement and make them appear out-of-place in the highly informal Israeli milieu.[32] Thus, the Emin appear to have drawn upon diverse religious and cultural sources only in order to deny fragmentation, to claim that they have the universal truth, and to defend the self by situating it within a strong group and grid.

Although religious developments among Israeli Jews during the last two decades have been in the direction of greater diversity and fragmentation, there is little (if any) postmodern religion in the sense of embracing discontinuity and fragmentation. The modernist socialist Zionist ideology and the identities associated with it have lost their power and attraction, and most secularised Israeli Jews have not sought a substitute. The search for a grand narrative and centred identity has been largely confined to the realm of religion. For some, the greater the diversity and ephemerality, the more pressing the need to discover a coherent and immutable truth. The revival of pilgrimages to saints' shrines has not been part of a comprehensive revival of the tradition of North African Jews, but the custom provides a sense of continuity with a valued past, and insofar as they constitute ceremonies of ethnic renewal, the participants celebrate their specific ethnic identities as part of the overarching Jewish identity. A more comprehensive reappropriation of the tradition is represented by the *haredim*, and those Jews from secular backgrounds who have joined them are portrayed as 'returning' to the 'essence' of traditional Judaism. In the case of Gush Emunim, both traditional religion and modern secular nationalism are encompassed within a single sacred narrative. The Emin move outside the Jewish tradition but only to construct their own overarching system which they present as entirely consistent with their identity as Israeli Jews. Thus, although the recent religious developments in Israel may be understood, in part, as products of postmodern society, they are not forms of postmodern religion.

Notes and References

1.   David Harvey, *The Condition of Postmodernity* (Oxford: Blackwell, 1989), pp. 30, 63, 124, 284, 327.

2. Benjamin Beit-Hallahmi, *Despair and Deliverance: Private Salvation in Contemporary Israel* (Albany: State University of New York Press, 1992).
3. Alex Weingrod, *The Saint of Beersheba* (Albany: State University of New York Press, 1990).
4. Yoram Bilu, 'Dreams and the wishes of the saints', in Harvey E. Goldberg (ed.), *Judaism Viewed from Within and from Without* (Albany: State University of New York Press, 1987), pp. 285–313.
5. Eyal Ben-Ari and Yoram Bilu, 'Saints' sanctuaries in Israeli development towns: on a mechanism of urban transformation', *Urban Anthropology*, vol. 16, 1987, pp. 244–72. See also: Yoram Bilu, 'Personal motivation and social meaning in the revival of hagiolatric traditions among Moroccan Jews in Israel', in Zvi Sobel and Benjamin Beit-Hallahmi (eds), *Tradition, Innovation, Conflict: Jewishness and Judaism in Contemporary Israel* (Albany: State University of New York Press, 1991), pp. 47–69; and Alex Weingrod, *The Saint of Beersheba, op. cit.*
6. Joseph Shilhav and Menachem Friedman, *Growth and Segregation – The Ultra-Orthodox Community of Jerusalem* (in Hebrew) (Jerusalem: Jerusalem Institute for Israel Studies, 1985).
7. Beit-Hallahmi, *Despair and Deliverance, op. cit.*, p. 60. See also: Janet Aviad, *Return to Judaism: Religious Renewal in Israel* (Chicago: University of Chicago Press, 1983); and Herbert M. Danzger, *Returning to Tradition: The Contemporary Revival of Orthodox Judaism* (New Haven, CT: Yale University Press, 1989).
8. Gideon Aran, 'From religious Zionism to Zionist religion: the roots of Gush Emunim', *Studies in Contemporary Jewry*, vol. 2, 1986, pp. 11–43.
9. Ehud Sprinzak, *The Ascendance of Israel's Radical Right* (New York: Oxford University Press, 1991), p. 107.
10. Gershon Shafir, 'Institutional and spontaneous settlement drives: did Gush Emunim make a difference?', in David Newman (ed.), *The Impact of Gush Emunim* (London: Croom Helm, 1985), pp. 153–71. See also David Newman, 'Spatial structures and ideological change in the West Bank', in ibid., pp. 172–82.
11. David Newman, 'Introduction: Gush Emunim in society and space', in ibid., p. 2.
12. David Schnall, 'An impact assessment', in ibid., p. 15.
13. Eliezer Don-Yehiya, 'Jewish messianism, religious Zionism, and Israeli politics: the impact and origins of Gush Emunim', *Middle Eastern Studies*, vol. 23, 1987, pp. 215–34.
14. Beit-Hallahmi, *Despair and Deliverance, op. cit.*, pp. 17–33, 115–31.
15. Jacob Katz, 'Traditional society and modern society', in Shlomo Deshen and Walter P. Zenner (eds), *Jewish Societies in the Middle East* (Washington: University Press of America, 1982: article first published in Hebrew in 1960), pp. 35–47. See also: Charles S. Liebman, 'The Reappropriation of Jewish Tradition in the Modern Era', in Jack Wertheimer (ed.), *The Uses of Tradition: Jewish Continuity in the Modern Era* (New York: Jewish Theological Seminary of America, 1992), pp. 471–7; Anthony Giddens, *The Consequences of Modernity* (Cambridge: Polity Press, 1991), pp. 22–40,

45–9; and Phillip A. Mellor, 'Reflexive Traditions: Anthony Giddens, High Modernity, and the Contours of Contemporary Religiosity', *Religious Studies*, vol. 29, 1993, pp. 111–127.

16. Stephen Sharot, *Judaism: A Sociology* (Newton Abbot: David & Charles, 1976), pp. 76–100. See also: Stephen Sharot, *Messianism, Mysticism and Magic: A Sociological Analysis of Jewish Religious Movements* (Chapel Hill: University of North Carolina Press, 1982), pp. 208–10; and Calvin Goldscheider and Alan S. Zuckerman, *The Transformation of the Jews* (Chicago: University of Chicago Press, 1984), 64–75.

17. James A. Beckford, 'Religion, modernity and post-modernity', in Bryan Wilson (ed.), *Religion: Contemporary Issues* (London: Bellew, 1992), pp. 11–23. See also Barry Smart, *Postmodernity* (London: Routledge, 1993).

18. Stephen Sharot, 'Religious fundamentalism: neo-traditionalism in modern societies', in Bryan Wilson (ed.), *Religion: Contemporary Issues, op. cit.*, pp. 24–45.

19. David Ellenson, 'German Jewish Orthodoxy: Tradition in the Context of Culture', in Jack Wertheimer (ed.), *The Uses of Tradition, op. cit.*, pp. 5–22. See also Michael K. Silber, 'The Emergence of Ultra-Orthodoxy: The Invention of a Tradition', in ibid., pp. 23–84.

20. Stephen Sharot, 'Israel; Sociological Analyses of Religion in the Jewish State', *Sociological Analysis*, vol. 52 (S), 1990, pp. 63–76.

21. On the relationship between ethnicity and religion among Israeli Jews see Eliezer Ben-Rafael and Stephen Sharot, *Ethnicity, Religion and Class in Israeli Society* (Cambridge: Cambridge University Press, 1991).

22. Issachar Ben-Ami, 'The folk veneration of saints among Moroccan Jews', in S. Morag, I. Ben Ami and N. Stillman (eds.), *Studies in Judaism and Islam* (Jerusalem: Magnes Press, 1981), pp. 283–345.

23. Shlomo Deshen, 'Tunisian hillulot', in Moshe Shokeid and Shlomo Deshen (eds), *The Generation of Transition* (Hebrew) (Jerusalem: Ben Zvi Institute, 1974).

24. Alex Weingrod, *The Saint of Beersheba, op. cit.*

25. Stephen Sharot, 'Religious fundamentalism: neo-traditionalism in modern societies', in Bryan Wilson (ed.), *Religion: Contemporary Issues, op. cit.*

26. Menachem Friedman, 'Life tradition and book tradition in the development of ultraorthodox Judaism', in Harvey E. Goldberg (ed.), *Judaism Viewed from Within and from Without* (Albany: State University of New York Press, 1987), pp. 235–55.

27. Aviezer Ravitzky, 'Religious radicalism and political messianism in Israel', in Emmanuel Sivan and Menachem Friedman (eds), *Religious Radicalism and Politics in the Middle East* (Albany: State University of New York Press, 1990), pp. 11–37. See also Menachem Friedman, 'The state of Israel as a theological dilemma', in Baruch Kimmerling (ed.), *The Israeli State and Society: Boundaries and Frontiers* (Albany: State University of New York Press, 1989), pp. 165–215.

28. Janet Aviad, *Return to Judaism, op. cit.*

29. Gideon Aran, 'Redemption as a catastrophe: the gospel of Gush Emunim', in Emmanuel Sivan and Menachem Friedman (eds), *Religious Radicalism*

and Politics in the Middle East, *op. cit.*, pp. 157–76. See also Stephen Sharot, *Messianism, Messianism, and Magic, op. cit.*, pp. 229–37.

30. Gideon Aran, 'Redemption as a catastrophe', *op. cit.* See also Janet Aviad, 'The contemporary Israeli pursuit of the millennium', *Religion*, vol. 14, 1984, pp. 199–222.

31. David Newman, 'Gush Emunim between fundamentalism and pragmatism', *Jerusalem Quarterly*, vol. 39, 1986, pp. 33–43.

32. Benjamin Beit-Hallahmi, *Despair and Deliverance, op. cit.*, pp. 17–33.

8 The Self and Postmodernity
Rex Ambler

One dilemma of deciding whether or not we have entered into postmodernity is the lack of a clear idea of what modernity itself is, or was, or indeed what it is we are supposed to have superseded. This chapter argues that there is more coherence in modernity than initially appears to be the case. This coherence derives from a specific attitude to the human self which pervades all forms of modernity. With that understanding it becomes clear that if the fundamental attitude of modernity becomes problematic, the whole of modernity is called in doubt. This is exactly our present situation. The typically modern relation to the self can no longer be sustained. In this sense, it is argued, we have entered a postmodern situation.

This point is similar to the argument that identifies modernity with the 'project of the enlightenment' and then regards that project as having failed.[1] But this argument has difficulties: it excludes many movements that claim the word 'modern' but which are opposed to the Enlightenment. It fails to explain the present cultural confusion signified in the term word 'postmodern'. For example, Habermas can attempt to 'answer' the French postmodernists by reconstructing the project of the Enlightenment as a genuinely social, democratic affair, but still relying on reason, albeit a 'communicative reason', to bring it about.[2]

What then is, or was, modernity? Answering this question involves a detour into the past of modernity, stopping first to consider two texts that are widely regarded as having defined modernity in their own time and place. These are Baudelaire's essay on 'The painter of modern life' (1863) and Kant's 'Answer to the question "What is Enlightenment?"' (1784).

Baudelaire's essay picks up on the etymology of the word 'modern', tracing it back to the Latin *modo*, 'now'. The modern, he claims, is concerned with what happens in the moment in which I as an observer exist. A truly modern art tries to capture that fleeting moment in a permanent form. Thus, 'by "modernity"', he means 'the ephemeral, the fugitive, the contingent, the half of art whose other half is the eternal and the immutable'.[3] But there is something curious in this description, because he immediately then distinguishes it from that other derivation of the Latin *modo*, 'la mode', fashion, modishness. Fashion goes with the flow of time. The modern artist he has in mind – specifically the journalistic traveller Constantin Guys – 'has an aim loftier than that of a mere *flâneur* (an idle spectator), an aim more general, something other than the fugitive pleasure of circumstance. He is looking for that quality called 'modernity [and] he makes it his business to extract from fashion whatever element it may contain of poetry within history'.[4]

What he is after, of course, is no less than the eternal in the present, the transient, the contingent for, like Daumier, 'he is the painter of the passing moment and of all the suggestions of eternity that it contains'.[5] It is a paradoxical view, but it is the specific task of the modern painter to be sufficiently sensitive and imaginative enough to be able to see the eternal in the moment, and then to convey that in his work of art. But this is to say that he himself escapes time in this moment and transcends it, so that from this unique position he can establish a meaning that will not be swept away immediately in the flow of time. The modern work of art is an affirmation of the artist's momentary experience as supremely valuable, but also, so that this work can be possible, it is an affirmation of the human artist himself as supremely able to determine this value.

Such a view would seem to be necessary once the authority of the received 'academic' tradition had been abandoned. Access to what is eternally valid could now only be reached through the creative imagination of the individual subject. For Baudelaire, 'every efflorescence [in art] is spontaneous, individual ... The artist stems only from himself ... He stands security only for himself. He dies childless. He has been his own king, his own priest, his own God.'[6] But if it is thought, as Baudelaire argues, that the forms of antiquity are no longer 'adapted or suitable to human nature'[7], then a distinctively modern art would be a great liberation. It was certainly thought to be so by the group of artists who later became known as the Impressionists, who were particularly inspired by this essay.[8]

Similarly in that other definitive text on modernity, 'What is Enlightenment?', the surface question is about the deployment of reason, which Kant says characterises the enlightened person. But the deeper question is about the courage to affirm oneself, through reason, for 'dare to know', *sapere aude*, is Kant's precise motto. The person who does so becomes mature. Thus, for Kant:

> enlightenment is man's emergence from his self-incurred immaturity. Immaturity is the inability to use one's own understanding without the guidance of another. The immaturity is self-incurred if its cause is not lack of understanding, but lack of resolution and courage to use it without the guidance of another. The motto of enlightenment is therefore: *Sapere aude!* Have courage to use your own understanding![9]

Kant takes the argument a step further: insofar as many individuals dare to think for themselves, by participating in the discourse of reason, humanity itself becomes mature. This is precisely the historical moment of

the Enlightenment. It is a collective bid for maturity, to overcome the
immaturity of depending on what others have said.

In his essay on this text, Foucault is right to argue that modernity is
fundamentally an attitude, an ethos, although one is less happy with his
precise description of it as a 'critical attitude'. Foucault had wondered
whether we may not envisage modernity rather as an attitude than as a
period of history. By 'attitude', Foucault means:

> a mode of relating to contemporary reality; a voluntary choice made by
> certain people; in the end, a way of thinking and feeling; a way, too, of
> acting and behaving that at once and the same time marks a relation of
> belonging and presents itself as a task. A bit, no doubt, like what the
> Greeks called an *ethos*. And consequently, rather than seeking to distin-
> guish the 'modern era' from the 'premodern' or 'postmodern', I think
> it would be more useful to try to find out how the attitude of modernity,
> ever since its formation, has found itself struggling with attitudes of
> 'countermodernity'.[10]

Foucault then suggests that 'the thread that may connect us with the Enlightenment is not faithfulness to doctrinal elements, but rather the permanent reactivation of an attitude – that is, of a philosophical ethos that
could be described as a permanent critique of our historical era'.[11] That
critical task describes Foucault's own work rather well, but it falls short
of an adequate description of the continuing thread of modernity. It is too
theoretical and loses precisely that moment of courage and self-affirmation
which Kant had thought to be essential.

Both these texts point to, and celebrate, a *new attitude of human self-
assertion*. In practice it is the self-assertion of the individual in the present
of an individual's life-span. But by implication it is also an assertion of
humanity – the 'enlightenment of *Menscheit*' is Kant's term – against the
claims of the collective past. Reason is a means only, and not the only one.
In Baudelaire, it is art that is sensitive to the eternal. These two means, the
rational and the expressive, suggest two ways in which modernity might
develop, and indeed has developed.

In this way, it would be possible to regard romanticism as no less
modern than the radical Enlightenment, though it was undoubtedly a strong
reaction against it. It would be misleading, however, to identify modernity
precisely with what Jürgen Habermas calls its 'project'. For him,

> the project of modernity formulated in the 18th century by the philo-
> sophers of the enlightenment [which] consisted in their efforts to develop
> objective science, universal morality and law, and autonomous art

according to their inner logic . . . The enlightenment philosophers wanted to utilize this accumulation of specialized culture for the enrichment of everyday life – that is to say, for the rational organization of everyday social life.[12]

This has undoubtedly been the dominant form of modernity, against which other forms have measured themselves. Ironically, it is everything which twentieth-century modernism has rejected: the integrity of the self, the rationality of the world, the unity of truth, the malleability of society. But not quite everything, because what modernism retained, and re-emphasised, was the ultimate validity of the subjective viewpoint.[13] In the face of disorder, fragmentation and change, there was a new strong affirmation of the human self: the unique, individual, isolated self. In that respect it had an equal right to the contested word modern.

Allowing this broad characterisation, Martin Luther, Christopher Columbus and Michel de Montaigne might be said to have initiated modernity, or at least to have marked symbolically its beginning. Each in their own way gave priority to their own experience, their own self-determination, in the discovery of a new reality. Of course, if we go back this far in our account of modernity we are going to have to include an even greater variety of stances, attitudes and ways of doing things: perhaps most of the innovations of the last 500 years. But remarkably the coherence remains, once we recognise modernity as a fundamental attitude to life rather than a very particular philosophy or social practice or 'period'. At the same time the fragmentation and dissonances of modernity seem to become more intelligible.

Luther's protest is especially important because, coming at the very beginning of the movement, it marks it off most dramatically from what came before, precisely that against which he protested. But again, to appreciate the 'modernity' of what he did, we have to look beneath the surface of his religious 'reformation' to the deeper attitudinal shift that it involved. In a sense he was pushed into it by the strong reaction to his initial complaints against ecclesiastical practice, the ninety-five theses of 1517 in particular. Like other humanists of his time, notably Erasmus, he had initially wanted to reform the Church in the light of the newly translated texts of the New Testament. His opponents argued forcefully that in so doing he would be rejecting the tradition of the church and in particular the decisions of its great councils and the authority of its popes. On that basis they only had to confront him with a simple question: was it even conceivable that he, as an individual, could be right and the whole Church throughout the centuries wrong?[14]

Luther himself would have been prepared to rest his case on the teaching of Scripture, which the Church itself recognised as the source of its authority. But at the famous Diet of 1521, when he was called by the imperial authority to recant, he was drawn by his skilful opponent, one John von der Ecken, to shift his ground more dramatically than he himself may have perceived at the time.

Von der Ecken rejected his simple appeal to Scripture by pointing out that Scripture needs interpretation and that interpretation needs sound judgement. He warned:

> do not deceive yourself, Martin. You are not the only one who knows the scripture, not the only one who has struggled to convey the true meaning of holy scripture – not after so many holy doctors have worked day and night to explain holy writ! Do not set your judgment over that of so many famous men.[15]

Luther's reply was unprecedented:

> since then your majesty and your lordships demand a simple reply, I will answer without horns or teeth. Unless I am convicted by scripture and by plain reason (I do not accept the authority of popes and councils because they have contradicted each other; my conscience is captive to the word of God), I cannot, and I will not, recant anything, for to go against conscience is neither right nor safe. Here I stand; I can do no other. God help me. Amen.[16]

His affirmation that he stood alone before God, addressed by Him through His Word (a minimal mediation) and answerable to him directly, was therefore in principle a decisive break with the whole world view of the ancients. It was implicitly an ontological affirmation, since his daring 'Here I stand' put him in the position of being able to determine himself what was ultimately true and good.

It also found expression in his central teaching of 'justification by faith', though we would have to say in a paradoxical form. It appears to be a doctrine of passivity, a prescription for simply believing what God has done. But this individual faith turned out to be vulnerable to the conscientious scrutiny that made it necessary in the first place as an alternative to 'works'. For how would a believer know that he had pure and genuine faith, especially if he was also aware of feelings of pride or uncertainty?

Luther's understanding of faith allows for this possibility, however, because he recognises God's hand in this ambivalence of human feeling: it is God who judges in the experience of guilt as well as God who justifies in the experience of forgiveness. It therefore becomes important for a believer to explore the depth of his wrongdoing with searching honesty in order also to discover the reality of God's forgiveness. Only in this way, says Luther, can a man judge himself as God would (*conformis deo est et verax et justus*).[17] By the same token, the experience of mental suffering this entails can be, for the believer, a participation in Christ's suffering where the guilt is finally taken away. This means that we can trace the workings of God within our own experience: *via dei est, qua nos ambulare facit.*[18] All the conflicts and confusions which characterise human experience, which Luther himself knew in a particularly acute form, are modes of God's paradoxical activity within us.

All that is required for us to know this liberation is to affirm our trust in God through Jesus Christ. It is now apparent that this act of passive submission is also an act of active self-affirmation, that attests experience of day-to-day life as the theatre of God's drama of salvation. The individual conscience is the chief witness of that drama.[19]

Yet this human self-affirmation before God carried with it a denial, the denial of everything that might intervene in a direct personal encounter with God. It was a very radical asceticism, a 'worldly asceticism' as Weber described it, because having rejected everything other than God as a means to attaining God, Luther was then able to reinstate everything as a way of serving God. The old medieval distinction between sacred and secular had been in principle removed.

The world, then, is suddenly open for human exploration and development: precisely what the later 'project of modernity' systematically carried out, both in science and in trade. This is not to say that Luther himself advocated an ethic of development, and certainly not the materialist form that came to dominate capitalism in later centuries. But it does mean that there is an important historical link between the early faith and the later ethic, in that the first makes the second possible.[20]

The radical implications of Luther's move are perhaps masked for us by the strongly religious form that it took. By comparison with even some contemporary renaissance figures, his preoccupation with faith seems to place him firmly in the premodern world. But this judgement leans too much on that interpretation of 'modern' which identifies it narrowly with the rationalist version of the Enlightenment.

Galileo, however, is a step in that direction. His own stand against the Church parallels Luther's in a number of ways, especially in his claim that his own experience offers a first criterion of truth. Like Luther, he was reiterating a view that had been propounded before, in this case by Copernicus and Kepler, but he was adding to it a new kind of authority. Nor was he original in pointing out the incongruence of recent observations with scientific theory. The new navigators and cartographers had been forced to think differently about the globe by their own practical experience, and their new thoughts often failed to harmonise with the official Ptolemaic theory.[21] As an English clergyman bluntly put it at the time, 'the thoughts of the philosophers have been contradicted by the unexpected observations of the navigators'.[22]

What was new was Galileo's insistence – at least until his recantation – that the truths of science had to be grounded in and verified by personal observations. This stand was no less outrageous than Luther's because it challenged the most fundamental principle of medieval culture, which not even the humanists had questioned: namely, that truth and value are determined by an appeal to authorities of the past. The church was not then being particularly stubborn or oppressive in asserting its own privileged position in relation to truth; it was merely expressing the generally accepted medieval view. Meanwhile, Galileo was being stubborn in asserting his right, as a mere individual, to exercise his own judgement independently and to do so on the basis of his own experiential observations.[23] What is more important even than the development of the experimental *method* for science is the assertion of his ontological position as an individual human being, or, to put it more concisely, his *ontological self-assertion*.

The method made an impact as well, not least as a way of demonstrating how ontological self-assertion could be carried through in practice. That was a point made strongly by his English contemporary, Francis Bacon, who regarded the experimental method as a tool, a *novum organum*, of a new historic venture which he described as 'the assertion of the mind's own authority, so that it may exercise over nature the power which properly belongs to it'.[24]

The specific results of the new science seemed to undermine the whole rationale of the medieval world picture. For example, one can note Galileo's observation of Jupiter's satellites apparently crashing through the crystal spheres of heaven. On the basis of observation it was possible to construct a picture of the world which looked more like a machine than the emanation of a universal mind. And the fact that it had to be constructed in order to fit experimentally implied that the ideas by which the world became intelligible were furnished by the human minds that investigated it, not by the Divine mind that created it. Scientists were not so obviously 'thinking God's thoughts after him', as Johan Kepler had said, but finding thoughts of their own to fit the world.[25]

This was certainly how Descartes came to see it, and the shock was profound. All of a sudden, it seemed, men were left on their own in

an empty, disenchanted world. Descartes' contemporary, Pascal, was able
to express this well, because he saw it as a warning that rationalists like
Descartes were getting it disastrously wrong. As Pascal noted, 'we burn
with desire to find a firm footing, an ultimate, lasting base on which to
build a tower rising up to infinity, but our whole foundation cracks and
the earth opens up into the depth of the abyss'.[26] This was the vertigo of
the new self-assertion. The trauma is surely still being felt, along with an
increasing sense of the human individual's isolation. We might, then, suggest that the attempt to overcome that isolation or abandonment, or rather
the very many different attempts to do this, have also been characteristic
of modernity. But this is to run ahead of the story.

Descartes' immediate problem was how to find an adequate basis for
our knowledge of the world once it was granted that we inevitably interpreted the world when we came to know it. His answer was fateful for
the direction modernity was to take,[27] because he grounded knowledge
in the human being's awareness of itself, in consciousness, thereby split-
ting the person into thinking self and material body, and alienating the
newly defined self from the world it knew. The scientific system which
Descartes then erected on this basis was far from successful. He attempted
to derive a complete and certain knowledge of the world from his direct
awareness of certain 'clear and distinct ideas', without much regard for
their verifiability in empirical observation. Given his anxiety about the
unreliability of observation, this retreat into the self was perhaps understandable. But despite the power of his arguments that our merely human
reasoning can be guaranteed by the certain knowledge of the existence of
God, his imaginary construction of the world was effectively demolished
by the new, empirical scientists, like Newton and Huygens,[28] and with it
the possibility of a purely rational philosophy. But significantly, the preoccupation with the self remained, and has stayed with philosophy ever
since.

He established the procedure that in order to test our knowledge of the
world and to determine whatever meaning or purpose or value it might
have, we have first to examine the competences of the individual human
mind. This typically epistemological idea also carries with it the (implicit)
ontological claim that the individual human mind, as a self-conscious
entity, is in the unique position of determining what is true and real and
valuable. It therefore gives priority to the self not only over the claims of
other human beings, both past and present, but also over the world and
over nature, precisely as Bacon had required.[29]

In looking at Descartes this way we can see him as attempting to further (the still implicit project of) modernity, rather than initiating it. He

resolved one profound problem that had been thrown up by the new cultural movement, but doing so in a way that gave a new impetus to the movement and helped to set it in a particular direction.

For one thing, he gave a new role to the philosophers, and a new task for independent human reason. Having established that human beings were essentially 'thinking things' it became clear that human life itself was to be developed by thinking. Other traditional sources of truth and wisdom, such as faith, custom and Church were to be subordinated to the one source of reason, because this alone was in keeping with man's essential nature. In its nature, truth was to be conceived as an experimental (re-)construction of the world. Reason was to provide the sure guide to knowing the world and knowing how to live in it, both in fact and value.

What was being proposed by the philosophers who followed Descartes was a complete overhaul of human thought and practice on the basis of a radical self-assertion by human beings through the instrumentality of reason. This became the Enlightenment, or what Habermas calls 'the project of modernity'. It is now the task of reason, according to the project, not only to understand the world, but also to shape it, to guide it. With reason, men would be able to determine their own goals and devise the appropriate means for achieving them, thereby gaining the maturity that Kant talked about as the essence of the Enlightenment, the freedom of people to think and to decide for themselves.[30]

The Enlightenment therefore pushed the self-affirmation of modernity even further, dispensing finally with all reference to the Other as a source of truth or value (heteronomy). If faith represents dependence on God or nature, reason represents independence. Reason is therefore the necessary condition and means for human beings to realise their freedom in reality and in the world.[31] From the time of the French Revolution, the time of Thomas Paine, the great liberators of mankind are all rationalists: Darwin, Marx and Freud especially. Faith and religion are then conceived as opposed to freedom, and this forms the basis of most of the major critiques of religion in the modern era.

The project of modernity can therefore be defined as follows: the historic attempt to gain freedom and autonomy for man by gaining control over nature and society, first by understanding them analytically, then by manipulating them technologically and organisationally. But this way of defining modernity also suggests how the project might falter. For human beings live in society; they are also part of nature, or so it once seemed and still seems to common sense. Their attempt to gain freedom from nature or gain control of society therefore seems to involve a contradiction.

At this point Descartes' philosophy came to serve another purpose, in that it managed to resolve, or perhaps only to cover up, this seeming contradiction. Human beings were essentially 'minds'. Therefore they were apart from nature, which is merely matter and were essentially individual entities in relation to one another, so that they were not essentially part of a community. But those ideas needed to be developed if they were to make the historical project seem plausible.

The ideas of the radical Enlightenment can be summarised:

1. The self is identical with consciousness, and is directly knowable through individual introspection.
2. The world, as essentially matter, can be identified with everything that is given through the senses, so that it can be thoroughly known, in principle at least, by the combined use of sensuous experience and rational mediation. The mind is a mirror of nature.
3. The ultimate truth of the world, and of ourselves, can be known by us: the ultimate truth is the sum total of all the true things we can say about the world on the basis of sense and reason.
4. In the world things change according to single, one-way causation, on the model of a machine.
5. Given (1) to (4) it follows that in principle we know how to control the world, and if necessary how to change it completely. All we need is the technical power to move the material levers of causation.
6. Finally, given an introspective knowledge of what we free individuals want, it is possible to transform the world so that it answers completely to our desires (alternatively, our sense of rightness).

Spelling out these entailments of the Enlightenment view of the world illustrates both its attractiveness and its inevitable shortcoming. It has affected every aspect of human thought and activity in the modern world, and has become indeed the dominant form of modernity itself. Certainly in the social sphere, modernity has come to mean the subjection of every aspect of life to a rational analysis, long-term planning and bureaucratic organisation with the aim of maximising human prosperity and freedom.[32]

Others have laid claim to the word modern who have a quite different understanding of what it should mean and who are often quite opposed to the Enlightenment version. But, as already suggested, a recognition of their right to the concept gives an insight into the deeper significance of modernity itself. This points to an understanding of its present crisis. Having now formulated the 'project' as a particular form of human self-assertion, we can also see how people like the Romantics or the socialists might perceive it as a form of oppression.

The argument of the Romantics always was that the rational view of the world imprisoned the human spirit.[33] Like the Rationalists they were also appealing to the ontological primacy of the individual human subject and to the supreme value of individual freedom. But they differed in their idea of how that primacy and freedom were to be realised. More specifically, the Romantics were exposing a contradiction in the Enlightenment project, or rather two contradictions. The first was that in using reason to affirm freedom it denied human nature and its participation in nature itself. It therefore denied what human beings *were*, and forced them to become something which they were not, a detached thinking substance. On this understanding freedom became impossible.

The second contradiction was that the Enlightenment affirmed human experience as the basis of our knowledge of, and relationship to, the world, but in then (re-)constructing a rational view of the world on this experiential basis, especially when it used the method of Newtonian science to do this, it created a picture of the world that contradicted ordinary human experience. Methodical reason gave objective reality, it was supposed, whilst personal experience yielded only a subjective view. Once again, by using reason in this way to realise human freedom, it actually denied human freedom. So the Romantic rejected the Enlightenment in the name of the very value it was meant to make real. It affirmed individual experience in its integrity, relying on the free expressive forms of art to make it real in the world.

The socialists did something similar, but they were reacting as much against the practical outworking of the project as against its theoretical formulation. The implementation of the project after all needed structures of power, just as the theoretical task needed structures of reason. It could not be carried out by individuals alone, even though individual enterprise and adventure were greatly admired and celebrated. They needed new technologies of transport and manufacture, new skills of navigation and discovery, and above all an economic system that enabled them to exploit natural and human resources to the full and beyond the limitations of premodern feudalism. The new economic structure was provided by capitalism, which promised not only to increase wealth massively for those individuals who invested in it, but also offered the opportunity of improvement to everyone, whatever their traditional status in society. It was the ideal economic device for implementing the modern dream, as Adam Smith in particular argued at the time, except, of course, that the structure had a dynamic of its own which was not subject to the control of individuals. Its workings were risky, fickle and unjust. It required a certain faith to believe that it would in the long run serve human interests; that, as Adam

Smith put it, 'a hidden hand' guided the market. This was a ghost of divine Providence.

Marx would have none of it. To him it was quite clear that capitalism did not and could not serve human interests because its dynamic was essentially exploitative. The only 'individuals' whose interests were served were that social group which already had the capital to invest in it. With such people the ideal of freedom and the view of the world that went with it was mere 'ideology'. It was a conception of the world which masked rather than disclosed its reality. It was not so much a rational representation of the world by independent human minds, as a distortion of the world created by the material interests of human collectivities, who were to be seen then as fully part of the material world they were trying to understand. And Marx claimed this to be true on the basis of a scientific study of collective human behaviour.

Marx was therefore exposing a second contradiction of classic modernity: its objective rational account of the world had disclosed that no such account was possible! But he was still able to affirm modernity. What better expression of it is there than Marx's stated article of faith that 'the supreme being for man is man himself?' He offered a new, collective version of the project which was aimed at harnessing the mechanism of the economy for humanly chosen purposes, transforming the goal of individual freedom into a generalised human emancipation. It is of course this version of the project, in a newly revised form, that Habermas seeks to defend.

It is not difficult to give an account of other, more recent, forms of modernity by showing how they coped with emerging tensions and contradictions in existing forms by finding new ways to express the fundamental affirmation of modernity. Nationalism and Fascism, for example, are self-affirmations of groups, rooted in some premodern sense of identity such as race or culture, but are characteristically modern in seeking freedom from outside control and protection for their own developing economies. In the realm of high culture, modernism can be seen as an affirmation of the human subject against the bland objectivities of the so-called modern world.[34] Existentialism in particular often made this affirmation in a notably stark form, that the world objectively is wholly empty of meaning and value, so that it is up to the individual subject to create and project meaning. But these are merely hints, intended to suggest how such different manifestations of modern life can still reasonably be called modern, and indeed how their very modernity can enable us to understand how and why they have emerged and have been in conflict with one another. Modernity is obviously rich and complex. What appear to be negations of it mostly turn out to be new versions of the same thing.

This very fact should make us wary of any talk of the end of modernity. The present crisis with the Enlightenment project might after all yield a new viable version of it, or at least a new mode of being modern. This is indeed possible, and many critics who characterise their own view as postmodern are prepared to consider it as a continuation rather than a denial of modernity.[35] But it is also possible that the crisis is so profound that we might have to talk after all of the end of modernity.

Consider where the argument has led us so far. It started with the idea that modernity is best understood as an expression and outworking of a fundamental *attitude* to the world, which also separates it from everything premodern. This attitude, referred to as ontological self-assertion, is associated psychologically with the bid for maturity as self-determination. Played out in the world, however, this defiant assertion, with its attendant denials and rejections, creates conflicts of various kinds which lead in turn to various 'crises' of modernity. These have usually been resolved by the invention of a new form of human self-assertion. But with all these, resolution was possible because the human self was still able to assert itself. The question then arises as to whether that is still possible, or whether there is now an unsurpassable limit.

One problem is quite practical. Our human self-assertion over nature is proving to be damaging to nature itself, so that it is becoming less and less able to support the human life that ultimately depends on it. Because of these newly discovered ecological limits to our human expansion, it now seems to be necessary to our survival as a species that we see ourselves precisely as a species: that is, as part of nature, rather than above it and distinct from it. Or, to put it another way, it has now become clear that there are ecological and economic limits to human self-assertion and that beyond a certain point it becomes not only dangerous but profoundly illusory. It is not wholly inappropriate – though it may be philosophically idealistic – that many ecological thinkers refer to Descartes as the source of our modern illusion.

Descartes solved the problem of grounding knowledge and self-identity in immediate self-consciousness, thereby setting up a radical dualism between the essential human being and nature in general. But Descartes' was only one of a number of attempts to make sense theoretically of the fundamental assertion of modernity. What is to be questioned now is not only a theoretical dualism of mind and body, but the underlying attitude that gives primacy and supremacy to human beings as subjects.

There is, however, another problem which is essentially theoretical, and which seemingly has nothing to do with the practical outworkings of the modern project. This is a philosophical problem about maintaining the notion of an individual, integrated, unique human subject. It arises from new developments in the human sciences which, ironically enough, have been zealously carrying forward the modern project of objective study into the field of human subjectivity. One obvious example is the psychoanalytical research of Sigmund Freud.

Freud wished to formulate a theory of the unconscious which was to be understood not only as an additional source of motivation to the conscious mind, but as present *in* the conscious mind and its activities. What appear to us, consciously, to be the rational utterances and actions of fully self-conscious beings, turn out on analysis to be conflicted, double-edged, multi-faceted actions whose full significance is mostly hidden from us. Another example is the linguistic analysis of our depth grammar by Wittgenstein – the similarity in language to Freud's psychoanalysis cannot surely be accidental[36] – which showed that speech conforms to many different rules and 'games' and practical requirements, locking the individual into many different social networks, so that language cannot be construed, even initially, as a representation of the individual human consciousness. Similarly, the structural analysis of Lévi-Strauss and the post-Freudian post-structuralist analysis of Lacan, Kristeva and others, in what is now being called a postmodern movement, point emphatically away from the idea that we can be directly aware of ourselves through immediate introspection. Rather than the world being reflected in, or constituted by, the self, it is more the other way round. In these researches the objective study characteristic of modern science is being turned back on the independent knowing subject to demonstrate that it is no such thing at all.

For those thinkers who take these researches seriously, the results can lead to a most alarming vertigo, not unlike Pascal's. Now the whole construction of knowledge seems to hover over an abyss. It appears that this way leads to nihilism and despair. But this need not be a necessary consequence. The end of this particular modern project need not mean the end of structure, value or meaning, any more than its initiation some few hundred years ago implied the absence of these things before. On the contrary the present crisis in our sense of reality and value is precisely the occasion to reconsider and perhaps recover that sense of the world that modernity itself rejected and (almost) finally displaced: to welcome, in Freud's terms, 'the return of the repressed'.

Of course, we could not recover the specific structures of the premodern world, which would be entirely inappropriate to the world in which we now live, the world that modernity itself has so radically transformed. But we can surely reinterpret the old in ways that are appropriate to the new situation, and in ways that do not in turn deny those truths and values of modernity to which we still want to hold (insofar, of course, as they too are still appropriate). The clues to this reinterpretation are already given in the recent discoveries which have brought about the crisis itself. These relate to our rediscovery of the many subtle ways in which we are still – despite our mighty efforts at liberation – enfolded in nature; and the discovery that – despite our efforts at individual liberation – we are still part of one another, still inescapably communal beings, even in our individual thought processes and private emotional experiences.

These discoveries, however, if they are to yield greater insights into what it now means for us to be human beings, seem also to require a new attitude, a new ethos, of openness to the other, of acceptance of difference and mystery, as the fundamental attitude of a new cultural outlook. To see it this way is to invest the situation with a great deal of hope.

Notes and References

1. I am thinking of: Jean-François Lyotard, *The Postmodern Condition*, trans. Geoff Bennington and Brian Massumi (Manchester: Manchester University Press, 1984); Alisdair MacIntyre, *After Virtue*, London: Duckworth Press, 1985; and John Milbank, *Theology and Social Theory* (Oxford: Blackwell, 1990).
2. Jürgen Habermas, *The Philosophical Discourse of Modernity* (Cambridge: Polity Press, 1987). See also his essay 'Modernity – an incomplete project', in Hal Foster (ed.), *Postmodern Culture* (London: Pluto Press, 1985), pp. 3–15.
3. Charles Baudelaire, *The Painter of Modern Life and other Essays*, trans. and ed. Jonathan Mayne (London: Phaidon Press, 1964), p. 13.
4. Ibid., p. 12.
5. Ibid., p. 5.
6. Ibid., 'Art in Paris', pp. 121–9. Marshall Berman ascribes this remarkable passage to 'Baudelaire's mercurial and paradoxical personality "where Baudelaire" leaps into a transcendence that leaves Kant far behind: this artist becomes a walking *Ding-an-sich*'. See *All That is Solid Melts into Air* (London: Verso, 1983), p. 139. I do not believe Baudelaire is being quite as absurd as Berman suggests. This leap into transcendence is precisely what is required if the artist is to be able to find something of universal or 'eternal' significance in the passing moment. And the logic here is probably not so far from that of Kant's deduction of the transcendental ego.
7. Charles Baudelaire, *The Painter of Modern Life, op. cit.*, p. 3.
8. The young Parisian artist Bazille wrote a letter to his parents in 1867 claiming that he and his friends, Manet, Renoir, Monet and others, 'knew what Baudelaire meant' in his essay 'The Painter of Modern Life'. Since they

'understood the modern era' they were happy to break with the tradition of the Academy which insisted on themes from Antiquity. See James Heard, *Art in the Making: Impressionism* (London: National Gallery, Video, 1990). Compare the reminiscence of a contemporary writer, Armand Sylvestre, specifically on the painter Manet. He wrote that:

> he was one of the first to brighten the French palette and bring light back into it. Less intense, less magisterial than Baudelaire, but with a much surer taste, he nevertheless affirmed in painting, what the writer had done in poetry, a sense of modernity, which though it was latent in many minds, had not till then seen the light of day. (1892)

See Bernard Denvir (ed.), *The Impressionists at First Hand* (London: Thames & Hudson, 1987), p. 71.

9. Immanuel Kant, 'An Answer to the Question: "What is Enlightenment?"' (first published 1784) in Hans Reiss (ed.), *Kant's Political Writings*, trans. H.B. Nisbet (Cambridge: Cambridge University Press, 1971), p. 54. The motto *sapere aude* is part of the opening words of the essay and is derived from Horace, Epodes, 1, 2, 40. See also reference to Hegel's 'spirit' which 'calls to every consciousness: be for yourselves what you all are in yourselves – reasonable' in G.W.F. Hegel, *Phenomenology of Spirit*, trans. A.V. Miller (Oxford: Oxford University Press, 1977), p. 328.

10. Michel Foucault, 'What is enlightenment?', in Paul Rabinow (ed.), *The Foucault Reader*, trans. Catherine Porter (Harmondsworth: Penguin, 1991), p. 39.

11. Ibid., p. 42.

12. Jürgen Habermas, 'Modernity – an incomplete project', *op. cit.* p. 9.

13. See for example, Michael Levenson, *Modernism and the Fate of the Individual* (Cambridge: Cambridge University Press, 1991).

14. Richard Marius, *Luther* (London: Quartet Books, 1975), p. 102.

15. Quoted in ibid., p. 154.

16. Quoted in ibid., pp.154f. Marius points out that the words 'Here I stand; I can do no other' were inserted, later, in the printed edition of the speech, but maintains that they 'do express his conviction'. Interestingly, Erik Erikson comments that:

> if Luther did not really say the words which became most famous: 'Here I stand', legend again rose to the occasion; for this new credo was for men whose identity was derived from their determination to stand on their own feet, not only spiritually, but politically, economically, and intellectually. No matter what happened afterward – and some terrible and most terribly petty things did occur because of it – Luther's emphasis on individual conscience prepared the way for a series of concepts of equality, representation, and self-determination which became in successive secular revolutions and wars the foundations not of the dignity of some, but of the liberty of all.

See *Young Man Luther* (London: Faber & Faber, 1959), pp. 224f.

17. Martin Luther, *Werke*, Weimarer Ausgabe 1883, III, Lectures on Romans, p. 289.

18. Ibid., p. 529.

19. Erikson's judgement is therefore surely right: 'a theological system of increasing self-assertiveness was founded on fragments of mood swings and intuitive thoughts which later found their climax, as well as their conceptual unification, in the "revelation in the tower"'. See *Young Man Luther, op. cit.*, p. 144. Erikson also notes that 'under these conditions [accepting inner conflicts as God's work of grace], apparent submission becomes mastery, apparent passivity the release of new energy for active pursuits'. See p. 211.

20. Max Weber, *The Protestant Ethic and the Spirit of Capitalism*, trans. Talcott Parsons (London: George Allen & Unwin, 1930), for example p. 45, but especially p. 154 which summarises his view, where he states:

> Christian asceticism, at first fleeing from the world into solitude, had already ruled the world which it had renounced from the monastery and through the church. But it had, on the whole, left the naturally spontaneous character of daily life in the world untouched. Now it strode into the market-place of life, slammed the door on the monastery behind it, and undertook to penetrate just that daily routine of life with its methodicalness, to fashion it into a life in the world, but neither of nor for this world.

21. Robert Mandrou, *From Humanism to Science, 1480–1700*, trans. B. Pearce (Harmondsworth: Penguin, 1978), pp. 48–50.

22. William Watts (1633), quoted in R. Hooykaas, *Religion and the Rise of Modern Science* (Edinburgh: Scottish Academic Press, 1973), p. 37.

23. I like the way Bertolt Brecht brings out this epistemological issue of how truth is to be judged in his *Life of Galileo*, trans. D.I. Vesey (London: Methuen, 1963), Act I, scene 3, p. 41, where the following dialogue appears:

> *Sagredo (a friend)*: Galileo, I have always regarded you as a shrewd man. For 17 years in Padua and for 3 years in Pisa you patiently instructed hundreds of pupils in the Ptolemaic system which the church supports and the Scriptures, on which the church is founded, confirm. You thought it untrue, like Copernicus; but you taught it.
> *Galileo*: Because I could prove nothing.
> *Sagredo (incredulously)*: And you believe that makes a difference?
> *Galileo*: All the difference in the world !

24. Francis Bacon, *Novum Organum*, in *The Works of Francis Bacon* (eds), J. Spalding, R. Ellis and D. Heath (London: Longmans, 1870), vol. IV.

25. Charles Taylor, *Sources of the Self* (Cambridge: Cambridge University Press, 1989), p. 144.

26. Blaise Pascal, *Penseés*, trans. A.J. Krailsheimer (Harmondsworth: Penguin, 1966), pp. 92f.

27. Richard Rorty suggests that Bacon had an implicit pragmatic alternative that was never developed, by Descartes or anyone else, until Pierce and Dewey in the twentieth century. See Richard Rorty, 'Habermas and Lyotard on postmodernity', in Richard Bernstein (ed.), *Habermas and Modernity* (Cambridge, MA: MIT Press, 1985), pp. 161–75.

28. R. Hooykaas, *Religion and the Rise of Modern Science, op. cit.*, pp. 44–6.

29. Descartes echoes Bacon's own rhetoric in his (Descartes') *Discourse on Method*, part 6, when he states:

some general notions in physics opened my eyes to the possibility of gaining knowledge which would be very useful in life, and of discovering a practical philosophy which might replace the speculative philosophy taught in the schools . . . We could use this knowledge – as the artisans use theirs – for all the purposes for which it is appropriate, and thus make ourselves, as it were, the lords and masters of nature.

Cited in John Cottingham, Robert Stoothoff and Dugald Murdoch (eds), *Descartes: Selected Philosophical Writings* (Cambridge: Cambridge University Press, 1988), p. 47.

30.   See for example Peter Gay, *The Enlightenment: An Interpretation*, vol. II, 'The Science of Freedom' (London: Wildwood House, 1973), ch. 2 'From experience to progress'.

31.   This is illustrated in a point of Condorcet, who noted that:

the time will come when the sun will shine only on free men who know no master but their reason . . . How consoling for the philosopher who laments the errors, the crimes, the injustices which still pollute the earth and of which he is often the victim, is this view of the human race, emancipated from its shackles, released from the empire of fate and from that of the enemies of progress, advancing with a firm and sure step along the path of truth, virtue and happiness .

Cited in W.T. Jones, *A History of Western Philosophy*, vol. 4, *Kant and the Nineteenth Century* (New York: Harcourt Brace Jonanovich, 2nd ed., 1975), pp. 2ff.

32.   This is broadly Weber's understanding. See the discussion by Bryan S. Turner, 'Periodization and Politics in the Postmodern', in his *Theories of Modernity and Postmodernity* (London: Sage Publications, 1990), pp. 6–10.

33.   See Theodore Roszak's 'romantic' account of the romantics in *Where the Wasteland Ends* (London: Faber & Faber, 1972), pp. 277–345.

34.   The paradox that modernism in our century has to be anti-modern is brought out well by Marshall Berman, *All That is Solid Melts into Air*, *op. cit.*, pp. 23–36.

35.   Charles Jencks, *What is Post-Modernism?* (London: Academy Editions, 1986).

36.   Robert Solomon, *Continental Philosophy since 1750: The Rise and Fall of the Self* (Oxford: Oxford University Press, 1988), pp. 139–51.

9 Postmodernity and Culture: Sociological Wagers of the Self in Theology

Kieran Flanagan

The Nine O'Clock Service at Ponds Forge Sports Complex in the centre of Sheffield attracted a large congregation. With the public support of the Anglican Bishop of Sheffield, the service took the form of a Planetary Mass. The atmosphere was described as 'a sea of paradox'. In the Mass, beat, dance, light and meditation were used to 'reconnect people with God'. The rite seemed filled with the unexpected. The offertory procession included the expected bread and wine, but also earth and a Big Mac, when prayers were said pointedly 'for integrity'. Sacraments were regarded as the 'epicentre of a new Big Bang' and were illustrated with dance, clockwise and anti-clockwise. The rite catered for those wrecked by the hard end of culture. A New Age Church, in sympathy with the creation theology of an ex-Dominican, Matthew Fox, sought a site of relevance in the field of cultural change. A searching for repentance and change in attitudes to creation was incorporated in a seeking for *Songs of Post-modernism*. Theories of postfeminism and deconstruction were also embodied in this form of rite that might seem to express all that a sociologist could hope for, signifying all his analytical dreams, with a priestly blessing of empowerment and sacralisation.[1]

Unfortunately, even the darkest satirical sociological thoughts become the experimental practice of Anglicanism whose endless permutations of liturgical forms, from Roman rites to Raves in the Naves, are under continual testing. The explosion of liturgical experimentation in the 1960s has become a ritely implosion in the 1990s. So many permutations of worship are made possible by the Alternative Service Book of the Church of England that a software programme called 'Worship Master' is available for liturgical planners. Reflecting on these decades of liturgical change, John Habgood, the former Archbishop of York and architect of the Alternative Service Book, 1980, felt that 'by throwing everything up in the air, you are undergoing a process of winnowing'. Noting that faith involves a continual process of testing, he concluded that 'what is solid will eventually fall back to the ground again'.[2]

Habgood's approach to liturgical reform provides a curious echo of a phrase of Marx, which Berman has popularised to characterise the experience of modernity, that 'all that is solid melts into air'.[3] Thus, in Anglican approaches to rite, solidity takes on a peculiar ambiguity of presumption and assumption, denoting what *might* fall back from heaven, but which, given the spirit of the times, *might* melt inconsequentially into the air. In the face of such brave efforts to inculturate postmodernity, a withering sociological response might seem ungracious. Visiting such rites, assuming a teflon thick spirituality, a sociologist might behold the importation of cultural presumptions of endless powers to self-actualise through the miracle of technology in a ritual order that affirms everything which postmodernity has led him to despise. Seeing is disbelieving, and if nostalgia hovers over the postmodern machine, then any sociologist of minuscule spirituality will flee affrighted to choral evensong at the nearest Cathedral. Better pastiches of the angels than those of McDonalds to envision escape from the tyrannies of the times.

Postmodernity sacralises the secular to provide an aura of mystification to hallow that which is endlessly commodified by globalisation and technology, fodder for the religion of consumerism. As the condition of postmodernity matures, the agenda of sociology has changed utterly. Issues of ethics, the self and authenticity have become embodied in an unsettled form of knowing that characterises the discipline. Postmodernity has changed sociology's sensibilities of itself. A disciplinary self-awareness, a reflexivity, has become entangled in its language of purpose. This complements a sense of precariousness in a culture, increasingly fractured and fragmented, where the self, its empowerment, its agency and its manufacture, have become foci of analytical concern. Increasingly, these issues relate to spirituality in a way that forces sociology into unfamiliar wrestling with an inchoate, if not unsustainable, division between theology and religion.

A decade ago, sociology knew where it was going. Laden with left-wing ideals, with critical analytical instruments that betokened the consensus of the trade, sociology found a conjunction between idealism and a vocation from which to debunk, where the latter fed the former. But times change, and as culture becomes a centre of its analytical concerns, so does the basis of sociological engagement. Scientific disembodiment has been replaced by an embodied angst less about critical engagements than about the understandings and meanings incarnated in life-styles in a culture offering prospects of limitless commodification. But this process has led to a diminishment of the quality of culture, and has engendered a sense of futility as to its basis. Now, sociological issues are about the making of meanings and not about their unmasking to effect their unmaking. Establishing meanings in a culture proximate to a cult of meaninglessness has placed sociology in the unusual position of witnessing to a crisis of moral ecology, an issue of spiritual conservation in the face of forces of calculation, commodification and disenchantment. It is the issue of the diminishment of the human spirit that increasingly engages sociological concerns. Estrangement points to a denial of spiritual ambitions. These changes have been forced on to sociology.

Postmodernity denotes a sociological sensibility of living beyond one's analytical means in a post-Enlightenment age. It has left sociology, the child of the Enlightenment, as an orphan in these uncertain times. Caught in an era of cultural politics, bereft of credible means of arbitration, sociology faces an identity crisis, less over its disciplinary remit than over its language of purpose. This seeking of meanings has generated renewed interest in the self and its relationship to culture, an unexpected pairing that poses unfamiliar dilemmas for sociology. These are embodied in the plenitude of options a culture of postmodernity presents for the endless manufacture of forms of self-actualisation. But these carry a price of narcissism and artifice. Entrapment rather than liberation seem near at hand in an arena where sociology finds it impossible to arbitrate between the authentic and counterfeit self on offer in the marketplace. New Age religions compete with supposedly dead theologies. In this mixing of manufacture and nostalgia, that effects so many selves, can sociology spot the difference?

The reflexivity surrounding postmodernity reveals a dual impotence in sociology in its dealings with this cultural diversity: it cannot manufacture beliefs of its own that reflect a transcendent critical position; and it lacks the means of rectifying unaided the spiritual deficiencies it now encounters in culture. This duality of analytical impotence is matched by a certainty that there is no Holy Ghost in the analytical machine of sociology, even in engagements with the self. Yet even this certainty is subject to a certain uncertainty.

It is difficult to understand why sociology should be fated to filial affiliation with nihilism unless it embodies some meta-narrative exempted by postmodernity. It can exercise choice anywhere but in constructing the opposite to nihilism; it can unmask any cultural arrangement save that of the discipline itself that makes disbelief a convention; and it can reflect any doubt, effect any affiliation with any belief system, except in the case of theology, where sociology becomes positively unreflexive. In dealing with theology, the grammar of sociology falls into stylistic confusion, where only the brave read between the lines. But elements that belong to theology have been incorporated unrecognised into recent sociology.

Aesthetics, self-identity, the efficacy of ritual and ethics now belong to sociology, but they belonged always to theology. Seldom have the sociological times seemed so propitious for playing Pascal's wager, for the tossing of the coin maybe to land the self safe on Canaan's side from these dreary shores of postmodernity. But there are further gloomy reasons for tossing coins borrowed from Pascal.

Risk, anxiety, the disembedding of institutions in a globalised culture, all operate to unsettle sociology in a manner that seems to accelerate. Doubt has become intensified as reflexivity has expanded into cultural awareness now admitting little division between sociologists and their laity. In reflexive terms, both are equally confused. Sociology now faces an unprecedented plight: it risks knowing too much about permutations of the cultural to decipher the plenitude of icons and images manufactured. Engulfment has become the occupational peril of postmodernity, thus paralysing the sociological imagination concerning potential objects and beliefs of affiliation. As the demands of service industries increase, in advertising, in marketing and in the commodification of images, the prospects for self-realisation in a culture of plenitude seem to have become unrealisable.[4] Opportunity combined with frustration is a postmodern variation on a theme in Simmel's tragedy of culture. Discovery of the capacity to realise what is elusive has unsettled the self for Beck and Giddens who have changed the agenda of late modernity. The construction of the self has become *the* project of a culture of postmodernity.

As Heelas and Birch indicate in this collection, concern with empowerment can lead to awareness of the god/goddess within. This tapping of wisdom might seem sufficient in a sociology where the self is a reflexive project seeking its own narrative, with all manner of choices to make it so.[5] But the quest for ontological security which Giddens sees as shaping the self in late modernity also carries theological prospects.[6] There is a risk that the unceasing constructions of the self in therapeutic forms can manufacture endless emptying themes of self-adulation. As Pascal notes, 'the nature of self-love and of this human self is to love only self and consider only self'. Both sociology and theology fear such a self. For the former, the egoism so effected subtracts from the social bond, whereas for the latter it signifies an imprisonment in pride and conceit. Sociology and theology can be understood to come to the issue of the self from differing expectations, for as Kreeft suggests, 'secular morality is a plan for the fulfilment of selfishness, Christianity is a plan for its destruction'.[7] For Christians, this is necessary for the task of putting 'on a new self, which is created in God's likeness, and reveals itself in the true life that is upright and holy' (Eph. 4: 23–4).

The seeking of a therapeutic self in communities and in self-help groups attracts sociologists, for these endorse the rootlessness that characterises postmodernity and the culture it portrays where imitation is possible without commitment. The *flâneur* desires to move with metaphysical impunity between reflexive communities. In Bourdieu's term, these are fields, reflexive sites for selves questioning the problem of their creation, for constantly re-inventing their basis over time and space with tools and products that are abstract and cultural and not material. They are places for the manufacture of reflexivity and its commodification.[8] There is a self-confirming property to the elective affinity embodied in these reflexive communities. If travellers do not like the cultural arrangements for the rendering of angst, they pass on to other sites of reflexive gathering.

This rootlessness, this seeking, combining aspirations for attachment but also means of escape, has given rise to a pilgrim metaphor in the culture of postmodernity. This form of seeking supposes a break with tradition. But, as Heelas suggests in this volume, even New Age religions have their own aspirations to tradition. There are other signs of a reappraisal of tradition unexpectedly arising as a means of emancipation from the tyranny of late modernity.

In his essay, 'Living in a Post-Traditional Society', Giddens provides a sensitive account of the functions of tradition, and the imperative to re-invent rituals of bonding. Re-thinking his way though the impasse of 'the end of history' and the slough of despond foreshadowed by the impending *fin de siècle*, the questioning of modernity points to a reappraisal of the basis of tradition. To some extent, Giddens is marking an analytical turn in this rehabilitation of tradition in the context of late modernity. For him, tradition 'is bound up with memory . . . ; involves ritual; is connected with . . . a *formulaic notion of truth*; has "guardians"; and, unlike custom, has binding force which has a combined moral and emotional content'.[9] Giddens recognises that modernity involves issues of choice, of making aspects of tradition new in life-style decisions. This notion of choice in late modernity is expressed in the context of religious fundamentalism by the assertion of a formulaic truth without regard for consequence.[10] At the end of his essay, Giddens sees post-traditional society as *not* being about a fated fragmentation and individualism, as an ending, but rather about a beginning, an escape from the compulsive repetitiveness of modernity to where there is a chance 'of developing authentic forms of human life that owe little to the formulaic truths of tradition, but where the defence of tradition also has an important role'.[11]

This seems a slightly equivocal ending to his essay. Formulaic truths of tradition are of consequence, to characterise fundamentalism, but inconsequential in the pursuit of authenticity. Giddens wants tradition but without the memory of the religious belief it might embody. He wants a believing without belonging, a faith without belief, a spirituality but without theological substance. This seems to place sociological reflexivity unexpectedly close to theological modes of reflection. A wanting, a seeking, an unsettlement, these are cultural matters that betoken a thirst for the spiritual, for forms of enchantment. But sociology is selective in what it admits from this implicit religious condition. Angsts of the New Age are permitted, but those seeking admission to re-invented traditions of Catholicism, such as monasticism, are off the sociological scale of reflexivity. Disciplinary convention suggests such zealots are those of a tribe for whom no sociological attachments are possible. What debate on religion and postmodernity has exposed are the conventions of sociological rhetoric trained to disbelief, but not to belief.[12] The issue of choice is on the agenda of a reflexive modernisation, an end product of postmodernity, but is not to be reflected upon in a manner that might risk corrupting the anxious sociologist into taking a theological turn. But then it depends what one wants sociology to say about the theological. What if Giddens' notions were arbitrarily re-cast to theological advantage?

What if the issue of the quest for ontological security is tied in with an *acceptance* of formulaic truths? Such a conjunction is not improbable, and neither is there anything in the rhetoric of sociology to preclude such a felicitous marriage in the face of the ills of late modernity. If nothing else, awareness of a reflexivity in sociology betokens the realisation that it suffers its own existential angst in the climes of postmodernity. Any question is possible and none is impossible. It is a characteristic of postmodernity that it has cleared the field of presumption, even of secularity, theology being assumed to have been long dispatched into the ditch. But if the field is so barren, where no stipulations preclude any belief system, bar that it deals with escape, the self and the balm of communal reflexivity, what precludes the resurrection of theology as an object of speculation on the site? It could be argued that postmodernity has its own theological imperatives which a sociological reflexivity uncovers.

Theology is faith seeking understanding. It provides formulae founded in revelation and tradition in a lineage of seeking to deepen understanding of the mystery of God. Sociological lineages, however, have been concerned with revealing this mystery as deceiving social projections whose illusory basis provides consolations to the unenlightened. This career of disbelief comes from a pantheon of sociological prophets, from Comte and Feurbach, to Marx and Durkheim, who saw religion as an impediment to a fullness of authentic realisation of social affairs. But this trumpeting of sociological prophecy now emits a very uncertain sound. If all meta-narratives can be contextualised, as tales with no transcending theme bar their fragmentation, then the sociologist's own story of the death of God is no exception. This account can also be contextualised for, in the last analysis, sociology is about the social arrangements of religious belief, not their substantive nature about which it is wise to be mute. In applying sociology to itself, its own contingent arrangements of disbelief can easily be read in terms of belief.

Sociology has no rhetoric to preclude such arbitrary re-readings, for we are told it is a discipline of consequence, not choice. But consequences generate choices, unsettlements, plights to be understood, for revelations of these are the peculiar fruits of the analytical calling of sociology in its dealings with a culture of postmodernity and the theodicy it uncovers. Disbelief has become an unreflexive conventional position of sociology, an arbitrary arrangement that can be adjusted in the direction of belief. The reflexivity of sociology enhanced in postmodernity reveals the unre-flective nature of this disbelief, its contingency and fragility. If postmodern-ity is about the contingency of ambiguities, the ambiguous nature of which leads to reflexive demands for community and modes of resistance to a rampant individualism, then sociology seems ripe and ready to consider Pascal's wager. Only disciplinary convention forbids it to spin that coin to declare if God exists or not. It might not want to, but the plights of postmodernity suggest to sociology the possibility of a spin in these climes of risk and anxiety.

The wager deals with the question: does God exist or not? The gamble is not about a proof of the existence of God – one starts with Aquinas for that – but about a probability that can be translated into a disposition to believe. If believing that God does exist, then the rewards are great and infinite, whereas if He does not, then nothing is gained, for disbelieving means gaining nothing but losing might risk eternal damnation.[13] Because reason cannot answer either way, the gamble is necessary and choice has to be made. This discussion is well known even if its sociological implica-tions are less so. But, for sociology, matters have changed. The ground upon which disbelief operated has become unsecured in the context of postmodernity, hence the prospect of the wager increasing as intolerance of nihilism develops and belief becomes an option, however reluctantly entered. Sociology is increasingly governed by issues relating to the price of disbelief for as Morris indicates the existential price of the atheist's wager is high, being increased wretchedness and unhappiness.[14] Such effects are far from ludicrous given public debate on the quality of culture, hedonistic individualism and increasing suicide rates for young males, for whom life has no purpose. Increasingly, there is a price to be paid in a society hell-bent on detachment from traditional forms of religious belief. There is a fine line between a social and a spiritual pathology, which sociology is unable to draw. Durkheim saw the problem, but drew the line in favour of positivism, to effect a commonality founded on reason. But postmodernity has dethroned these gods of positivism, so now what is left but to wager?

For Pascal, disbelief does not rest on reason, but on the failure to regulate the passions that legitimise the rejection of God. Pascal shares with Durkheim a worry over regulation of the individual, but seeks a different solution through means of the social in imitating the belief of others, in acting as if believing by taking holy water and having masses said, all of which diminish passions, the root of disinclination to believe. In so acting, one comes to virtue.[15] Clearly, this is not Durkheim's solution. Pascal seeks to move man away from the risk of engulfment with self into a loving and transcendent relationship. This relates to the plight of postmodernity, of the self seeking what is beyond actualisation, that transcends what can be commodified. The self oscillates between indifference over difference and a searching for a difference that will confound indifference. Endless diversions combined with indifference are theological enemies of belief, but they are also, precisely, the cultural characteristics of postmodernity. They disable prospects of belief, by disguising its necessity. But then as Pascal observed 'if our condition were truly happy we should not need to divert ourselves from thinking about it'.[16] The unhappiness signified in postmodernity indicates the amount of time thinking about it.

That sociology has a characteristic analytical insufficiency in dealing with culture arises in Georg Simmel in the disjunction between form and content where the capacity to grasp the tangible exceeds that of the intangible. In this discrepancy lies the tragedy of culture. There is a limitation in sociology which Blondel realised; it 'has a scientific nature only if it is not a science like others'. Later he suggests that the distinctive nature of the social sciences derives from the character of life itself.[17] This echoes debate on the autonomy of the cultural sciences. It also raises the issue of locating ephemeral properties of spirit within the social and the capacity of sociology to accomplish this task without reference to theology. At present the grammar of placement seems lost in the endless permutations of a tragedy of culture played out more by consumers than sociologists. Thus, as von Balthasar observes:

> man cannot place himself – not only because, like all finite beings, he is suspended at the level of being within the infinite, but also because,

at the epistemological level, he hovers as a spirit in a void that he cannot understand, and therefore is unable to root his (real) knowledge in the Absolute.

This relates to an aphorism of Pascal that characterises the dilemma reflexivity effects on the imagination of a sociologist dealing with a culture of postmodernity: 'I see too much to deny and not enough to affirm.'[18]

The purposelessness of a culture, especially a civilisation that can fail to see the evil of the Holocaust, might well pose unavoidable moral questions to sociology.[19] It might well force sociology into wagers it might not desire, for the issue of 'God is dead' takes on a different character when located in the concentration camp as against the academic's study. But sociology's theological questions lie nearer home. They lie in the area where sociology is strongest, in the relationship between action and self. This also reflects a point of convergence between theology and sociology.

Issues of action bear extension into theology in the understandings of the French Catholic philosopher, Maurice Blondel, which complement Pascal's wager. Many of Blondel's themes relate to issues of postmodernity. In his approach to action, the irresistible nature of choice is juxtaposed to the imperative to exercise will. A continual theme of his writing is that man is insufficient to himself. Thus Blondel notes, 'we would will to be self-sufficient; we cannot be'.[20] In the need to act in, through and with others, a consciousness of the universal can be found. Blondel pursues the reflexive implications of action through sociology into theology, and this gives him an unexpected contemporary relevance. For Blondel 'the role of action, then, is to develop being and to constitute it'.[21] This insight might start in symbolic interaction, but only convention dictates that this reflexivity should not be extended in a theological direction. Revolt against the intolerant limitations of nihilism invites a compensatory response to admit holy possibilities in action. At some point the 'mere' in action is ignoble and a transcendent leap is demanded to realise something deeper of the human, but also of the divine.

For Blondel, enactment relates to self-realisation, but in expectations and contradictions that mark a division between those of New Age religion and those of theology. Finding the *goddess within* means tapping the self for a wisdom of empowerment and independence. The self seems sufficient when re-born in the supportive groups which Birch describes. But theology makes a more radical demand on the self, one exemplified in the saying of Christ that 'he that findeth his life shall lose it; and he that loseth his life for my sake shall find it' (Matt. 10: 39). Blondel gives this a more direct expression when he states 'the sacrifice of self-will is the road of life for man'. This adventure involves mortification 'the true metaphysical experiment, the one that touches on being itself'.[22] It is in this setting that action can be understood as having a social function but also as the 'organ of spiritual reproduction'.[23]

Finding God involves the application of discipline to the social, to its structure, by sticking to the letter, to rituals that specify, for central to Blondel's link between theology and action is that 'the *act of faith* should inspire *faith in acts*'.[24] Inadvertently, Catholic reform of liturgy after Vatican II effected a disjunction of these properties, so that forms of rite that belonged to memory and tradition (now so valued) were arbitrarily jettisoned. In the interests of accommodation to modernity, these forms were deemed by ecclesial authority *not* to be capable of so inspiring this *faith in acts*. But with postmodernity, and the passing of modernity, sociology is saying and asking otherwise, for rites of resistance to the perils of globalisation and technology; these can be found in newly invented traditions which involve re-making new of what was old. In the perils of ambiguity postmodernity yields, sociology stumbles on theological issues. As Blondel noted, the 'secret of hearts is revealed through these ambiguities'.[25]

Echoing later comments of Ricoeur, Blondel discerns a surplus in the human act that affects and effects choice.[26] In dealing with what *cannot* be manufactured, man encounters a dilemma of will and action, but also the choice of a gift for, as Latourelle suggests, 'we effectively will the supernatural without however being able to bestow it on ourselves'.[27] This marks the end of sociology and the beginning of its theological wisdom, its new task of speaking to the self about how to effect a social construction of belief, when a culture of postmodernity conspires to speak otherwise. As Blanchette suggests, Blondel's philosophy demonstrated the need for an understanding of the subject in relation to human action and its destiny.[28] Affirming that action points beyond itself is not to impoverish sociology; rather it is to point to its significance within theology. Sociology gives witness to the contingent nature of belief, the means of discerning mechanisms that structure, social forces that shape and facets of action which achieve a condensed role in the social construction of sacred, but which can be given a comparative reading that enhances their significance. It is indicative of the impoverishment of theology's dealings with culture that feminist and liberation accounts were promoted as far as they have been. But sociology has other expectations in dealing with theology.

Sociology needs a site for the unfolding of action, a field that relates to culture, a setting for acting with recognisable purpose where meanings and understanding are to be performed for interpretation by an audience.

The orthodox Catholic Swiss theologian, Hans Urs von Balthasar, has unexpectedly supplied a theology well fitted for these sociological needs. He sought to formulate an aesthetic dimension to theology in an awesome range of writings which almost embodies a faculty of arts in one man.[29] He wrote the five-volume *Theo-Drama* describing how relationships between God and man can be understood in the language of the theatre. These volumes have a small but important section on sociology with an unexpected reading of Goffman. He also used a theatrical metaphor to inform his sociological understandings of the self.

The excursion of such an orthodox theologian as von Balthasar to the theatre to find his theology is as unexpected as the rich description of nature produced by Gerald Manley Hopkins, who as a Jesuit novice was taught to exercise a preventive custody of the eyes to realise a spiritual discipline. In Catholicism, there has been a long-standing suspicion of theatre and its potential for deception and corruption. Prior to Vatican II, there was prohibition in canon law against priests attending the theatre.

Von Balthasar argued that 'theatre springs from existence and is characterized by it'.[30] It draws on a distinctive trait of man: the capacity to act in a way that can be understood both by his self and those who behold his act. Through drama, public and private relations can be expressed and staged in a narrative that engages attention but also creates an affiliation with what is being unfolded, whether the play is a tragedy or a comedy. The theatrical metaphor in von Balthasar in *Theo-Drama* is used to understand a game played out before God, one that is dramatic in that it arouses a curiosity as to the purpose of the play. For von Balthasar, man plays a role before God that makes present a theological relationship (a game that also can be played in sociological terms). The staging of this drama involves a play, a director and an audience, the given props of human destiny sufficient to achieve self-understanding before the Divine. Deciphering the script, seeking the director's instructions and wondering over the ultimate audience of all – God – all these form a central theme in *Theo-Drama*. It is sometimes easy to feel that sociology's approach to self never had a theological dimension, but this is to forget sociology's own history.

Charles Horton Cooley made a seminal contribution to symbolic understandings of action in a way that influenced George Herbert Mead and many other sociologists since. Cooley stressed a fullness of self, one tied into theology and literature, that found itself in its imaginative dealings with symbols. The finding of an ideal self in this process humanises the actor but it also relates to the social aspects of conscience. Cooley's notion of self was directed to the issue of the cultivation of virtue, a moral dimension neglected up until recently. In this context he observed that 'an

unhealthy self is at the heart of nearly all social discontent'.[31] Speaking
of Cooley's sociology, George Herbert Mead observed that 'the gospel of
Jesus and democracy were of the essence of it, and more fundamentally
still it was the life of the spirit'.[32]

Cooley bequeathed to sociology a pivotal term: the looking glass self.
Its implications for reflexivity in the context of a culture of postmodernity are obvious. This concept denoted the way the self defines itself in
response to the actions of others. It finds its identity in and through their
responses.[33] Blondel echoes this concept, when he noted that 'action is the
mirror that offers us a visible image of our character. It is performed to
be seen.'[34] The concept fulfils a dual purpose for the self, of knowing and
being known. In the social process of life, the looking glass self, embodied in a role, achieves a temporary refuge, the partial sight of one caught
in a play without being asked.[35] It involves a fleeting image. In drama,
the looking glass self is given more systematic inspection. Drama offers
an artificial means of expressing a truth about life. Through masks and
ambiguous disguises, the actor realises a role that is make-believe, but
'real' in that it represents the essence of the human condition in public
dramatic form.

Von Balthasar makes passing reference to Cooley, referring to what he
terms his description of 'the self as a mirror reflex'.[36] Earlier, he noted the
way that 'functioning as a mirror, the theatre retains its ambiguity'. He
goes on to add that 'existence has a need to see itself mirrored (*speculari*)
and this makes the theatre a legitimate instrument in the pursuit of self-
knowledge and the elucidation of Being – an instrument, moreover that
points beyond itself'. But, as von Balthasar suggests, while the mirror
enables ultimate understanding of existence to commence, this will eventually take second place to the truth which it reflects only indirectly.[37]

Von Balthasar might have been surprised at the highly original reading Creelan has given of Cooley and Goffman which tries to establish
the theological significance of their work. Creelan suggests that there has
been a cognitive blindness to the critical moral and religious aspects of
their writings, aspects of which are interlinked. According to Creelan, the
notion of the looking glass self metaphor is derived from Adam Smith's
Theory of Moral Sentiments. Smith used the notion of sympathy as a
moral gauge, a form of consideration, where we become spectators on our
behaviour. This notion of sympathy and moral responsibility was related
to a Protestant notion of individuality. Creelan argues that Cooley gave the
metaphor a much wider use than sociologists have realised. His concern
with the concept was with self-transcendence rather than self-interest. Stress
on individuality as a vehicle for deeper generosity and self-giving relates

to a mystical tradition which had become obscured and which exists only as fragments in an age when economic man dominates.[38]

Creelan also suggests that Cooley was concerned with the social construction of an ideal character which the self could imitate and appropriate. The implications for theology of such ambitions attract sociological considerations. Cooley was interested in qualities of disinterested love and this related to the cultivation of a self-transcending moral affection. As with Goffman, selfishness and egoism represent failures that subtract from the social. This echoes Durkheim's concern with egoism as being a form of social pathology leading to an individualism, a loosening of bonds, expressed in high suicide rates. Egoism is the enemy both of sociology and theology for it subtracts from the need for self-realisation in a giving into the communal bond, where for both, with differing interpretations, the sacred is to be found. Both Cooley and Goffman show the way self-love leads to a degeneration of sacred symbols. For Cooley, the ideology of self-interest 'is less a grand cultural achievement of modernity than an intellectual and spiritual failure of the highest order'.[39] This ideology masks and overshadows greater and richer forms of cultural expression.

However, Creelan's most interesting point is to show the effect of Thomas à Kempis' *The Imitation of Christ* on Cooley's notion of the looking glass self when related to a mystical tradition. This points to a convergence of interest between Blondel, von Balthasar and Cooley, but also between theology and sociology. Creelan suggests that in reading à Kempis, Cooley found the fullness of what had been degraded and was fragmentary in the economic man: the shadow of his substance. The restoration of the soul as the mirror of God pointed back to a mystical synthesis in a way that roots a key concept of sociology, the looking glass self, within a spirituality. Reflexivity is given a contemplative turn. Furthermore, the self is seen in a theologically enhanced manner without eroding its distinctive sociological use. Creelan argues that Cooley's central distinction between self-love and disinterested love finds its root in à Kempis and parallels the mystic's endeavour.[40] This reading points to the narrowness of expectation, both theological and sociological, of what can be read from current concerns with reflexivity and image.

The value of linking Cooley with Goffman is that Creelan draws attention to the way individuals display and recognise moral qualities in ritual display in a quest for authenticity. Ritual is linked to the self being enlarged. Idolatry and egoism are the twin enemies of the ritual order and its endeavour to manifest the sacred. When rites become vehicles for the worship of the self they are doomed to fail, a point that emerges in Creelan's reading of Goffman through the Book of Job.[41] This was a test of the inexhaustible nature of the social. Job was involved in a wager, one that seems also to characterise sociology in its dealings with culture. Sociology cannot exhaust meanings in culture in climes of postmodernity. This is the witness sociology makes to theology. But another witness it makes is the degree to which there is an implicit theology in the disproportions the self uncovers reflexively in dealings with the culture of postmodernity. It is the numbness to theological feeling that precludes Pascal's wager being played.

Goffman's worry was about how unfeeling the actor could become when the sacred bond was ruptured by unfettered egoism that admitted no sense of tragedy in its life. Rendering the actor an object outside the remit of tragedy relates also to a crucial theme in *Theo-Drama* that 'tragedy, shorn of transcendence, shorn of "faith" annihilates itself'.[42] It is this worry over the extinction of the self that also worries sociologists dealing with postmodernity. It leads to issues of identity which Beck has formulated, but which von Balthasar considered earlier in his prolegomena to *Theo-Drama*, one which he repeats through the book: 'Who am I?'[43] That question can be answered only in the dramatic form of human existence, a ground upon which belief and disbelief are to be constructed, that supposes the use of social resources and cultural trappings to make self-recognition before the Divine possible. But, again, this relates to issues of choice, of advance or retreat. As von Balthasar argues, 'the condition in which man finds himself can only be one "scene" within a dramatic action; it points back to his origins and forward to a destination, however hidden these may be and however impossible to construct'.[44]

It is only in performance that man actualises the incompleteness of his essence but in a way that permits a self-reflection that is redemptive. In a striking passage, von Balthasar suggests that

> the incompleteness of human existence is the ultimate reason for the actor's essential ambiguity as he stands between humility and vanity, between the power to mediate a higher truth of existence and the power to obstruct it through intrusive self-affirmation.[45]

The answer only incompletely lies within sociology. In his reading of Simmel, von Balthasar feels that only in the 'vertical axis of biblical revelation' can a positive answer be found. Only through the 'name' with which God addresses the individual can the uniqueness of the person be found. Thus, 'neither pre-Christian thought nor mysticism and idealism; neither psychology nor sociology were equipped, or even authorized to give this answer'.[46] This reflects an earlier insight of Blondel.

Such an antinomy has a decided theological reference point, but the value of von Balthasar's *Theo-Drama* is that he manages to place it also in a sociological ambit. In dealing with issues of the self, role and performance, von Balthasar finds a useful theological foil in the writings of Goffman.

Goffman was a handicapped Canadian Jew, an outsider in American sociology, yet he left an indelible mark on the discipline. His central interest was in giving a sociological characterisation to the fragile link between the actor, his self and the structure in which his role is to be realised. In his writings, a quality of the sacred is awarded to the intangible and inexhaustible nature of that link, one that echoes Durkheim's approach to the social. Goffman lacked a method and did not form a school for heirs to follow. His analyses are populated with the bizarre, the stigmatised and those who use appearances cynically to manipulate small worlds, such as in the restaurant or the asylum. Street knowledge is elevated into the realm of the theoretical as Goffman gets below the texture of social intercourse to capture how sophisticated life is enacted.[47] If his actors have accomplishments, they involve deceptions which hardly seem a basis for edification or use by a theologian such as von Balthasar, whose concerns could not be further removed from those of Goffman, at least at first glance.

The brief section on sociology in volume 1 of *Theo-Drama* forms part of a chapter entitled 'role as the acceptance of limitation'. Whereas the preceding section treats Freud, Jung and Adler under separate headings, the sociological section is presented as a coherent essay remarkable for the extensive literature cited.[48] Von Balthasar seeks to move from existentialism to sociology as the site where his theology of drama can be constructed. Through its concern with roles and with socialisation, sociology aids in understanding issues of identity. In an extended footnote, von Balthasar gives a critical reflection on *The Presentation of Self in Everyday Life*. He found that Goffman had relativised the system of concepts he had borrowed from the world of the stage. Unlike the structures of social encounter which constituted a montage, von Balthasar observed that Goffman found theatrical action an artificial illusion. Anticipating later critics, von Balthasar was worried by Goffman's failure to flesh out the self behind the role. He felt that 'the means of producing and affirming a self do not lie with the peg on which it is hung'.[49]

Von Balthasar is concerned with the ambiguity of the link between self and role which sociology exposes. Characteristically, his treatment of sociological sources is exhaustive and has a remarkable completeness, again indicating von Balthasar's capacity to work in any literature. He spots a weakness in sociology's dealings with roles, an ambiguity that emerges as it places a foot in philosophical anthropology. Roles manifest either properties of freedom, of enablement, or of alienation of the self in the structures forms of actualisation require. This tension echoes the dilemma Simmel encounters between form and content. But the ambiguity penetrates further into the division between *homo sociologicus* and *homo absconditus*.[50] This points to a dilemma Dahrendorf noted, of the artificial basis of roles for sociology, that this generated a moral problem of risking masking the real being of the actor in the interests of achieving a scientific respectability. The more precise the analysis becomes, the more it threatens the man seeking authenticity and individuality in society, a point von Balthasar also grasps. For sociology, 'society is the alienated persona of the individual, *homo sociologicus*, a shadow that has escaped the man to return as his master'.[51] There is a dimension to role which transcends the aggregate of public positions, that Dahrendorf sees as inaccessible to sociology. Dahrendorf has drawn attention to an issue, oddly neglected in the context of the recognition of a reflexive dimension to sociology. What is the social image of man sociology uses? Reification of roles leads to an inauthenticity. A moral and sociological defence against such a risk is to stress the elusive nature of the essence of man. But to follow the latter course is to propel sociology in a theological direction.

With characteristic insight, von Balthasar has entered sociology into a competition it cannot win. There is a price in the artificial constructions, the concepts and forms, which sociology of necessity has to use, to enable its analysis to proceed, a point von Balthasar owes to Simmel. Within this antinomy that oscillates between limits and the limitless in roles, sociology speaks against itself. Roles realise the intentions of the self, but they are merely the form of its expected manifestation. A problem which runs through sociology, from Simmel to Giddens, is the antinomial nature of the social means of manifesting an act in relation to its structure of realisation, that it enables and disables, in a way that places a burden of choice on the actor. This opacity, this indeterminacy, in sociology is a weakness that points to a theological strength. Wagers are a humanistic but also a theological necessity which sociology needs to confront. Using Berger, von Balthasar wishes to set up sociology to deal with an issue of freedom, a property that leads to 'society as drama' where a human communion is possible.[52] Von Balthasar recognises the fruitfulness of sociology for theology, but also marks out its limitations as to how far it can go before it stumbles into the theological realm.

It is within Goffman's work, in the concept of role distance, that von Balthasar finds the gap where the self can escape and realise its own authentic meanings.[53] This gap between self and role points to an area of ambiguity, one that also realises properties of freedom. Miller argues that the concept of role distance has defensive functions that permit a personality to be uncovered, but one which Goffman has neglected to flesh out.[54] The self comes to realise itself in performance by using the social as a foil and, if need be, has the freedom to escape threats of reification and artificiality. Clearly, structures will vary according to the room given to escape, but Goffman's writings suggest that, even in a total institution, the self can find light in the cracks sufficient to survive.

Beneath the trivia of Goffman's actors lies an issue of tragedy, a property of self-deception, a blindness to social forces whose artifice and artificial basis are continually misrecognised. In their ploys, Goffman's actors flee but seem to find no safe sanctuary. It might seem as if in postmodernity Simmel's tragedy of culture has become a playful farce, or has it? What does tragedy signify in relation to the self?

Steiner argues that 'drama is the most social of literary forms. It exists fully only by virtue of public performance'.[55] This is a view von Balthasar would share, and probably he would also share Steiner's point that 'the increase in scientific and resource and material power leaves men even more vulnerable' to their tragic condition.[56] The death of tragedy is related to a retreat from public communal values into those that affirm the construction of the ego, a private venture, whose narcissistic qualities so vex a reflexively inclined sociology.

Steiner sees this movement of autonomy and self-actualisation occurring in the context of the discovery of belief in perfectibility and the responsibilities for overcoming imperfections which mark the writings of Rousseau and the Romantic movement. The self is invented as a site of self-inspection, reflecting little but the narcissism it can mirror. But this site could be illusory, for in mirroring but itself, the self might miss the risk which the tragedy betokens, which the audience sees, but to which the hero is blind. Tragedy involves great risks. In a point that Pascal might have approved, Steiner suggests that 'in authentic tragedy, the gates of hell stand open and damnation is real'.[57]

When forces of secularity effect a blindness, an unfamiliarity in the audience to deepest issues of grace and damnation implicit in classical and Shakespearian approaches to drama, when these elements form a diminishing part of what he terms 'active belief', then in like manner tragedy is diminished.[58] Steiner presupposes a social complement between a cultural milieu and discernment of the basis of a tragedy enacted.

At the end of his work, when dealing with Claudel (an interest he shares with von Balthasar), Steiner pulls his punches in relation to Christianity for reasons that are understandable. Damnation has to be absolute in his reading of tragedy. Because of the prospect of mercy, which occurs for

Faust, Steiner argues that 'there has been no specifically Christian mode of tragic drama even in the noontime of the faith'.[59] But in Claudel he glimpses the notion of partial tragedy, that affected by waste, the sense of havoc wrought by a careless life that detours from God's purpose. In the end, Steiner eloquently suggests that with His shadow no longer falling as on past dramatic heroes, God seemed to turn away during the seventeenth century. When He turned his back (and the advent of Benjamin's angel signifies this abandonment) the possibility of tragedy also seemed to pass, for it is 'that form of art which requires the intolerable burden of God's presence'.[60]

But the whole thrust of von Balthasar's *Theo-Drama* is to suggest the *persistent* presence of God acting within tragedy, even in that of the blindness of a culture of postmodernity. It is the social circumstances of the time that have killed a sense of tragedy. Part of that tragedy is that the belief in God has died. But it would be a ludicrous God who passed away leaving a vacuum known as the postmodern dilemmas of sociology. In any time there is a scandal of particularity attached to belief, that all times are ludicrous to affirm faith. But none are or have been so ludicrous as the time of postmodernity. It represents a sense of a tragedy of culture which sociology is peculiarly gifted to discern, where the making of theological wagers seems more and more a credible response to the times. In this context, sociology seeks its own ontological security that derives from its own reflexive circumstances.

Dahrendorf noted the myth of sociology, that in the aggregate of roles it had somehow discovered man's nature.[61] But sociology also faces a choice between affirming a reified *homo sociologicus*, or the belief that this is a caricature of humanity.[62] All postmodernity has done with its cultural creatures is to widen and to intensify this issue of choice. In the rampant commodification that follows, eternal dilemmas are transmuted into pastiche. All dilemmas, eternal or transient, serious or trivial, can be resolved in the dreams manufactured by the culture industry.

The value of von Balthasar's brilliant *Theo-Drama* is that he wrote a theology for a reflexive sociologist before it became fashionable. The self is given a place both within theology and sociology. Von Balthasar claimed that, 'if a time should come when all divine visiblity in the world should cease, when all questioning of God – even in the form of revolt or despair – should fall absolutely silent, drama would have lost its most essential dimension'.[63] But so would sociology fall, left to be locked in a culture of postmodernity desperately seeking solace in reflexive communities, with manufactured selves pursuing counterfeit images of themselves re-birthed by therapists but imprisoned by them also. Reflexivity is about seeing too much in the culture of postmodernity to live at ease with it. This unease of sight disturbs and therein lies the theological question that ultimately unsettles sociology, on its particular stage, in its particular tragedy unfolding in postmodernity. Perhaps sociology might learn that 'the fear of the Lord *is* the beginning of wisdom and the knowledge of the holy is understanding' (Prov. 9: 10). This is what was misunderstood at Sheffield, and perhaps sociology only can understand the folly of the venture.

Notes and References

1. *The Church Times*, 23 July 1993. Two years later, in the last week of August 1995, the English mass media were filled with graphic accounts of a tragedy surrounding these rites, with charges of sexual abuse made against the leader of the group, an Anglican priest, Chris Brain. He was suspended from preaching anywhere in the country, the services were closed down and he entered a psychiatric hospital as a private patient, amidst charges that a cult had been formed within the Diocese. A member of the Church of England Liturgical Commission had helped Brain write his services. This liturgical experiment, part of a parcel of house church worship styles and other radical Evangelical ventures, attempts to mirror cultural trends that have a self-evident cultural relevance to the young. The result is often a liturgical ghetto, with a young middle-class congregation, aged between 18 and 25, on a permanent high of praise, with a low understanding of theology. Few sociological studies exist of the turnover rate amongst these styles of worship. Manufactured feel-good emotions should not be confused with a hard-won spirituality that emerges from a sacramental theology to be found only in Catholicism.
2. *The Church Times*, 26 May 1995. It is difficult to know if Habgood had in mind the Sheffield experiment.
3. Marshall Berman, *All That is Solid Melts Into Air* (London: Verso, 1983), pp. 35–6.
4. For a comprehensive overview of this state of affairs, see Scott Lash and John Urry, *Economies of Signs and Space* (London: Sage, 1994).
5. Ibid., see especially ch. 3, pp. 31–59.
6. For his two pivotal works relating to these issues see Anthony Giddens, *Modernity and Self-Identity. Self and Society in the Late Modern Age* (Cambridge: Polity Press, 1991), especially ch. 2, pp. 35–69; and *The Transformation of Intimacy. Sexuality, Love and Eroticism in Modern Societies* (Cambridge: Polity Press, 1993).
7. Peter Kreeft, *Christianity for Modern Pagans. Pascal's Pensées, Edited, Outlined and Explained* (San Francisco: Ignatius Press, 1993), pp. 148–9.
8. Ulrich Beck, Anthony Giddens and Scott Lash, *Reflexive Modernization.*

Politics, Tradition and Aesthetics in the Modern Social Order (Cambridge: Polity Press, 1994), pp. 159–61.

9. Anthony Giddens, 'Living in a Post-Traditional Society', in Ulrich Beck, Anthony Giddens and Scott Lash, *Reflexive Modernization, op. cit.*, p. 63. Giddens refers to memory in its collective form in a way that seems similar to its use by Hervieu-Léger in relation to religion, as discussed in Grace Davie's contribution to this volume.

10. Ibid., pp. 100–1.

11. Ibid., p. 107.

12. Some of these themes are discussed in Kieran Flanagan, *The Enchantment of Sociology: A Study of Theology and Culture* (London: Macmillan, 1996).

13. Blaise Pascal, *Pensées*, trans. A.J. Krailsheimer (Harmondsworth: Penguin, 1966), pp. 149–53.

14. Thomas V. Morris, 'Wagering and the Evidence' in Jeff Jordan (ed.), *Gambling on God. Essays on Pascal's Wager* (Lanham, MD: Rowman & Littlefield, 1994), pp. 52–3.

15. Blaise Pascal, *Pensées, op. cit.*, pp. 152–3.

16. Peter Kreeft, *Christianity for Modern Pagans, op. cit.*, pp. 167–206. For the quotation, see p. 169. See also Jacob Meskin, 'Secular Self-Confidence, Postmodernism, and Beyond: Recoving the Religious Dimension of Pascal's *Pensées*', *The Journal of Religion* (Oct. 1995), vol. 75, no. 4, pp. 487–508.

17. Maurice Blondel, *Action (1893) Essay on a Critique of Life and a Science of Practice*, trans. Oliva Blanchette (Notre Dame, IN: University of Notre Dame Press, 1984), pp. 239–40. For a useful assessment of the influence of Blondel see the introduction to *Maurice Blondel. The Letter on Apologetics and History and Dogma*, trans. Alexander Dru and Illtyd Trethowan (London: Harvill Press, 1964), pp. 13–116; and James Le Grys, 'The Christianization of Modern Philosophy according to Maurice Blondel', *Theological Studies*, vol. 54, 1993, pp. 455–84.

18. Hans Urs von Balthasar, *The Glory of the Lord. A Theological Aesthetics*, III. *Studies in Theological Style: Lay Styles*, trans. Andrew Louth, John Saward, Martin Simon and Rowan Williams (Edinburgh: T. & T. Clark, 1986), pp. 207–8. Pascal's aphorism is cited in ibid.

19. Zygmunt Bauman, *Modernity and the Holocaust* (Cambridge: Polity Press, 1991).

20. Maurice Blondel, *Action, op. cit.*, p. 302.

21. Ibid., p. 425.

22. Ibid., pp. 352–3.

23. Ibid., p. 222.

24. Ibid., p. 375. It is in this context that sociology finds its theological mandate. If culture is a ground of faith, enabling or disabling the viability and authenticity of belief and its reception, then sociology has a characterising function in regard to this ambiguity. Contrary to Ayres, in Chapter 10 of this volume, the sociology proposed does not reach a 'theological dead-end' because of a lack of attention to the 'complex structure of theological discourse' (p. 184). This is just an imperialising trump card that can be played by theologians against a sociology with no pretensions to covering the gamut of theology. It also misses the point of sociological ambitions regarding engagement with theology, one where a viability of faith is sought. Sociological

intervention into theological discourse exists to force theologians to examine the ground upon which a flight into faith *can* be constructed in a hostile climate. The vacuity of culture forces sociology into a theological wager, one derived from an understanding of inductive circumstance and tyranny of detail, one that arises not from the cerebral treatment of texts, but from living within a cultural climate that militates against religious belief. Some of these issues have been explored in Kieran Flanagan, 'J.-K. Huysmans: The First-Post-Modernist Saint?', *New Blackfriars*, vol. 71, no. 838, May 1990, pp. 217–29.

25. Maurice Blondel, *Action, op. cit.*, p. 50.

26. Ibid., p. 287. See T.M. van Leeuwen, *The Surplus of Meaning. Ontology and Eschatology in the Philosophy of Paul Ricoeur* (Amsterdam: Rodopi, 1981). It is a pity that some of Blondel's insights have not been given adequate sociological recognition. There are many sociological resonances in his writing in *Action* (see especially pp. 241–84). His comment on the meaning and ambition of the ritual act, as 'the finite infinite, the infinite possessed and used' (p. 286) relates to themes explored in Kieran Flanagan, *Sociology and Liturgy, Re-presentations of the Holy* (London: Macmillan, 1991).

27. René Latourelle, *Man and his Problems in the Light of Jesus Christ* (New York: Albe House, 1983), p. 169.

28. Oliva Blanchette, introduction to Maurice Blondel, *Action, op. cit.*, p. xxi.

29. For an overall assessment of his work, see Peter Henrici, 'Hans Urs von Balthasar: A Sketch of His life', in David L. Schindler (ed.), *Hans Urs von Balthasar. His Life and Work* (San Francisco: Ignatius Press, 1991), pp. 7–43.

30. Hans Urs von Balthasar, *Theo-Drama. Theological Dramatic Theory*. 1: *Prolegomena*, trans. Graham Harrison (San Francisco: Ignatius Press, 1988), p. 259.

31. Charles Horton Cooley, *Human Nature and the Social Order* (New York: Schocken Books, 1964), p. 260. See also ch. 10, 'The Social Aspect of Conscience', pp. 358–401. For a useful appraisal of Cooley, see Edward C. Jandy, *Charles Horton Cooley. His Life and His Social Theory* (New York: Octagon Books, 1969).

32. George Herbert Mead, foreword to Charles Horton Cooley, *Human Nature and the Social Order, op. cit.*, pp. xxxvi–xxxvii. For an interesting theological reflection on Mead's approach to the self, see H. Richard Niebuhr, *The Responsible Self. An Essay in Christian Moral Philosophy* (New York: Harper & Row, 1978), pp. 69–74.

33. Ibid., pp. 183–7 and 196–9.

34. Maurice Blondel, *Action, op. cit.*, p. 218.

35. Hans Urs von Balthasar, *Theo-Drama. Theological Dramatic Theory*, 2: *Dramatis Personae: Man in God*, trans. Graham Harrison (San Francisco: Ignatius Press, 1990), pp. 341–2.

36. Hans Urs von Balthasar, *Theo-Drama*, 1, *op. cit.*, p. 532.

37. Ibid., pp. 86–7.

38. Paul Creelan, 'The Degradation of the sacred: approaches of Cooley and Goffman', *Symbolic Interaction*, vol. 10, no. 1, 1987, p. 33.

39. Ibid., p. 39.

40. Ibid., pp. 40–6.
41. Paul Creelan, 'Vicissitudes of the Sacred. Erving Goffman and the Book of Job', *Theory and Society*, vol. 13, 1984, pp. 663–95.
42. Hans Urs von Balthasar, *Theo-Drama*, 1, *op. cit.*, p. 430.
43. Ulrich Beck, *Risk Society. Towards a New Modernity* (London: Sage, 1992), see ch. 4, ' "I am I": Gendered space and conflict inside and outside the family', pp. 103–26. See also Hans Urs von Balthasar, *Theo-Drama*, 1, *op. cit.*, pp. 481–91. It is noteworthy that von Balthasar felt that there was one thinker at the end of the Christian and idealist periods who deserved special mention for endeavouring to answer the question 'Who am I?', and that was the German sociologist, Georg Simmel, whom von Balthasar seems to have admired and respected. See pp. 605–25.
44. Hans Urs von Balthasar, *Theo-Drama*, 2, *op. cit.*, pp. 335–7.
45. Hans Urs von Balthasar, *Theo-Drama*, 1, *op. cit.*, pp. 295–6.
46. Ibid., p. 628.
47. For a useful appraisal of Goffman, see Phillip Manning, *Erving Goffman and Modern Sociology* (Cambridge: Polity Press, 1992).
48. Hans Urs von Balthasar, *Theo-Drama*, 1, *op. cit.*, pp. 493–544. The section on sociology is on pages 531–44.
49. Ibid., p. 541.
50. Ibid., pp. 534–5.
51. Ralf Dahrendorf, 'Homo Sociologicus. On the History, Significance, and Limits of the Category of Social Role', in *Essays in the Theory of Society* (London: Routledge & Kegan Paul, 1968), p. 44. In dealing with sociology's image of man, Dahrendorf recognises a pocket of elusiveness in dealings with role and self. He notes that 'sociology has paid for the exactness of its propositions with the humanity of its intentions and has become a thoroughly inhuman, amoral science': p. 77. See also pp. 74–7.
52. Hans Urs von Balthasar, *Theo-Drama*, 1, *op. cit.*, p. 543.
53. Ibid., p. 541.
54. For a useful discussion of the implications of role distance, see Thomas G. Miller, 'Goffman, Positivism and the Self', *Philosophy of Social Science*, vol. 16, 1986, pp. 177–95. See especially p. 186–7.
55. George Steiner, *The Death of Tragedy* (London: Faber & Faber, 1961), p. 113. See also Graham Ward, 'Tragedy as Subclause: George Steiner's Dialogue with Donald MacKinnon', *The Heythrop Journal*, vol. 34, 1993, pp. 274–87.
56. Ibid., p. 6.
57. Ibid., p. 128.
58. Ibid., p. 197.
59. Ibid., p. 331.
60. Ibid., p. 353.
61. Ralf Dahrendorf, 'Homo Sociologicus. On the History, Significance, and Limits of the Category of Social Role', in *Essays in the Theory of Society*, *op. cit.*, p. 79.
62. Ralf Dahrendorf, 'Sociology and Human Nature', in ibid., p. 98.
63. Hans Urs von Balthasar, *Theo-Drama*, 1, *op. cit.*, p. 359.

10 Theology, Social Science and Postmodernity: Some Theological Considerations

Lewis Ayres

In a survey of the history of relations between sociology and theology, Robin Gill sees the current context as one in which an increasingly hermeneutically aware social science, somewhat chastened about its earlier universalist rhetorics, is now matched by a theology aware of the complexity of social scientific discourse and more ready to understand, use and struggle with its products.[1] Similarly, accepting the challenge of some basic postmodernist strategies of thought, Kieran Flanagan points to the possibility of the reintroduction of the sacred into sociology as a basis of religious belief and to the need for categories which will help in providing a nuanced description of the place of the self. In the postmodern context of a relativisation of the meta-narratives which penetrate all discourses, theological wagers within sociology are now possible, and are perhaps vital, if nihilistic relativism is to be opposed in theory and in society.[2]

The aim of this chapter is to ask, from the theological side, some fundamental questions about the nature of this dialogue between disciplines.[3] Although this contribution is that of a theologian, not a social scientist, the exploration of what is actually at issue – both philosophically and through attempting to reconstrue that dialogue theologically – has relevance to *both* partners in the debate.

The discussion begins with John Milbank's recent critique of the relationship of social theory and theology. Although social theory is at the centre of his investigation it is also the focus for a consideration of many different social sciences. Despite the critical response of some social scientists to his work, Milbank has a serious and vital point to make: the discourses of the social sciences and the discourse of theology are in conflict. While accepting some of Milbank's 'theses on theology', this chapter attempts to outline the possibility of a deeper and more fundamental dialogue between theology and the social sciences. The second section examines the nature of theological discourse and the true area of conflict between these disciplines. In the third section a possible reconstrual of the hermeneutical nature of theology is explored which both offers the foundation of a deeper and more fruitful dialogue and a critique of the attempt of Flanagan to use von Balthasar's work within sociology. The last section sketches something of the complexity of the different dialogues between theology and the social sciences that need to be envisaged. Throughout the chapter the question of postmodernism as the stimulus for and as the situation of this new and more fundamental dialogue between disciplines is explored.

Milbank's critique of the social sciences is based on a few basic and interrelated themes, the most important of which is his accusation that there is in the social sciences an implicit 'policing of the sublime'.[4] This 'policing' results from the attempt of secular social theorists to describe society in ways which locate the divine as a second-order representation of prior social forces, or as a misconstrued grappling with a factor of experience best explained by other means. According to this criticism, the social sciences, and social theory in particular, have been allowed by the theological world to usurp a central part of theology's role through claiming explicitly or implicitly that the networks of social and symbolic relations we see around and between us are most properly the subject of social scientific methods of investigation. But by following the methods of social scientific investigation and speculation, theologians simply delude themselves that they are taking into account the social situation of late- or post-modernity. In fact they are simply allowing their investigations to be skewed and distorted by other equally comprehensive sets of overarching narratives ('comprehensive' is used here as an alternative to 'theological' to avoid for the moment the complication in vocabulary involved in the latter).

Theology will benefit not from entering into a mutual dialogue with these sciences, but through inaugurating the uncovering of the *theological* 'social science' contained *within* theology (and specifically within ecclesiology). In an excellent summary of the argument, Fergus Kerr traces the dual nature of Milbank's programme. Kerr asserts that for Milbank

> there is no need to bring theology and social theory together, theology is already social theory, and social theory is already theology. The task is to lay bare the theology, and anti-theology, at work in supposedly non-theological disciplines like sociology, and, analogously, to uncover the social theory inscribed in theology.[5]

Many discussions critical of Milbank's *Theology and Social Theory* have focussed on the diversity of approach in modern social science and on the impossibility of tarring all social science with the same brush in such an indiscriminate fashion. Thus, Gill points to the example of David Martin and asks how can one accuse all sociologists of being trapped in Kant's legacy when so much of the work of someone like Martin seems aimed at offering a critique of that tradition. Similarly Flanagan notes the example of Berger, whose lifetime's work attempts in different ways to find a place for the sublime in social scientific thought. But Milbank argues that this style of criticism simply misses the point because it fails to understand the nature of theological discourse and of Christianity.[6]

For Milbank the problem with modern social science only begins with those theorists who follow an openly Kantian or neo-Kantian line. From criticism of those positions he follows a line through other current styles of social thought, always connecting back to some fundamental charges, which in part draw many unsuspecting other thinkers into the 'Kantian' net. The idea that all modern sociology can ultimately be spoken of as Kantian is intended as much to point to a possible theological archaeology of modern sociology as it is to indicate direct theoretical relationships. To understand this, it is important to follow through a brief outline of this sort of Milbankian archaeology. To begin with Berger, it is clear that his famous theological appendix to *The Social Reality of Religion* is founded on the idea that religious explanation applies to the 'existential' situation of the individual while sociology describes the workings of empirical society. Sociology does not raise questions which theologians need to answer because an empirical discipline is not susceptible to non-empirical answers. The threat to theology comes when the sociology of knowledge attempts to place the theoretical work of the theologian in a particular socio-historical situation and begins to offer an alternative account of the reasons for holding particular beliefs. The particular notion of the divine possible in Berger's thought is only ever a general absolute, bearing little relation to the structures of Christian discourse.[7]

Although the majority of interpretative social scientists of the 1970s and 1980s, strongly influenced by hermeneutics, would be much more wary of easy divisions between the private – the 'existential' – and the social, a similar underlying conception of human existence and society remains. One has only to look to the anthropological practices of such giants as Jonathan Z. Smith, whose work is overtly tied into a Kantian paradigm of knowledge, and Clifford Geertz, where religion or culture functions as a text which addresses something fundamental and inexpressible about the 'human'. In both cases, emphasis on the 'ordinary, recognisable features of religion as negotiation and application',[8] which has been so fruitful in developing the nature of social observation (and in the case of Geertz which has had such a deep effect on a number of theologians), is actually tied into a conception of the cultural system theological in scope and with the characteristics Milbank identifies. Here one should note the continuity between Milbank's antipathy to social scientific styles and his antipathy to the philosophy of hermeneutics. The latter also relies on a separation between empirical knowledge and an *a priori*, inviolable sphere of 'humanity': a distinction between explanation and understanding (*verstehen*).[9]

The largely neo-Kantian structures in these understandings of the task of social science, the distortion of Kant's more subtle understanding of categorical cognition in favour of grounding knowledge of an empirical realm in a sphere of 'value' neither purely platonic nor purely formal, are relatively clear.[10] Already, they point towards one other theme besides the 'policing of the sublime' key to Milbank's argument: a strong critique of any theory which rests on the supposition of an ultimate, or 'natural', ontological violence. For Milbank, if the 'empirical realm' is open to purely sociological analysis and if that analysis claims at least to work towards accurate description of the forces 'naturally' at work, then the empirical realm is one in which there is ultimate violence and discord. This is a theological (virtually gnostic) theme which is opposed by the Christian supposition of an ultimate non-violent peaceful process of difference. Milbank draws out this theme particularly strongly in the case of postmodern thought.

At the beginning of his chapter 9 in this volume, Flanagan points to the uncertainty of sociology in the 1990s, an uncertainty brought on by postmodern doubts about the mechanistic and analytic rhetoric so beloved of previous generations of sociologists. The three factors which Flanagan identifies at the core of this postmodern attitude are fairly uncontroversial: the loss of faith in meta-narratives; the 'sacralisation' or 'mystification' of the endless commodification of modern culture; and the increased individualistic focus in society which has its theoretical counterpart in uncertainty about the nature of the self, its roles and identity formation. However, whereas for Flanagan this stimulus finally makes possible a theological wager within sociology and a supposition of the divine, for Milbank – whatever the wagers that become possible in the wake of postmodernist trends – the assertion of an absolute historicism and an ontology of difference lead postmodernism only into the creation of a new metaphysics, a new meta-narrative. Thus the nihilist philosophical and semantic trends upon which so many postmodernists draw only serve to emphasise their following of intellectual strategies which can also be drawn out from openly modernist thought. The move from modernism to postmodernism becomes simply a shift within a larger tradition of secular thought.

In fact it is the rise of postmodernist thinking that has provided key theoretical support for Milbank's attack: not through providing a set of philosophical tools which can be used for theological ends to deconstruct social theory, but by providing a dialogue partner whose observations and speculations stimulate, parallel and develop Milbank's own. For Milbank postmodernism exposes the character of the many incommensurable languages games other than theology, and provides a stimulus which turns theology back to its own fundamental claims. Postmodernism does not create a situation in which some sort of intellectual wager in favour of the divine becomes possible in quite the same way as it does for Flanagan. The radicalism of postmodern thought enables Milbank to see that there are no 'arguments' against nihilism and modern culture. As a consequence, theologians must simply attend to their own story and their own modes of narration. This point is perhaps clearest in his attempt to radicalise MacIntyre.[11] For Milbank, the different modes of knowledge we tend to take for granted should all be understood as forms of 'narrative knowing', in which explanation and understanding are replaced by renarration, by non-identical repetition. All narratives construct. They do not explain, however much they like to deceive themselves that they do. Christianity is simply more persuasive, a better, more consistent story and practice.

Milbank has identified as secular that tradition of thought which, underneath the direct discussion of social theory in the post-Enlightenment context, follows a line from the emergence of the individual absolute owner of property in the late antique world, through Kant's philosophy of right to the postmodern assumption of an ultimate violence. In contrast to this tradition, Milbank offers a picture of Christianity as a transformative social discourse which naturally adapts and surpasses the Classical philosophical tradition. Christianity contains the resources for its own metaphysics and ontology within its narrative structure, and envisions a state of ultimate peaceful difference created by God. This picture (openly) has significant Hegelian overtones, perhaps most obvious in the extent to which Milbank portrays the history of Christianity not as a witness to some transcendent Other but as the gradual description and evolution of the true transformative, redemptive practice. The narrative of Christianity is one which contains its own speculative moment and the way in which this moment represents ultimate truth enables Christianity to be an alternative discourse which is not ultimately concerned with its own power. Thus Milbank asserts that '[a narrative] has to assume an ever fully representable synchronic setting, which means that it always in a fashion anticipates the speculative task of ontology and theology. Narratives only identify God because they simultaneously invent the unrepresentable "idea" of God.'[12]

While Hegel himself is ultimately guilty for Milbank of not getting past the 'secular' removal of the absolute as the ground of religion as a cultural practice, this very particular retrieved Hegelianism is a vital part of the Milbankian programme. It allows Milbank to concentrate on the arena of actual social negotiation and narrative existence as the place where the Kingdom of God is made real. Although Gillian Rose castigates Milbank for insufficient Hegelianism and too much idealism, the Hegel with which she castigates him is one who sees the negotiations of ordinary existence as the place where our lives find their meaning. It may well be that there are more parallels between Milbank's stated aim and Rose's philosophy than either care to admit.[13]

Attacking Milbank's thesis on the grounds that it does not respect the diversity of modern sociology and social science is mistaken. This is partly because there is actually some continuity in the particular attitudes and assumptions that Milbank chooses to criticise, but also, more importantly, because his attempt to outline an archaeology and typology of modern social science is incorporated always within a *theological* perspective of his own. His philosophical positions on narrative and on the structure and intent of social science are intended to contribute towards a picture of the nature of theology and of theology as a discourse. Milbank creates a vision of competing discourses in which theological discourse is the only one that can provide a foundation for Christians. His message is in large part addressed to theologians who have, in his eyes, failed to see the nature of the theological perspective that should motivate their work. Theologians who wish to disagree with his work cannot just contradict his view of social science itself; they need to come to terms with his theological perspective and offer a different account of theological discourse.

Similarly, social scientists who wish to argue against him are faced with the task of finding ways to enter on a new and more complex dialogue with theology in which they become aware of the nature of theological discourse. Because of Milbank's linking an understanding of the untranslatable nature of discourses (based on the lack of a medium of universal meaning) with a picture of theological discourse as competent to deal with all the areas traditionally left to the social sciences, social scientists who wish to engage with his thesis, and with theology, need to explore the actual structure of theological discourse itself. So far, both theological and social scientific responses to his thesis have failed to do this.

In this chapter, our task now is to look more closely at the nature of theology as a discourse, to examine that discourse in a little more density, and to see how such an examination makes clearer what exactly is at issue. This will show that Milbank's thesis, under the stimulus of postmodernism, does point towards the correct area of conflict between theology and social science, but also indicates the possibility of an alternative construal of the dialogue between the disciplines. This investigation will involve examining the nature of Christianity as a discourse within a tradition close to Milbank's and suggesting some negotiations within that tradition. This leads us to our second section.

There are similarities between Milbank's attitude to sociological explanation and the attitude of the Swiss Reformed theologian Karl Barth to secular disciplines. For Milbank, these disciplines are ultimately theological, partly because they represent a bastardised version of theological questions, partly because they can be seen to have developed from theology and hence take up a 'heretical' stance to it. For Barth, such disciplines must be subjected to an *a priori* theological meta-perspective, locating them as 'fallen' precursors to a legitimate theological understanding.[14] Only by first locating them within that perspective is it possible for Barth to create and to form the right attitude, one formed around invocation of God. Only this attitude will allow someone to participate in the world of fallen human knowing while learning to attend to the paradox of revelation.[15] There are great differences between these two thinkers, especially in terms of their philosophical foundations, but there is a parallel in their concentration on the need for a theological meta-perspective, and a specifically theological discourse in which to ground dealings with non-theological disciplines. Only thus can a hermeneutic for the world be formed, and only thus can Christianity as a *practice* be formed.

Understanding Christianity as a practice formed through a particular discourse perhaps indicates why something of the density of that discourse needs to be made clear. The conflict between social science and theology concerns the nature of 'reality', the role of perceived 'reality' in the development of personal life and the nature of the discourse which one should use to describe the basis of 'reality'. Putting these three points in specifically theological dress, one might say that the conflict comes first because theology attempts to offer an account not simply of a greater reality 'elsewhere', but a re-structuring of the world of human life. Second, theology attempts to offer accounts of how this re-structuring should be understood as a call for a new process of reading the world, as a reconsideration of the style of our thought about and interaction with the world. Third, theology, and specifically doctrinal and systematic theology, explores the nature and structure of the discourse which will promote this re-reading of the world.

In this context, discourse refers to a *style* of speaking about, and reacting to, things from the perspective of an understanding of existence where our selves are formed and exist within a complex of semi-autonomous textual structures (using to some extent the links made by Ricoeur in his 'action as text' paper). Thus, a discourse is a style or way of existing, including a conception (amongst other things) of selfhood. The emphasis in this usage is on a discourse as a place in which particular styles of interaction are formed and developed, rather than on a discourse as an excluder of certain, possibly positive, other options (and in this sense is far more related to MacIntyre's notion of tradition than to the rationality of Habermas). But if a discourse is also an account of selfhood it is an account of the place of the self, its styles of interaction and so forth. The meaning of 'self' is clear only by looking at the place of that 'self' in a particular discourse. To explore the nature of Christian discourse and the Christian notions of selfhood is thus to explore the relationship between our selves, the life of Christianity and the call of God.

Following this analysis it can be said that Christian discourse and thus Christian accounts of selfhood should be exercises in Trinitarian theology. Christian discourse is an attempt to think and act towards a description of reality by attempting to work within a belief that God is represented in history. God's representation has a form that demands continual appropriation and is structured not simply by the story of God's intervention in Christ, but by the story of God's intervention which is part of a narrative told by the Church as it responds to that intervention. The process of response is one in which God is present (as we might expect given an incarnational revelation of his *presence*): an account of the difference between Son and Spirit, between representation and appropriation or re-representation, lies at the core of Christian discourse.[16]

This difference between Son and Spirit and the process of our life within it lies at the core of Christian discourse, for it is in this process that we begin to understand the life of progress towards re-envisioning the world as the creation of God. This appropriation, mentioned earlier, takes the form of an attempt to live as if the narrative of God's threefold intervention provides a model which will lead us back towards a true interpretation of the world as created. Thus the idea of 'Trinitarian theology' is not simply an attempt to offer a different model of God; it is first an attempt to structure the process of Christian life as a representation and appropriation of the Christ-event and, second, it seeks to indicate that the Christ-event is a revelation of a God who is involved in the world as creator *and* redeemer. The traditional language of immanent and economic Trinities is thus seen to be unhelpful when it is taken to indicate a Trinitarian structure to revelation from which we then deduce our way to an immanent picture or model of God in Godself. Instead, the theology of the Trinity is designed to build upon the simple belief that in Christ God is revealed as God. In so doing, notions of God as simply one or as simply a transcendent 'divine' are deconstructed. To a large degree, the idealist legacy within theology has hidden the extent to which the Christian notion of God is closely related to the structure of Christian discourse. Christian discourse thus invokes a practice and calls for a transformation of our reading of the world.

An account of the basic structure of Christian discourse highlights the key areas of conflict between theology and social science more accurately than simply referring to conflicts over the verifiability or otherwise of social 'facts'. Such an account also helps to make clear the importance (and theological dangers) of postmodernist thinking in exploring this conflict. Earlier fears within theology about the reductionism of sociology tended to focus particularly on the belief that sociology wished to follow through a programme of identifying immanent, empirically testable, causal networks which would leave no place for God. While in many cases the dialogue between the two disciplines may have been that harsh, in most cases the position is much more complicated.

When we begin to think about the conflict in the light of sociologists influenced by hermeneutics and the various streams of postmodern (and especially deconstructive) trends, that complication is revealed much more clearly. Once theologians are aware of the close interaction between methods and the results of description in the social sciences, and once we examine these hermeneutical trends in the light of a postmodern challenge which characterises all these self-perpetuating disciplines as totalising rhetorics, then theologians are forced into a close examination of their own discourse and its characteristics. Once the full force of this postmodern challenge is faced – faced but not necessarily *accepted* – the conflict between social science and theology can be seen to be a more subtle conflict between different patterns of life and selfhood, all of which involve conflicts over the interpretation of existence and over styles of interpretation and possible threads of explanation. The nature, place and style of the adaptation and re-reading which Christian discourse proposes in the world become key areas of conflict. Our notions of reality, our theologies of God and of creation, and our theologies of causality – and perhaps our flirtings with Hegelianism – all need to be viewed within a more complex picture of discourses and their interaction.

There is no room here to indicate concrete lines of inquiry for investigating dialogue over notions of 'empirical reality' and 'causality'. At this juncture, the task is to sketch out the 'space' within which such an investigation should occur. The subtlety and complexity of the possible dialogue will only become clear once theologians so engaged become more aware of the complex structure of theological discourse and social scientists also explore that complexity. The more theologians (and social scientists) come to understand the subtlety of the dialogue, the more they will find themselves pushed into endeavouring to understand the structures of Christian discourse in the search to comprehend the complexity of the problem. For social scientists the question is, of course, more complex; nevertheless, for the dialogue between the disciplines to proceed more fruitfully there must be a deeper appreciation of the need to explore the complexity of theology's structure if more than superficial points are to be made. This leads on to our third section.

Having offered a brief sketch of the purpose of Christian discourse, the next stage is to see how theologians might refound the dialogue between these two disciplines. Flanagan's own attempt to highlight the possible structures of a postmodern sociology centre around the reintroduction of the category of drama as a means for rethinking the concepts of self and role. In Chapter 9 of this volume, Flanagan follows Giddens' lines of thought in his 'Living in a Post-Traditional Society', but then goes on to highlight the ambiguity of Giddens' call for tradition without traditional forms of religiosity: Giddens strays on to theological territory but refuses the dialogue. Flanagan himself, more deeply influenced by postmodernism, sees sociology drawn into a Pascalian wager because of its ability to contextualise its own accounts and prescriptions. Wagering on the existence of God, Flanagan turns to Blondel's philosophy of action and von Balthasar's account of drama in order to find an account of the self founded on symbolic and purposive accounts of action. Sociology can now provide accounts of particularity, of the structuring mechanisms and social forces which are vital in the social representation of the sacred, while making a theological wager that allows an account of the self which has deep theological resonances. Von Balthasar uses the theatre to develop a theology in which humanity plays out a drama before God. The theme of drama is used because it takes account of humanity's need to see itself 'mirrored'. Drama as a form begins to enable understanding of existence, although it can do so in only a shadowy way. The essential ambiguity of human existence can ultimately be played out and understood only against the 'vertical axis' of biblical revelation. Only the incompleteness of human existence is properly mirrored in human drama.

Building on von Balthasar's use of secular models of drama to describe human mirroring of itself, Flanagan is then able to distinguish between a 'sociological' analysis of human existence carried out in the sphere of drama (von Balthasar's dialogue with sociology is taken to mean that there must necessarily be a specifically sociological section of von Balthasar's discourse) and a 'theological' account of the ultimate purpose of the drama. Flanagan's outline of his position both here and in *Sociology and Liturgy* is extremely suggestive, and, as will become clear, has *some* links with the alternative proposed here. Flanagan's analysis, however, eventually reaches something of a theoretical dead-end because of his lack of attention to the complex structure of theological discourse.

At key points in his attempt to set out a *Theodramatik*, von Balthasar describes our role as actors in the drama of life, which is also a drama of God, through the use of the category of transposition.[17] Von Balthasar uses this category as part of his description of the basic structure of the Church and specifically to provide an account of the relationship of post-Easter Christians to the historical life of Christ. For von Balthasar, two transpositions are involved. First, the apostles have to draw an analogy between their post-Easter experience of God and their life with Jesus the man (whose talk of the coming 'hour' they now understand through concentrating on the function of His life); second, non-Christians and non-apostolic Christians must draw a similar analogy between their situation and that of those first post-Easter Christians.

In the first transposition the apostles must play 'in a new key' the actions and responses developed during their time with Jesus. Statements about the presence of Christ and about His life among them are made not as historical record, but as testament to the meaning of Christ and His function. The giving of testimony in turn emphasises the role of the Spirit as interpretative guide. To begin to understand what has happened (beginning to create a 'space' in which the process of coming to understand may be structured) the apostles start to speak of Christ and the Spirit, which necessitates both setting out the uniqueness of Christ and the problematic role and nature of the Spirit. If post-Easter life and interpretation is to be found in something like this space, then the repetition of Christ's actions, the living out of His commands, and the active interpretation of the parabolic material from His lifetime becomes a non-identical repetition aimed always at discovering the presence of Christ and the intention or direction of that presence.

The second analogical leap is made by subsequent generations of Christians who equate their own experience with that of the first apostles. At this point the post-Easter synchronicity of all Christians brings into full focus the structure of transposition. The Spirit acts to reverbalise the Son. The language of Spirit creates communities in which the deeds of the Son can be non-identically repeated: in so doing the character of God is revealed in historical practice. The moment of theoretical representation is deeply embedded in this process of identification. Again, the doctrine of the Trinity offers not simply a doctrine of God's objectivity *per se*, because it also and always indicates the 'shape' of our reception of revelation. We learn the nature of the relationship between Spirit and Son not simply by searching for an analogical *tertium quid* in our Trinitarian language, but through seeing the relationship between founding action and our talk of repetition in the Spirit.

Both the virtue of von Balthasar's description and the problems of the project Flanagan proposes can now become clear. In the second volume of his *Theodramatik*, von Balthasar makes more use of this theme of transposition, attempting to set out rules for the 'transposition of horizons'.[18] Here we find very strong emphasis placed not simply on the synchronicity of all post-Easter Christians, but on the need for transposition to be seen as functioning always against an ultimate horizon. Only against such a horizon will it remain clear that our repetitions are non-identical. The nature of the ultimate horizon and the way it has been made known to us radically influences the nature of our transposition and repetition. Hence, von Balthasar develops his account of how that ultimate horizon is lost through an account of spiritual discernment whose character is closely dependent on relating images of Christ to particular socio-historical circumstances.

At this point, von Balthasar's theme can be extended a little further, and its relation to a necessary 'discipline of the world' within Christian discourse discussed. From my sketch of Christian discourse as Trinitarian, it should be only a short step to the statement that the created world itself is a discipline, a practice, an *askesis* for Christians. Seeing the created world as the creation of God, and our actions within the created world as representations of God's self-presentation to us, is a practice which we have lost through our fallenness (one does not have space in a short study to explore the meaning of 'fallenness' in Christian discourse). This practice is recovered through the *imitatio Christi* and through the complex process of negotiation and judgement constituted by that imitation. To sustain this negotiation (which, contrary to Flanagan, is truly apophatic in that it involves a *dynamic* of apophatic and cataphatic) a metaphysics is necessary to secure the possibility of negotiation and engagement. This metaphysics will be one which can accommodate both relationship *and* the reality of external relations, for without these we will not be able to secure the full reality and difficulty of the process of transposition. Thus our theology finds a place for the world as our 'situation' in an attempt to secure the reality of the structure of limits within which the complexity of transposition can be understood. Theology's discipline of the world is central to its Christological and redemptive practice.[19]

In the world, we encounter and are involved in a variety of discourses, 'readings' of its structure. Many of these readings are founded on theoretical conceptions of the world's actuality and possibilities which may contradict some fundamental structures of Christian discourse: not simply a result of our modern, late-modern or postmodern condition, but a result of our fallenness. The correlation between the theologies of fallenness, redemption and creation has a long history, and at many points through that history these themes have been drawn together in the prism of our discipleship in the world, the practice of Christian life being the place where Christian discourse is articulated and formed. One can usefully point here to the changing attitude of the Christian community towards 'heresy'. Whether theologians have founded their positions in some sort of socio-historical criticism, in some form of *Tendenzkritik*, or even in some variety of the deconstructionists' account of *différence*, there has been an increasing understanding of the difficulty involved in the *a priori* dismissal of the other's fallen experience of the world. This might be seen simply as the crumbling of theology under the weight of modernity, but alternatively one might look upon it as theology's extension of the principles of Christian discipleship to new areas of Christian existence. The connection between *humilitas* as the ultimate discipline (Augustine) and the theme of continual transposition into *this* situation means that the presentation and search for orthodoxy must be conducted as essentially and necessarily linked to *humilitas* in its presentation.

Christian discourse exhibits a fundamental structure which aims to promote practices of interpretation, adaptation and transposition. The narrative at the base of this process is one which functions anagogically, leading us into an engagement with our place in the fallen mysterious world. That world is explored through the retelling of the Gospel story as a key to the other stories we tell. The engagement on a theoretical level between theology and social science is simply one sophisticated example of this process. And yet, if it is so, then a failure to see the complexity of the process of Christian life and discourse means a failure to see the nature of the possible dialogue: and this is my accusation against Flanagan. His dialogue still refuses to see what role the divine plays in *Christian* discourse (there is only a situation insofar as there is also an account of the meaning and purpose of that situation) and thus fails to explore the full possibility – and danger for a social scientist – of the dialogue.

Finally, it should be noted that general remarks about the conflict and possible dialogue between disciplines remain highly theoretical without an attempt to take account of the many different dialogues that occur between different areas of theology. The virtue of the foundation for dialogue proposed in this chapter is that it is able to support the discussion of a number of these levels. It allows the consideration of the theoretical dialogue between disciplines that has been the central concern of this exploration but, also, it may provide a foundation for considering the description of actual practical Christian life as a negotiated narrative between the many different narratives and discourses that are the inevitable situation of life in our world (and it provides a theological account of why we must expect this) in any event.

This conception may also be useful in examining the study of Christian history; it calls those who investigate Christian history from within theology to think through more carefully the theological purpose of their investigations (and thus accept some of Milbank's description of the un-theological interaction between Biblical studies, Church history and social thought). At the same time, however, it may perhaps contribute towards the outlining of a hermeneutic which is self-critical, and more confident in its openness to the difficulty of reading the world.

The theme of transposition points clearly towards the need for a theology of the limits of understanding as a fundamental structure of Christian discourse. In the light of postmodern thought the need to attend to the particular structure of Christian discourse has become more evident. Milbank is thus right to say that turning to the nature of Christian discourse results in a severe critique of postmodern meta-narratives however much it detracts from their styles and strategies. However, turning back to examine the structure of Christian discourse also results in a severe questioning of the nature of 'a' discourse and how one discourse is related to another. Christianity as a discourse reveals itself to be a highly complex structure which already provides a place from which these questions may be examined. The dialogue between theology and the social sciences must – at least for theologians – begin from this place, in a strange borderland between theology, spirituality and the theology of creation. That borderland paradoxically turns out to lie at the centre of Christian life and thought. Even for social scientists, the failure to explore this structure, talking simply of 'resacralising social science' actually misses the possibility of a fundamental and challenging dialogue for all sides.

Notes and References

1. Robin Gill, 'Theologians and Sociologists – A Comparison', *Christian Ethics in Secular Worlds* (Edinburgh: T. & T. Clark, 1991), pp. 23–41.
2. Kieran Flanagan, 'Postmodernity and Culture: Sociological Wagers of the

Self in Theology', in this volume (pp. 152–73). See also his *Sociology and Liturgy: Re-presentations of the Holy* (London: Macmillan, 1991).

3.   I would like to thank Fr David Moss, St Stephen's House, Oxford, and Dr Jonathan Dyck, Trinity College, Dublin, for their discussions of earlier versions of this chapter.

4.   John Milbank, *Theology and Social Theory* (Oxford: Blackwell, 1990), pp. 101ff. Milbank provides a clear account of his view of the postmodern project in his 'Problematizing the Secular: The post-modern project', in Phillipa Berry and Andrew Wernick (eds), *Shadow of Spirit: Postmodernism and Religion* (London: Routledge, 1992), pp. 30–44.

5.   Fergus Kerr, 'Simplicity Itself: Milbank's Thesis', *New Blackfriars*, vol. 73, no. 861, June 1992, p. 307.

6.   Robin Gill, 'Theologians and Sociologists – A Comparison', *op. cit.* See also Kieran Flanagan, 'Sublime Policing: Sociology and Milbank's City of God', *New Blackfriars*, vol. 73, no. 861, June 1992, pp. 333–41. For a critique of Milbank from within theology, see Richard Roberts, 'Transcendental Sociology: A Critique of John Milbank's *Theology and Social Theory*', *Scottish Journal of Theology*, vol. 46, 1993, pp. 527–35. In this essay, Roberts fails to explore the nature of theological discourse and does not offer an account of how the modernist perception of the world remains theological. This is not say such an account is doomed to fail, but that Roberts' criticism presents yet another example of a theologian failing to enter into the discussion theologically.

7.   Peter L. Berger, *The Social Reality of Religion* (Harmondsworth: Penguin, 1973), pp. 181–90. Milbank offers a discussion of the influence of sociology on Biblical criticism and church history in terms of the natural sociological trend to explain religion in terms of society. See *Theology and Social Theory, op. cit.*, pp. 110 ff.

8.   The phrase belongs to Jonathan Z. Smith and appears in *Map is Not Territory* (Chicago: Chicago University Press, 1993), p. 308.

9.   John Milbank, *Theology and Social Theory, op. cit.*, pp. 269ff.

10. My own understanding of the foundations of neo-Kantianism and that of Milbank, ibid., p. 98, follow closely Gillian Rose. See her *Hegel Contra Sociology* (London: Athlone, 1981), ch. 1.

11. John Milbank, *Theology and Social Theory, op. cit.*, pp. 326–79.

12. Ibid., p. 385.

13. See Gillian Rose, 'Shadow of Spirit', *Judaism and Modernity* (Oxford: Blackwell, 1992), pp. 37–51.

14. Ingolf Dalferth, 'Karl Barth's Eschatological Realism', in Stephen Sykes (ed.), *Karl Barth: Centenary Essays* (Cambridge: Cambridge University Press, 1989), pp. 14–45.

15. Fundamental to my understanding of the theological structure of Barth's ethics is John Webster, *Barth's Ethics of Reconciliation* (Cambridge: Cambridge University Press, 1995).

16. My sketch here is closely related to the brief account in John Milbank's two papers, 'The Second Difference: For a Trinitarianism Without Reserve', *Modern Theology*, vol. 2, 1986, pp. 213–34, and 'The Name of Jesus: Incarnation, Atonement, Ecclesiology', *Modern Theology*, vol. 7, 1991, pp. 311–33.

17. I am particularly concerned with the second and third volumes of Hans Urs von Balthasar, *Theo-Drama. Theological Dramatic Theory*, 2: *Dramatis Personae: Man in God*, trans. Graham Harrison (San Francisco: Ignatius Press, 1990) and 3: *The Dramatis Personae: Persons in Christ* (1992). My exploration of this theme in von Balthasar is closely related to a much longer discussion in Lewis Ayres, John Milbank, David Moss and Graham Ward, *Balthasar at the End of Modernity* (Edinburgh: T. & T. Clark, forthcoming).

18. Hans Urs von Balthasar, *Theo-Drama*, 2, *op. cit.*, pp. 96ff.

19. This attempt to outline a theological account of the place of the world within theological discourse, in the light of postmodernism but in resistance to it, has a parallel in two papers of Rowan Williams, 'Postmodern Theology and the Judgement of the World', in Frederick Burnham (ed.), *Postmodern Theology* (San Francisco: HarperCollins, 1988), pp. 92–112, and 'Between Politics and Metaphysics: reflections in the Wake of Gillian Rose', *Modern Theology*, vol. 11, 1995, pp. 3–22. The relation between Hegel, postmodern thought and apophatic theology is explored in Rowan Williams' 'Hegel and the Gods of Postmodernity', in *Shadow of Spirit: Postmodernism and Religion, op. cit.*, pp. 72–80.

11 Between Postmodernism and Postmodernity: The Theology of Jean-Luc Marion
Graham Ward

This chapter seeks to place the theological work of Jean-Luc Marion[1] in the context of what the French sociologist, and Marion's contemporary, Pierre Bourdieu would call its field of cultural production. This notion refers to the complex web of power relations, reinforced and disseminated by the play of institutions and the play of discourses within a competitively determined social field. It defines a double space, a 'space of stances (conceived as a space of forms, styles and modes of expression as much as of contents expressed)' and a 'space of positions held by their authors'.[2] It is Bourdieu's belief that 'knowing the overall space in which they are situated enables us to put ourselves so to speak *in their place* in the social space'.[3]

Thus the attempt is made here to outline Marion's theology in terms of the rhetorical and institutional context within which his thinking is legitimated and valued. What emerges is a picture of a theologian working both with and against the strategies and concerns of postmodernism in the social realities characterising postmodernity. These terms will be clarified later. For the moment it is only necessary to emphasise that the field is complex, far from homogeneous and the relationship between postmodernism and postmodernity is not simply one of correlation. Let me begin, then, by situating Marion's theological work ecclesiologically, philosophically and sociologically.

Marion is a Roman Catholic influenced by the anti-liberal and Neopatristic theology of Daniélou, du Lubac and von Balthasar. He began publishing theological essays in the international Catholic journal *Communio* in 1975, while working as an Assistant at the University of Paris IV. Prior to this, while a student at the prestigious Ecole Normale Supérieure (Ulm), he had already published several theological essays on Augustine, the patristic doctrine of the Incarnation, Pseudo-Dionysus and Maximus the Confessor in the conservative Catholic French journal, *Résurrection*.

Subsequently, while holding positions in philosophy faculties at Poitiers and, since 1988, Paris X-Nanterre, Marion has held visiting professorships at the Catholic University of Leuven (1987), the Gregorian University at Rome (1993) and the Catholic Institute of Paris (1994).

His Catholic roots are profound and conservative in contrast to those of some leading, and older, French postmodern figures, such as Lacan (whose brother and intimate friend, Marc-François, entered the monastery of Abbaye de Hautecombe in 1926), Foucault (who spent the last decade of his life working in the Dominican library of Saulchoir in Paris on a book concerned with the genealogy of Christian sexuality), Kristeva (whose pronounced nostalgia for the Catholic church has led one of her foremost commentators to write that her work 'privileges and recreates the Christian imaginary'),[4] and Irigaray (whose concern to articulate a 'sensible transcendental' returns us to an examination of Jesus Christ, Mary and the age of the Spirit).

Nevertheless there remains, between Marion and these postmodern thinkers, a Catholicism which, having declined following its revival in France in the 1920s and 1930s, is re-emerging from the ashes of exist-entialism and the slow demise of socialism after 1968. But what charact-erises these older, postmodern figures is their radical anti-institutionalism and their academic marginality (in terms of the academic power relations within the French university system); of which, more later.

Marion is one of the central figures in a new Catholic theological move-ment in France that took its impetus from Heidegger's later work on the phenomenology of Being. Of course, Rahner developed (rather sketch-ily) the theological resources in the Heidegger of *Sein und Zeit*. But, as Heidegger's complete works were being published in German and avail-able from 1975, and following in the wake of the French phenomenological tradition of Merleau-Ponty and Levinas, the theological question of Being took on new life in Catholic academic circles. Furthermore this new inter-est in ontology came in the wake of the radical critique of metaphysics in the form of structuralism and poststructuralism. The main drive behind this interest in Heidegger and God was Etienne Gilson who, in 1952, pub-lished his *Being and Some Philosophers* and then, in 1972, his important *Etre et Essence*. With Gilson, Heidegger was brought into dialogue with Thomas Aquinas. The most important French commentator on Heidegger at this time was Jean Beaufret, an influential philosopher who had paved the way for the reception of the German tradition into French universities after 1945. Beaufret was used by Heidegger post-1945 to re-establish his reputation in France following allegations of his involvement in National Socialism. It was at an important seminar in Scrunch with Heidegger and

Beaufret, in 1951, that direct questions were asked of Heidegger concerning the identity of Being and God.[5] This followed an earlier correspondence with Beaufret, one letter of which, *Lettre à Jean Beaufret sur l'Humanisme*, composed in 1947, is almost fifty pages long. The letter contains one of Heidegger's most important and influential discussions, in the light of Beaufret's interest in Holderlin, on the space of the sacred and the divine.

Between them, Gilson and Beaufret influenced a generation of Catholic philosophical theologians of whom Marion is one of the most widely known, particularly outside France. In France, his *métier* is understood to be Cartesian philosophy, for which he was awarded in 1992 the Grand Prix de Philosophie de l'Académie Française. A number of these scholars (including Beaufret) contributed to the volume *Heidegger et la question de Dieu*,[6] but since that work in the 1970s and early 1980s several have moved beyond Neothomism to wider investigations into phenemonology, Being, time, religious experience and the revelation of God.[7] A new line of theological and philosophical inquiry was and still is being established. Few of the works, as yet, have been translated into English. Of the most important, for Marion, would be the work of Remi Brague, who examined Aristotelean ontology, like Marion and Ricoeur, in the 1980s and recently has been analysing the work of St Bernard; Jean-Louis Chrétien, whose work also concerns revelation, the promise and phenomenology; Jean-François Courtine, who has examined the development of metaphysics from Suarez' reinterpretation of the *analogia entis*; and Jean-Yves Lacoste, who began exploring the Platonism of the Early Church Fathers and more recently turned to a phenomenological inquiry into the religious experience of hope and memory, despondency and the unforgettable. Many of the concerns of these new Catholic theologians find echoes in Marion's work. But some of their themes (and Marion's) find echoes in the work of postmodern thinkers like Levinas, Derrida and Lyotard.

Having outlined the ecclesiological and theological context of Marion, we turn to examine the postmodern implications of his writings. Marion himself alerts his readers to these in the 'Preface to the English Edition' of *God Without Being*. In meditating upon the first and highest of the divine names and arguing for the radical reversal of the relations between Being and loving, Marion's stand is at once theological and philosophical. The philosophical position, he tells us, 'takes place within the framework, perhaps, of what is conventionally called "postmodernism". If we understand by modernity the completed and therefore terminal figure of metaphysics, such as it develops from Descartes to Nietzsche, then "postmodernity" begins when, among other things, the metaphysical determination of God is called into question.' Thus, he asserts, 'my enterprise remains "postmodern" in this sense, and, in this precise sense, I remain close to Derrida'.[8] Jacques Derrida, a *normalien* himself, taught Marion at the Ecole Normale Supérieure (as did Louis Althusser). Emmanuel Levinas's university career bears a remarkable similarity to Marion's. Levinas also went from the University of Poitiers to a professorship at Paris X-Nanterre in the department where Marion now works. It is these two philosophical figures, Derrida and Levinas, along with Nietzsche and Heidegger, who constitute the postmodern horizons of Marion's work.

Marion's philosophical and postmodern project is the critique of what Heidegger termed onto-theology. For Heidegger, onto-theology is the unspoken theology of modernity's project. From as early as 1936, Heidegger equated onto-theology with metaphysics.[9] The question of universal Being (*das Seiende im Ganze*) is recognised to be a theological question which has become correlated to the question of any particular being. The relationship between Being and beings (that there is an relationship) is the project of ontology. In exploring ontological difference rather than correlation, Heidegger's project was the overcoming of metaphysics and therefore onto-theology. Beings issue not from Being as *causa sui*, but from an *Abgrund*, a place of Nothing. Nothing is the same as Being when Being is considered in its ontological difference: Nothing is the other face of Being. Here, stepping back from the strictly phenomenological analysis of *Dasein*, Heidegger pushes at the very boundaries of the thinkable in an attempt to create a space in which the unthinkable is thought. The *Destruktion* of metaphysics, which is not a project that can be over once and for all, but a project which has constantly to be in operation since it is only manifested in time and historicality, is where Marion begins. The Derridean 'de-construction' of the logocentric totality is a variant of this project. Levinas's exploration of *illeity* and the 'otherwise than Being' (*autrement qu'être*) is another attempt to push the phenomenological inquiry to its utmost possibilities.

Marion rightly associates this trajectory with the 'death of God' announced first by Hegel and subsequently Nietzsche: 'what is called, following the last . . . metaphysical word, the "death of God", does not mean that God is out of play, but rather it points up the *modern* face of his immediate and eternal fidelity'.[10] As we will see, Marion's concern is with thinking through the premodern face of God for a postmodern agenda. He attempts to do this by examining the contemporary concern with difference in terms of trinitarian 'distance': the distance between the Father and the Son whereby the 'death of God' is comprehensible in terms of the events of the Passion.

Two other aspects of philosophical postmodernism are also evident in Marion's concerns; aspects that he remains blind to because they present the most immediate interface with his cultural context. They arise from meditations subsequent to *Destruktion* and *deconstruction* and we can name them: alterity and the ethics of love. For the first, Heidegger's work provided material for a radical critique of the Hegelian subject of desire. It presented an Other which could not be negated or sublated. The phenomenological method had already examined the Other as constitutive to the identity of the ego. It has done so first in Hegel's *Phenomenology of Spirit* which became a fashionable and influential philosophical text in post-war France through the work of Alexandre Kojève and Jean Hyppolite. Simone de Beauvoir points to its significance when she recalls her own turn to Hegel in 1945, observing 'we had discovered the reality and weight of history; now we were wondering about its meaning'.[11]

Phenomenology is concerned with elucidating the appearance, the meaningfulness and relation of this Other which always remains external and yet constituted by the 'I'. Hence, phenomenology has always concerned itself with intention, desire and the conflict of identity. For with desire and conflict, the Other emerges as the condition for experience. What interested these philosophers in Heidegger's work was a certain anti-foundationalism that proposed in the movement towards identity a fundamental aporia between being as an existent and grasping the meaning of being as an existent. The aporia forestalled the operation of Hegel's *aufhebung*. Heidegger's work encouraged an examination of a radical alterity which remains outside, marginal, unresolved and is thus forever in question. The philosophical investigation into the overthrow of the Hegelian dialectic work remains important for Marion. He also wishes to employ a phenomenological method, pushing it to its utmost limit where, for him, aporia provides insight into an original donation: the gift of God's presence, His self-revelation. Marion suggests that 'God gives Himself to be known insofar as He gives Himself – according to the horizon of the gift itself. The gift constitutes at once the mode and the body of his revelation. In the end the gift gives only itself, but in this way it gives absolutely everything.'[12] Such a phenomenology was bound to read the structuralist and poststructuralist attention to semiotics in terms of incarnation: the body of the sign as the body of Christ.[13]

For several postmodern thinkers, the concern with alterity and aporia has led to a new model of selfhood and an emphasis upon the ethics of loving in and through difference. The split subject, the subject in hostage to and/or responsible for the Other, is a familiar theme in Levinas, Lacan, Kristeva and Irigaray. In such a scenario, Hegelian desire, read theologically as *eros* (and aided here by Blondel's concept of 'action') becomes part of an unfolding drama of love. It is a drama constituted by sexual difference and as such it plays a major part in the ethics and philosophies of French feminism. It is a drama already examined by von Balthasar in his explorations into the role of Mary as prototype for the Church. For Marion, the logic of the gift is inextricably implicated in the logic of divine intra-Trinitarian love. 'The Last Rigor', the final chapter of *God Without Being*, is a preliminary analysis of the 'rigor of love' as 'the economy of salvation'.[14] In 1986, a more complete analysis was to follow in *Prolégomènes à la charité*. Here, in a characteristic postmodern and anti-Sartrean move, Marion announces that Hell, is the absence of all otherness and that 'the logic of evil destroy[s] the space within itself for alterity [distance]'.[15]

Despite these other two postmodern traits of Marion's work – alterity and the ethics of desire in and through difference – there is no better work than *Prolégomènes à la charité* to reveal the profound differences between Marion's work on love and the approaches of Kristeva or Irigaray to the same issue. Marion's text is a sustained phenomenological account of love, difference and the revelatory gift of presence, comparable to Kristeva's *Tales of Love* or Irigaray's *An Ethic of Sexual Difference*, but the philosophies of Hegel, Marx and Neitzsche are interpreted through and alongside expositions of Scripture, references to the early Church Fathers and Pope John Paul II's 'Message to the French People'. John Paul II's notion of our age as a time of crisis chimes well with Marion's depiction of 'the test of nihilism which, in France, marked the years dominated by 1968'.[16] This was a nihilism in which 'the obscuring of God in the indistinct haze of the "human science" was paramount'. Hence Marion's assertion that 'my enterprise does not remain "postmodern" all the way'.[17]

His enterprise, in fact, began by investigating the work of a philosopher who stood at the brink of modernity: Descartes. Six of his books so far are dedicated to exploring aspects of Descartes' work. His primary concern lies with Cartesian metaphysics, both Descartes' ontology (which he terms '*ontologie grise*') and Descartes' theology (which he terms '*théologie blanche*'). At base, Marion offers a critique of Descartes as the father of philosophical modernism, committed to describing the correlation between one kind of Reasoning and one kind of Reality. With reference to the work on analogy and being in Aquinas, Catejan, Suarez and Galileo, Marion first attempts to show that Descartes criticises the univocity of *ens*. Being, then, with Descartes, remains in question. Rather like Heidegger (who stands on the brink of postmodernism), 'Descartes opens up the question of the foundation . . . because he opens up the foundation as a question'.[18]

Descartes' ontology is therefore ambivalent or grey (*grise*). Six years later, a year before publishing *God Without Being* (his only book in English at the moment), Marion developed his argument in *Sur la théologie blanche de Descartes*. Here, having outlined a controversy among Cartesian scholars about whether the *ego cogito* is a reflection of the *causa sive ratio* of God (i.e., constitutes an *imago dei*) or autonomous and ontologically divorced from God, Marion concludes that it is both, that Descartes is being deliberately ambivalent. He develops what he had already hinted at in his earlier book, that the 'ambivalence of *eadem facultas* discovers, by its very anonymity, what declares itself as a blank theology [*théologie blanche*]'.[19] In this aporia a theology becomes possible which is outside human conception and construction (analogy) and what Levinas terms 'otherwise than Being' (*autrement qu'être*).[20]

At this point, and throughout his important book, *L'Idole et la distance*, philosophical analysis, historical research, phenomenological method and Catholic theology are worked constructively together. After *God Without Being*, in a project that was clearly aiming to establish theology beyond metaphysics (in the manner of Aquinas), philosophy and theology could no longer work in tandem. In his more recent work, his theological inquiry (developed in *Prolégomènes à la charité* and *La croisée du visible*) has proceeded through Scriptural exegesis to confirm the insights of the Church Fathers. His philosophical inquiry has continued to examine the relationship between the rise of metaphysics and Descartes and the phenomenological method of Husserl and Heidegger. The two inquiries are quite distinct, although at the end of *Réduction et donation. Recherches sur Husserl, Heidegger et la phénoménologie* we have arrived at 'a point of reference all the more original and unconditional'.[21] But this point 'no longer issues from the horizon of Being (nor objectivity) but from the pure form of the summons itself'. It is a summons which 'gives the gift itself'.[22] The theology of the gift (an important theme throughout his work) lies beyond a phenomenological inquiry.

The important work at the centre of this shift towards a division of the philosophical and theological projects is *God Without Being*. In that book two unsatisfactory moves are evident in which we see philosophy and theology no longer working together and supplementing each other. The first is a slide from the material to the metaphorical. The second, a consequence of the first, is a slide towards privileging revelation and immediacy above analysis; a privileging sanctioned and legitimated by an ecclesial authority which evades thorny hermeneutical issues. These can be briefly sketched.[23]

The inquiry in *God Without Being* rests fundamentally upon an analysis of the idol and the icon. The idol is self-consuming. It merely presents a mirror for the beholder's gaze. Like Narcissus, it allows no room for critique since the gaze is dazzled and dazed by its own reflection. The icon, on the other hand, summons the gaze of the beholder to surpass itself. While strictly speaking showing nothing, it steers the gaze away from the finite to the infinite. What is important is that the analysis of the idol and the icon issues from two forms of antithetical visibility. It is only because of this that Marion can institute a phenomenological inquiry; an inquiry into the 'conflict between two conflicting phenomenologies'.[24] A certain slippage is evident, then, when Marion moves from discussing material idols and icons to conceptual idols and icons. For example, with a conceptual idol we are told 'the measure of the concept comes not from God but from the aim of the gaze'.[25] But 'gazing' here can only be metaphorical, and likewise the use of 'idol'.

This move away from the concrete (the realm of the phenomenological) to the metaphorical occurs throughout *God Without Being*. It happens most profoundly in relation to the icon and the eucharist in Chapter 6. The material body and blood of Christ parallels the material bread and wine of the liturgy. But the priest as *persona Christi* affects the transformation whereby the material bread and wine becomes again the body of Christ, a sacramental body which, according to Catholic teaching, completes the oblation of the historical body of Jesus. This sacramental body is then assimilated into the 'ecclesiastical body' which is 'more real – than any physical body', for it constitutes the 'mystical body'. An implicit Platonism is evident here which continually moves us beyond phenomena to theological mystery; and hence beyond philosophical logic of a phenomenological inquiry to theology's 'own radical *theo*logical logic'.

This is another aspect of that second move and it is towards constructing an analysis upon the basis of faith and revelation. As Marion writes, *'the eucharistic present is deduced from theological, mystical "reality" alone'*.[26] The deduction of this present, this divine Being which issues from 'a difference more essential to being that ontological difference itself' is founded upon 'biblical revelation'.[27] Marion investigates the biblical revelation in Chapters 3 and 4. The analysis of such a revelation lies outside phenomenology's concern with the hermeneutics of intention. In fact, no science for the interpretation of biblical revelation is outlined, for the authority to interpret Scripture lies with the theologian and *'only the bishop merits, in the full sense, the title of theologian'*.[28] With an inquiry based upon revelation we have shifted to 'a discourse held about faith and on the basis of faith'.[29] It is a discourse sanctioned and safeguarded by the ecclesiastical hierarchy. As Heidegger observed, 'faith does not need the thought of Being'.[30] In moving beyond Being, Marion has moved beyond metaphysics and the basis for philosophy is detatched from theological *a priori* detailed in the Scriptures, Creeds, traditions and Catholic councils. His move beyond metaphysics is a move within postmodernism, but his Catholic theological conclusions are a move beyond postmodernism also.

Marion's distinctively conservative Catholicism evidently acts as the final interpretative framework within which his postmodern philosophical and phenomenological analyses are drawn. He re-reads Heidegger's concept of *Ereignis* as revelation; this becomes the gift of the Father to his Son, the Word. Postmodern concerns with textuality are coupled with a privileging of the Scriptures (and their exegesis) as the Word of God and the Body of Christ as both Church and eucharistic site for the presence of God. At the very centre of this postmodern theology lies the bishop as mediator, interpreter and priest *par excellence*. But a rather curious displacement has occurred.

The politics and ethics of postmodernism – influenced by French socialism and Althusserian Marxism – aimed at speaking up from or for the margins. It protested loudly against authorities, universals and totalities, were they political, theological or metaphysical. Its appreciation of and its desire to safeguard against the domestification of the other and the marginalised led to a championing of that which was being forgotten, surplus, repressed: whether it be the body of the sign, speaking as woman, the infinite, the chora, the sublime or as black South Africans, political dissidents under Franco or the rights of homosexuals. It saw itself, following the failure of the student riots of May 1968, as the necessary antidote for rightwing politics and policing, particularly under the last months of Charles de Gaulle's Presidency and the years of George Pompidou and Giscard d'Estaing. With its influence in the academy and media, the postmodern voice forced and fostered democracy. Perhaps then the climate was bound to change when it was proclaimed that Mitterrand and the Socialist Party had won an absolute majority in the National Assembly one late evening in May 1981. Marion belonged to a younger generation and thirteen years earlier, in May 1968, he was still a pupil of the Ecole Normale Supérieure whose director, Robert Flacelière, was 'one of the main targets of student protest'.[31]

There are other, more sociological, explanations for Marion's fraught marriage of postmodernism and Catholic ecclesial orthodoxy. The work of Pierre Bourdieu on the nature of the French Academy offers one such explanation. The work of certain British sociologists, such as Zygmunt Bauman, Ernst Gellner and Akbar Ahmed, on the characteristics of postmodernity offers another. We can recognise the importance and relevance of Bourdieu's analysis when he informs us that:

> positions in the university space . . . are so closely linked to 'political' declarations. Indeed . . . the associations and the distances correspond very closely to the 'political' affinities and antagonisms of the conflicts of May 1968 *and after* (thus, for instance, all the signatories of a motion supporting Robert Flacelière held positions in the university space very close to that of their 'threatened' colleague).[32]

Bourdieu's works sets out to plot the various positions in this university space and their political affiliations. What emerges from his study is that most of the major postmodern voices who came to the fore in the Seventies as 'prophets of extremity'[33] (several gaining an international reputation) belonged to peripheral academic institutions. For all its kudos as promoter of the *avant-garde*, the Ecole des Hautes Etudes (home to Althusser, Derrida, Barthes – and Bourdieu) on the eve of May 1968 'was a marginal institution, but prestigious and dynamic'.[34] As Bourdieu notes: '*structural dissonance* is written into the institutional regulations, in terms of the dependency of the Ecole des Hautes Etudes on other faculties (at least until recently) for granting degrees'.[35] The same is said of the Collège de France (home of Lévi-Strauss, Benveniste, Foucault – and now Bourdieu) which is also 'more or less totally deprived of social weight'[36] and political power within French University education. In these two institutions, journalism and media attention (in terms of radio and television interviews) mixed easily with scholarship. The University of Vincennes (earlier home of Foucault and Irigaray) was created in the wake of the student riots of 1968. *It* institutionalised political and intellectual dissidence and reaction. Its teachers and its students participated in sit-ins. All Vincennes' courses were interdisciplinary and modular, where students were examined and awarded credits. But from its earliest days there was an 'increasing conviction that a Vincennes degree was quite worthless'.[37]

There is a question that arises here concerning what happens when the marginalised and the reactionary are suddenly given power and take centre-stage in the political arena. It was hoped that this would occur with the election of Mitterrand to the Presidency. But it did not take place. What did take place was a change in the intellectual climate, which Marion's work reflects. Philosophically, whatever the vitality of deconstruction and poststructuralism in America (and to some extent Britain), throughout the 1980s new emphases emerged in France. As Peter Dews observes (though somewhat hyperbolically), 'from the late 1970s onwards it became possible to pose *philosophical* questions about the foundation of ethics, the nature of political principles, and the universal status of legal rights, in a manner which would have been unthinkable during the heady-years of "anti-humanism" and "post-philosophical" experimentation'.[38] There was a return to metaphysical thinking and it accorded with a renewed interest in the work of Merleau-Ponty and Emmanuel Levinas, and a deepening interest in the work of Paul Ricoeur and Jurgen Habermas. Both Levinas and Ricoeur belonged to faculties at the University of Paris X-Nanterre. Nanterre is subordinate to, but in the same league as, the Sorbonne (Levinas moved from one to the other), and as Bourdieu notes it is in these universities (upholders both of the establishment) that symbolic capital in French academic circles is accumulated. What the Collège de France is to the Ecole des Hautes Etudes, the Sorbonne is to Nanterre.[39]

This new philosophical climate of the late 1970s and early 1980s is reflected in Marion's detailed, analytic and scholarly work on Descartes, especially his metaphysical outlook. His Catholic conservatism parallels the political and academic conservatism of the specific Parisian academic circles within which he moved and developed his career. The question still remains why the philosophical climate changed in France. Why was there a return to more traditional modes of philosophical analysis, to a political (and ecclesial) conservativism?

Evidently, any answer to that question must be multi-faceted. This chapter suggests a direction for examination, one emerging from several British sociologists who have studied the phenomena of postmodernism and the eclectic cultural order to which it has given rise: postmodernity. In particular, Bauman, in his book *Intimations of Postmodernity*, argues that the defiance of order, the overall impression of disorientation and chaos, reality itself as soft, trivial and manipulable is both a product of, and fosters consumerism. We have become consumers rather than producers[40] and this is the legacy of late capitalism which postmodernism reflects and postmodernity encourages. Bauman argues that 'reality, as the consumer experiences it, is a pursuit of pleasure. Freedom is about the choice between greater and lesser satisfactions and rationality is about choosing the first over the second'.[41] This dissolution of the universal and this exaltation of consumer choice, which characterises the postmodern, 'shifts the focus on to the . . . agency of community. More precisely, the focus shifts to communities.'[42] Pronounced fragmentation has led to neo-tribalism or the 'obsessive search for community'[43] and 'imagined communities' which exist solely through individuals choosing to give their allegiance to them. 'Neo-tribes' are described by Bauman as 'the vehicles (and imaginary sediments) of individual self-definition'.[44] In the wake of postmodernism 'we console ourselves and summon our wilting determination by invoking the magic formula of "tradition" '.[45] Although they would not articulate their sociological observations within the purview of a late-Marxist and Jamesonian ideology (Bauman's position), the work of Ernest Gellner and Akbar Ahmed concurs with the correlation between postmodernity and fundamentalism. Gellner, in his book *Postmodernism, Reason and Religion*, defines postmodernism as 'a kind of hysteria of subjectivity' in which identity collapses and so self-affirmation groups flourish.[46] In particular, his work, like Ahmed's *Postmodernism and Islam*, examines the rise of Islamic fundamentalism. Both agree that in the face of postmodernism there is a return to the 'modernist position',[47] only less naïvely; with a profound awareness of the enemy without, those abjected,[48] those whose abjection marks the boundaries of the camp. That this is evidently occurring in France today is made manifest in a recent collection of essays by the French psychoanalyst and feminist, Julia Kristeva. In her *Nations Without Nationalism*, a concern of the French intellectuals with what she calls 'the polyphonic community that is today called France' dominates every page.[49] She observes that:

> the disarray as to identity, which just recently added to the membership and votes of the National Front, has henceforth found a positive countenance: one need only look and read in order to notice the proud return to the eighteenth century . . . [There is] a resurgence of the French national spirit.[50]

She herself is turning towards 'the inherent wealth of the Enlightenment's secularism' for a model to integrate the conflicting drives of tribalism and globalism, fundamental nationalisms and the demands of immigration.[51] Marion's postmodern (yet nevertheless Cartesian) Catholicism emerges from this very context.

From this analysis of Marion's theological work in terms of its symbolic field of cultural production – its ecclesiastical, philosophical and sociological matrix – there emerges the figure of an intellectual working at some complex interface between postmodernism and postmodernity. Despite the way the terms are frequently used in sociological, cultural and philosophical analyses, postmodernism and postmodernity are not coterminous. The relationship between any ideology and the cultural field of both its production and promotion remains highly complex.

The specific relationship between postmodernism and postmodernity has as yet received little attention. This is partly because of the great freight of meanings borne by the term 'postmodernism'. Since its first use (in

Germany in the 1930s) it has come to be associated with eclecticism in architecture (where buildings quote from a variety of established styles), self-ironisation in fine art and literature and late capitalism in Marxist economics. Its rampant interdisciplinary nature – where each intellectual discipline is a field of signs, a text interwoven with other texts – means that philosophical postmodernism has penetrated academic practices as widely diverse as psychology and law. The ideology of postmodernism is difficult to delineate. Furthermore, earlier delineations (such as Marion's characterisation of poststructuralism as nihilism) have been much criticised. Bauman is not the only thinker to point to the re-enchantment of the world (following the disenchantment of the Enlightenment's advocacy of scientism and technocracy) that has issued from postmodern philosophy. Postmodernism can be viewed as opening the world up again to the possibilities of transcendence, venturing new models for incarnation. Derrida is not alone in repudiating claims that he is a relativist, a nihilist and linguistic idealist. There are similar difficulties with postmodernity.

Bourdieu, like Foucault, would wish to examine the discourses of postmodernity (that is, those discursive practices which define and describe a certain set of social criteria instantiating postmodernity). They would wish to point out that postmodernity has been produced. It, too, is an ideology: an attempt to codify, formalise and, therefore, stabilise certain social phenomena. Such an attempt is an employment of power in the creation of a specific body of sociological knowledge, and any such attempt is never politically and institutionally innocent. Studies in postmodernism and postmodernity constitute big publishing business; they make, and can still sometimes break, academic careers. There is a market for these terms, the ideas and the *Zeitgeist* they seem to conjure. It is the fact that there is a market (although why there is a market is a significant question) that such accounts of postmodernity become believable or, at least, taken seriously. A certain correspondence exists between the desires of the market and those accounts of the cultural situation which feed and promote that market. Furthermore, postmodernity as a sociological notion is not without its paradoxical tensions. The move towards self-defining, self-inventing, self-selecting groups suggests a social fragmentation (in fact, the localisation of sociological analysis itself), which runs counter to the move towards greater globalisation and the dissolution of cultural differences. An account of the rapid growth of the fundamentalist house church movement has also to recognise that the hamburgers which members of that group eat, the cokes they drink and the clothes they wear are marketed internationally. Nevertheless, however complex such an investigation would be, there is an important study to be made of the relationship between postmodern thinking and the culture of postmodernity, a body of contemporary knowledge, its production and symbolic power. The theology of Jean-Luc Marion points to a need for such an investigation; it marks a textual site where the work might begin.

The French historian, Michel de Certeau, has undertaken such an investigation with reference to sixteenth- and seventeenth-century mystical writings and the ascent of the science of mystics. He has attempted to map out the symbolic power relations whereby a 'new epistemological "form" appears at the threshold of the modern era'.[52]

A similar mapping of postmodern theology in terms of postmodernity has yet to be done. In such an investigation, the sociology of religion has an important role, simply because the belief-system and its practices, which constitute the basis for commitment to a religious community, run counter to the sceptical anti-foundationalism, the cult of the *flâneur*, which characterises postmodern thought. This chapter is an attempt to begin that reflexive process.

Notes and References

1. The principal theological and philosophical works of Jean-Luc Marion are as follows: *Sur l'ontologie grise de Descartes* (Paris: Vrin, 1975); *L'Idole et la distance* (Paris: Grasset, 1977); *Sur la théologie blanche de Descartes* (Paris: PUF, 1981); *Dieu sans l'être* (Paris: Fayard, 1982); trans. T.A. Carlson, *God Without Being* (Chicago: Chicago University Press, 1991); *Sur le prisme métaphysique de Descartes* (Paris: PUF, 1986); *Prolégomènes à la charité* (Paris: la Différence, 1986); *Réduction et donation. Recherches sur Husserl, Heidegger et la phénoménologie* (Paris: PUF, 1989); *La croisée du visible* (Paris: la Différence, 1991). See also the special issue on Jean-Luc Marion's *God Without Being*, New Blackfriars, vol. 76, no. 895, July/August 1995.
2. Pierre Bourdieu, *Homo Academicus*, trans. Peter Collier (Cambridge: Polity Press), 1988, p. xvii.
3. Ibid., p. xix.
4. Kelly Oliver, *Reading Kristeva: Unravelling the Double-Bind* (Bloomington: Indiana University Press, 1993), p. 125.
5. This seminar is referred to and quoted by Marion in *God Without Being, op. cit.*, p. 61f.
6. Richard Kearney and J.S. O'Leary (eds), *Heidegger et la question de Dieu* (Paris: Grasset, 1980).
7. See D. Dubarle (ed.), *L'être et Dieu* (Paris: Cerf, 1986).
8. Jean-Luc Marion, *God Without Being, op. cit.*, pp. xx–xxi.
9. See Heidegger's *Schellings Abhandlundung uber der menschlichen Freiheit,*

Band 42 (Frankfurt: Klostermann, 1988), p. 6. I thank Lawrence Hemmings for this reference.

10. Jean-Luc Marion, *L'Idole et la distance*, *op. cit.*, p. 11.
11. Simone de Beauvoir, *Force of Circumstance*, trans. Richard Howard (London: Deutsch, 1965), p. 34.
12. Jean-Luc Marion, *God Without Being*, *op. cit.*, xxiv.
13. Luce Irigaray makes the same connection, calling for a new understanding of incarnation in her essay 'Egales a qui?', *Critique*, 480 (May 1987), pp. 420–37 and the last part of her book, 'The Crucified One,' in *Marine Lover*, trans. Gillian C. Gill (New York: Columbia University Press, 1991).
14. Jean-Luc Marion, *God Without Being*, *op. cit.*, p. 192.
15. Jean-Luc Marion, *Prolégomènes à la charité*, *op. cit.*, p. 31.
16. Jean-Luc Marion, *God Without Being*, *op. cit.*, p. xix.
17. Ibid., p. xxi.
18. Jean-Luc Marion, *Sur l'ontologie grise de Descartes*, *op. cit.*, p. 23.
19. Ibid., p. 207.
20. See Emmanuel Levinas, *Otherwise than Being or Beyond Essence*, trans. A. Lingis (The Hague: Martinus Nijhoff, 1981).
21. Jean-Luc Marion, *Réduction et donation*, *op. cit.*, p. 303.
22. Ibid., p. 315.
23. I have detailed these slippages more extensively in my essay 'Marion's Postmodern Theology', in Phillip Blond (ed.), *Theology Before Philosophy* (London: Routledge, forthcoming). See also my essay 'Theology and the Crisis of Representation', in Robert Detweiler (ed.), *Literature and Theology at Century's End* (Atlanta: Scholar's Press, 1994), pp. 131–58, for a discussion of Marion's idol/icon theme compared to Barth's *analogia fidei*.
24. Jean-Luc Marion, *God Without Being*, *op. cit.*, p. 7.
25. Ibid., p. 16.
26. Ibid., pp. 178–82.
27. Ibid., p. 85.
28. Ibid., p. 153.
29. Ibid., p. 87.
30. Cited by Marion in ibid., p. 61.
31. Pierre Bourdieu, *Homo Academicus*, *op. cit.*, p. 81.
32. Ibid., p. 125–6.
33. Allan Megill, *Prophets of Extremity* (Berkeley: University of Califonia Press, 1985).
34. Pierre Bourdieu, *Homo Academicus*, *op. cit.*, p. 110.
35. Ibid., p. 111.
36. Ibid., p. 103.
37. David Macey, *The Lives of Michel Foucault* (London: Vintage, 1994), p. 229.
38. Peter Dews, *The Logics of Disintegration: Post-Structuralist Thought and the Claims of Critical Theory* (London: Verso, 1987), p. xii.
39. Pierre Bourdieu, *Homo Academicus*, *op. cit.*, p. 109.
40. Zygmunt Bauman, *Intimations of Postmodernity* (London: Routledge, 1992), p. 49.
41. Ibid., p. 50.
42. Ibid., p. 36.

43. Ibid., p. 136. Bauman derives this phrase from the work of the French sociologist Michel Maffesoli.

44. Ibid., p. 137.

45. Ibid., p. 138.

46. Ernest Gellner, *Postmodernism, Reason and Religion* (London: Routledge, 1992), p. 27.

47. Ibid., p. 3. See also Akbar Ahmed, *Postmodernism and Islam* (London: Routledge, 1992).

48. The term 'abjection' and its importance in defining societies is extensively explored in the work of Julia Kristeva, particularly *Powers of Horror*, trans. Leon Roudiez (New York: Columbia University Press, 1982).

49. Julia Kristeva, *Nations Without Nationalism*, trans. Leon Roudiez (New York: Columbia University Press, 1993), p. 63.

50. Ibid., p. 39. Two major works by French intellectuals illustrate Kristeva's point. See Roger Muchembled, *L'invention de l'homme moderne: Sociabilité, moeurs et comportements collectives dans l'Ancien Régime* (Paris: Fayard, 1988); and Jacques Domenech, *L'Ethique des Lumières: les fondements de la morale dans la philosophie française du XVIIIe siècle* (Paris: Vrin, 1989).

51. Julia Kristeva, *Nations Without Nationalism*, *op. cit.*, p. 62.

52. Michel de Certeau, *The Mystic Fable*, trans. Michael B. Smith (Chicago: University of Chicago Press, 1992), p. 16.

Bibliography

Adams, Richard and Janice Haaken, 'Anticultural Culture: Lifespring's Ideology and Its Roots in Humanistic Psychology', *Journal of Humanistic Psychology*, vol. 27, no. 4, autumn 1987, pp. 501–17.

Adlam, Diana, Julian Henriques, Nikolas Rose *et al.*, 'Psychology, Ideology and the Human Subject', *Ideology and Consciousness*, no. 2, October 1977, pp. 4–56.

Adler, Margot, *Drawing Down the Moon: Witches, Druids, Goddess-Worshippers, and Other Pagans in America Today* (Boston, MA: Beacon Press, 1986).

Ahmed, Akbar S., *Postmodernism and Islam, Predicament and Promise* (London: Routledge, 1992).

Anon., 'Charles: the Private Man, the Public Role', Granada TV, 29 June 1994.

Anon., 'Love, Marriage, and Beyond', *Heart*, autumn 1983, pp. 29–33; 100–3.

Anthony, Dick, Bruce Ecker and Ken Wilber, *Spiritual Choices* (New York: Paragon House, 1987).

Aran, Gideon, 'From religious Zionism to Zionist religion: the roots of Gush Emunim', *Studies in Contemporary Jewry*, vol. 2, 1986, pp. 116–43.

Aran, Gideon, 'Redemption as a catastrophe: the gospel of Gush Emunim', in Emmanuel Sivan and Menachem Friedman (eds), *Religious Radicalism and Politics in the Middle East* (Albany: State University of New York Press, 1990), pp. 157–76.

Aviad, Janet, *Return to Judaism: Religious Renewal in Israel* (Chicago: University of Chicago Press, 1983).

Aviad, Janet, 'The contemporary Israeli pursuit of the millennium', *Religion*, vol. 14, 1984, pp. 199–222.

Ayres, Lewis, John Milbank, David Moss and Graham Ward, *Balthasar at the End of Modernity* (Edinburgh: T. & T. Clark, forthcoming).

Bacon, Francis, *Novum Organum*, in *The Works of Francis Bacon*, eds J. Spalding, R. Ellis and D. Heath (London: Longmans, 1870), vol. IV.

Bahr, Howard, 'Shifts in the Denominational Demography of Middletown, 1924–1977', *Journal for the Scientific Study of Religion*, vol. 21, no. 2, 1982, pp. 99–114.

Balthasar, Hans Urs von, *The Glory of the Lord. A Theological Aesthetics*, III. *Studies in Theological Style: Lay Styles*, trans. Andrew Louth, John Saward, Martin Simon and Rowan Williams (Edinburgh: T. & T. Clark, 1986).

Balthasar, Hans Urs von, *Theo-Drama. Theological Dramatic Theory*. 1: *Prologomena*, trans. Graham Harrison (San Francisco: Ignatius Press, 1988).

Balthasar, Hans Urs von, *Theo-Drama. Theological Dramatic Theory*, 2: *Dramatis Personae: Man in God*, trans. Graham Harrison (San Francisco: Ignatius Press, 1990).

Balthasar, Hans Urs von, *Theo-Drama. Theological Dramatic Theory*, 3: *The Dramatis Personae: Persons in Christ*, trans. Graham Harrison (San Francisco: Ignatius Press, 1992).

Barker, David, Loek Halman and Astrid Vloet, *The European Values Study 1990–1991. Summary Report* (London/The Netherlands: The European Values Group, 1993).

Bartley, William, *Werner Erhard* (New York: Clarkson N. Potter, 1978).

Bataille, Georges, *Eroticism, Death and Sensuality*, trans. Mary Dalwood (San Francisco: City Lights Books, 1986).

Bataille, Georges, *Theory of Religion*, trans. Robert Hurley (New York: Zone Books, 1989).

Bataille, Georges, *On Nietzsche*, trans. Bruce Boone (New York: Paragon House, 1992).

Baudelaire, Charles, *The Painter of Modern Life and other Essays*, trans. and ed. Jonathan Mayne (London: Phaidon Press, 1964).

Bauman, Zygmunt, *Legislators and Interpreters* (Cambridge: Polity Press, 1987).

Bauman, Zygmunt, *Modernity and Ambivalence* (Cambridge Polity Press, 1991).

Bauman, Zygmunt, *Modernity and the Holocaust* (Cambridge: Polity Press, 1991).

Bauman, Zygmunt, *Intimations of Postmodernity* (London: Routledge, 1992).

Bauman, Zygmunt, *Postmodern Ethics* (Oxford: Blackwell, 1993).

Beauvoir, Simone de, *Force of Circumstance* trans. Richard Howard (London: Deutsch, 1965).

Bebbington, David, *Evangelicanism in Modern Britain* (London: Unwin-Hyman, 1989).

Beck, Ulrich, *Risk Society. Towards a New Modernity* (London: Sage, 1992).

Beck, Ulrich, Anthony Giddens and Scott Lash, *Reflexive Modernization. Politics, Tradition and Aesthetics in the Modern Social Order* (Cambridge: Polity Press, 1994).

Beckford, James A., *Religion and Advanced Industrial Society* (London: Unwin-Hyman, 1989).

Beckford, James A., 'Religion and power', in Thomas Robbins and Dick Anthony (eds), *In Gods We Trust* (New Brunswick, NJ: Transaction Publishers, 1990), pp. 43–60.

Beckford, James A., 'Religion, Modernity and Post-modernity', in Bryan Wilson (ed.), *Religion: Contemporary Issues* (London: Bellew, 1992), pp. 11–23.

Beckford, James A., 'Ecologie et religion dans les sociétés industrielles avancées', in Danièle Hervieu-Léger (ed.), *Religion et Ecologie* (Paris: Cerf, 1993), pp. 239–49.

Beckford, James A., 'Religion, self-help and privatization', in W. Sprondel (ed.), *Die Objectivitat der Ordnungen und ihre kommunikative Konstruktion* (Frankfurt: Suhrkamp, 1994), pp. 318–341.

Beckford James A. and A. Suzara, 'A new religious and healing movement in the Phillipines', *Religion*, vol. 24, 1994, pp. 117–41.

Beit-Hallahmi, Benjamin, *Despair and Deliverance: Private Salvation in Contemporary Israel* (Albany: State University of New York Press, 1992).

Bellah, Robert, Richard Madsen, William Sullivan, Ann Swidler and Steven Tipton, *Habits of the Heart* (London: University of California Press, 1985).

Ben-Ami, Issachar, 'The folk veneration of saints among Moroccan Jews', in S. Morag, I. Ben Ami and N. Stillman (eds), *Studies in Judaism and Islam* (Jerusalem: Magnes Press, 1981), pp. 283–345.

Ben-Ari, Eyal and Yoram Bilu, 'Saints' sanctuaries in Israeli development towns: on a mechanism of urban transformation', *Urban Anthropology*, vol. 16, 1987, pp. 244–72.

Ben-Rafael, Eliezer and Stephen Sharot, *Ethnicity, Religion and Class in Israeli Society* (Cambridge: Cambridge University Press, 1991).

Berger, Peter L., *The Precarious Vision: A Sociologist Looks at Social Fictions and Christian Faith* (Garden City, New York: Nelson Doubleday, 1961).

Berger, Peter L., *The Social Reality of Religion* (Harmondsworth: Penguin, 1973).

Berger, Peter L., *The Heretical Imperative* (New York: Anchor/Doubleday, 1980).

Berger, Peter L., 'From the crisis of religion to the crisis of secularity', in Mary Douglas and Stephen Tipton (eds), *Religion and America: Spirituality in a Secular Age* (Boston, MA: Beacon Press, 1983).

Berman, Marshall, *All That is Solid Melts into Air* (London: Verso, 1983).

Berry, Phillipa, and Andrew Wernick (eds), *Shadow of Spirit: Postmodernism and Religion* (London: Routledge, 1992).

Bharti, Ma Satya, *Death Comes Dancing* (London: Routledge & Kegan Paul, 1981).

Bibby, Reginald, *Fragmented Gods* (Toronto: Stoddart, 1987).

Bilu, Yoram, 'Dreams and the wishes of the saints', in Harvey E. Goldberg (ed.), *Judaism Viewed from Within and from Without* (Albany: State University of New York Press, 1987), pp. 285–313.

Bilu, Yoram, 'Personal motivation and social meaning in the revival of hagiolatric traditions among Moroccan Jews in Israel', in Zvi Sobel and Benjamin Beit-Hallahmi (eds), *Tradition, Innovation, Conflict: Jewishness and Judaism in Contemporary Israel* (Albany: State University of New York Press, 1991), pp. 47–69.

Blanchette, Oliva, introduction to Maurice Blondel, *Action (1893) Essay on a Critique of Life and a Science of Practice*, trans. Oliva Blanchette (Notre Dame, IN: University of Notre Dame Press, 1984), pp. xi–xxx.

Maurice Blondel. The Letter on Apologetics and History and Dogma, trans. Alexander Dru and Illtyd Trethowan (London: Harvill Press, 1964), pp. 13–116.

Blondel, Maurice, *Action (1893) Essay on a Critique of Life and a Science of Practice*, trans. Oliva Blanchette (Notre Dame, IN: University of Notre Dame Press, 1984).

Bourdieu, Pierre, *Homo Academicus*, trans. Peter Collier (Cambridge: Polity Press, 1988).

Brecht, Bertolt, *Life of Galileo*, trans. D.I. Vesey (London: Methuen, 1963).

Brochure, 'About the Life Training'.

Brochure, The Breakthrough Centre, 1993.

Brochure, the Theosophical Society, Adyar, Madras.

Brown, J.A.C., *Freud and the Post-Freudians* (Harmondsworth: Penguin 1985).

Bruce, Steve (ed.), *Religion and Modernisation* (Oxford: Oxford University Press, 1992).

Bry, Adelaide, *est* (London: Turnstone Books, 1976).

Bull, Malcolm, 'Secularisation and Medicalisation', *The British Journal of Sociology*, vol. 41, no. 2, June, 1990, pp. 245–61.

Burkitt, Ian, *Social Selves. Theories of the Social Formation of Personality* (London: Sage Publications, 1991).

Calhoun, Craig (ed.), *Social Theory and the Politics of Identity* (Oxford: Blackwell, 1994).

Carter, Lewis, *Charisma and Control in Rajneeshpuram* (Cambridge: Cambridge University Press, 1990).

Certeau, Michel de, *The Mystic Fable*, trans. Michael B. Smith (Chicago: University of Chicago Press, 1992).

Champion, Françoise and Danièle Hervieu-Léger, *De l'emotion en religion: renouveaux et traditions* (Paris: Centurion, 1990).

Cohen, Stanley and Laurie Taylor, *Escape Attempts: The Theory and Practice of Resistance to Everyday Life*, 2nd edn (London: Routledge, 1992).

Cohn, Norman, *The Pursuit of the Millennium* (London: Granada, 1970).

Collinson, Patrick, 'Reformation or Deformation', *The Tablet* (22 January 1994).

Cooley, Charles Horton, *Human Nature and the Social Order* (New York: Schocken Books, 1964).

Cottingham, John, Robert Stoothoff and Dugald Murdoch (eds), *Descartes: Selected Philosophical Writings* (Cambridge: Cambridge University Press, 1988).

Crawford, Robert, 'Healthism and the Medicalisation of Everyday Life', *International Journal of Health Services*, vol. 10, no. 3, 1980, pp. 365–88.

Creelan, Paul, 'Vicissitudes of the Sacred. Erving Goffman and the Book of Job', *Theory and Society*, vol. 13, 1984, pp. 663–95.

Creelan, Paul, 'The Degradation of the sacred: approaches of Cooley and Goffman', *Symbolic Interaction*, vol. 10, no. 1, 1987, pp. 29–56.

Crook, Stephen, Jan Pakulski and Malcolm Waters, *Postmodernization: Change in Advanced Society* (London: Sage, 1992).

Crowley, Vivianne, *Wicca: The Old Religion in the New Age* (Wellingborough: Aquarian Press, 1989).

Dahrendorf, Ralf, 'Homo Sociologicus. On the History, Significance, and Limits of the Category of Social Role', in *Essays in the Theory of Society* (London: Routledge & Kegan Paul, 1968), pp. 19–87.

Dalferth, Ingolf. 'Karl Barth's Eschatological Realism', in Stephen Sykes (ed.), *Karl Barth: Centenary Essays* (Cambridge: Cambridge University Press, 1989), pp. 14–45.

Danzger, Herbert M., *Returning to Tradition; The Contemporary Revival of Orthodox Judaism* (New Haven, CT: Yale University Press, 1989).

Davie, Grace, 'God and Caesar: religion in a rapidly changing Europe', in Joe Bailey (ed.), *Social Europe* (London: Longman, 1992), pp. 216–38.

Davie, Grace, 'The religious factor in the emergence of Europe as a global region', *Social Compass*, vol. 44, no. 1, 1994, pp. 95–112.

Davie, Grace, *Religion in Britain since 1945. Believing without Belonging* (Oxford: Blackwell, 1994).

Davison Hunter, James, *Culture Wars: The Struggle to Define America* (New York: Basic Books, 1994).

Denvir, Bernard (ed.), *The Impressionists at First Hand* (London: Thames & Hudson, 1987).

Deshen, Shlomo, 'Tunisian hillulot', in Moshe Shokeid and Shlomo Deshen (eds), *The Generation of Transition* (Hebrew) (Jerusalem: Ben Zvi Institute, 1974).

Dews, Peter, *The Logics of Disintegration: Post-Structuralist Thought and the Claims of Critical Theory* (London: Verso, 1987).

Dobbelaere, Karel and Liliane Voyé, 'From Pillar to Postmodernity: The Changing Situation of Religion in Belgium', *Sociological Analysis* (51(S), 1990), pp. 1–13.

Domenech, Jacques, *L'Ethique des Lumières: les fondements de la morale dans la philosophie française du XVIIIe siècle* (Paris: Vrin, 1989).

Don-Yehiya, Eliezer, 'Jewish messianism, religious Zionism, and Israeli politics: the impact and origins of Gush Emunim', *Middle Eastern Studies*, vol. 23, 1987, pp. 215–34.

Dubarle, D. (ed.), *L'être et Dieu* (Paris: Cerf, 1986).

Duffy, Eamon, *The Stripping of the Altars. Traditional Religion in England 1400–1580* (New Haven, CT, and London: Yale University Press, 1992).

Durkheim, Emile, 'Individualism and the Intellectuals', in Robert Bellah (ed.), *Emile Durkheim. On Morality and Society* (London: University of Chicago Press, 1973), pp. 43–57.

Dury, Nevill, *Elements of Human Potential* (Dorset: Element Books, 1989).

Eliade, Mircea, *Occultism, Witchcraft, and Cultural Fashions* (Chicago: University of Chicago Press, 1976).

Elias, Norbert, 'On Human Beings and their Emotions: A Process-Sociological Essay', in Mike Featherstone, Mike Hepworth and Bryan S. Turner (eds), *The Body* (London: Sage Publications, 1981), pp. 103–25.

Ellenson, David, 'German Jewish Orthodoxy: Tradition in the Context of Culture', in Jack Wertheimer (ed.), *The Uses of Tradition: Jewish Continuity in the Modern Era* (New York: Jewish Theological College of America, 1992), pp. 5–22.

Erikson, Erik, *Young Man Luther* (London: Faber & Faber, 1959).

Feibleman, James K., *Understanding Oriental Philosophy*, revised edition (New York: Meridian Books, 1984).

Ferry, Luc, *Homo Aestheticus: L'Invention du Goût l'Âge Démocratique* (Paris: Grasset, 1990).

Flanagan, Kieran, 'J.-K. Huysmans: The First Post-modernist Saint?', *New Blackfriars*, vol. 71, no. 838, May 1990, pp. 217–29.

Flanagan, Kieran, *Sociology and Liturgy, Re-presentations of the Holy* (London: Macmillan, 1991).

Flanagan, Kieran, 'Sublime Policing: Sociology and Milbank's City of God', *New Blackfriars*, vol. 73, no. 861, June 1992, pp. 333–41.

Flanagan, Kieran, *The Enchantment of Sociology: A Study of Theology and Culture* (London: Macmillan, 1996).

Foucault, Michel, *The History Of Sexuality, The Care of the Self*, trans. Robert Hurley (Harmondsworth: Penguin, 1990), vol. 3.

Foucault, Michel, 'What is enlightenment?', in Paul Rabinow (ed.), *The Foucault Reader*, trans. Catherine Porter (Harmondsworth: Penguin, 1991), pp. 32–50.

Fox, Nicholas J., *Postmodernism, Sociology and Health* (Buckingham: Open University Press, 1993).

Friedman, Menachem, 'Life tradition and book tradition in the development of ultraorthodox Judaism', in Harvey E. Goldberg (ed.), *Judaism Viewed from Within and from Without* (Albany: State University of New York Press, 1987), pp. 235–55.

Friedman, Menachem, 'The state of Israel as a theological dilemma', in Baruch Kimmerling (ed.), *The Israeli State and Society: Boundaries and Frontiers* (Albany: State University of New York Press, 1989), pp. 165–215.

Gay, Peter, *The Enlightenment: An Interpretation* (London: Wildwood House, 1973).

Gehlen, Arnold, *Man in the Age of Technology* (New York: Columbia University Press, 1980).

Gellner, Ernest, *Postmodernism, Reason and Religion* (London: Routledge, 1992).

Giddens, Anthony, *Modernity and Self-Identity. Self and Society in the Late Modern Age* (Cambridge: Polity Press, 1991).

Giddens, Anthony, *The Consequences of Modernity* (Cambridge: Polity Press, 1991).

Giddens, Anthony, *The Transformation of Intimacy. Sexuality, Love and Eroticism in Modern Societies* (Cambridge: Polity Press, 1993).

Giddens, Anthony, *Beyond Left and Right: The Future of Radical Politics* (Stanford, CA: Stanford University Press, 1994).

Giddens, Anthony, 'Living in a post-traditional society', in Ulrich Beck, Anthony Giddens and Scott Lash, *Reflexive Modernization. Politics, Tradition and Aesthetics in the Modern Social Order* (Cambridge: Polity Press, 1994), pp. 56–109.

Gilbert, Alan, *Religion and Society in Industrial England* (London: Longmans, 1976).

Gill, Robin, 'Theologians and Sociologists – A Comparison', *Christian Ethics in Secular Worlds* (Edinburgh: T. & T. Clark, 1991), pp. 23–41.

Goldscheider, Calvin and Alan S. Zuckerman, *The Transformation of the Jews* (Chicago: University of Chicago Press, 1984).

Goudzwaard, Bob and Harry de Lange, *Beyond Poverty and Affluence: Towards an Economy of Care* (Toronto: University of Toronto Press, 1995).

Grys, James Le, 'The Christianization of Modern Philosophy according to Maurice Blondel', *Theological Studies*, vol. 54, 1993, pp. 455–84.

Habermas, Jürgen, 'Modernity – an incomplete project', in Hal Foster (ed.), *Postmodern Culture* (London: Pluto Press, 1985), pp. 3–15.

Habermas, Jürgen, *The Philosophical Discourse of Modernity* (Cambridge: Polity Press, 1987).

Hadden, Jeffrey, 'Towards desacralizing secularization theory', *Social Forces*, vol. 65, no. 3, 1987, pp. 587–610.

Harris, Martyn, 'A Meeting of Mind and Body', *The Daily Telegraph*, 24 May 1993.

Harvey, David, *The Condition of Postmodernity* (Oxford: Blackwell, 1989).

Heard, James, *Art in the Making: Impressionism* (London: National Gallery, Video, 1990).

Heelas, Paul, 'Californian Self-Religions and Socialising the Subjective', Eileen Barker (ed.), *New Religious Movements: A Perspective for Understanding Society* (New York: Edwin Mellen Press, 1982), pp. 69–85.

Heelas, Paul, 'Cults for Capitalism. Self Religions, Magic and the Empowerment of Business', in Peter Gee and John Fulton (eds), *Religion and Power, Decline and Growth* (London: British Sociological Association, Sociology of Religion Study Group, 1991), pp. 28–42.

Heelas, Paul, 'The Sacralization of the Self and New Age Capitalism', in Nicholas Abercrombie and Alan Warde (eds), *Social Change in Contemporary Britain* (Cambridge: Polity Press, 1992), pp. 139–66.

Heelas, Paul, 'The New Age in Cultural Context: the Premodern, the Modern and the Postmodern', *Religion* (special issue on 'Aspects of the New Age', ed. P. Heelas), vol. 23, no. 2, 1993, pp. 103–16.

Heelas, Paul, 'The Limits of Consumption and the Post-modern "Religion" of the New Age', in Russell Keat, Nigel Whiteley and Nicholas Abercrombie (eds), *The Authority of the Consumer* (London: Routledge, 1994), pp. 102–15.

Heelas, Paul, 'On Things not Being Worse: the Ethic of Humanity', in Paul Heelas, Scott Lash and Paul Morris (eds), *De-traditionalization: Critical Reflections on Authority and Identity* (Oxford: Blackwell, 1995), pp. 200–22.

Heelas, Paul, *Celebrating the Self. The New Age Movement and the Sacralization of Modernity* (Oxford: Blackwell, 1996).

Hegel, G.W.F., *Phenomenology of Spirit*, trans. A.V. Miller (Oxford: Oxford University Press, 1977).

Heidegger, Martin, *Schellings Abhandlundung uber der menschlichen Freiheit*, Band 42 (Frankfurt: Klostermann, 1988).

Henrici, Peter, 'Hans Urs von Balthasar: A Sketch of His life', in David L. Schindler (ed.), *Hans Urs von Balthasar. His Life and Work* (San Francisco: Ignatius Press, 1991), pp. 7–43.

Hervieu-Léger, Danièle, *De la mission à la protestation. L'évolution des étudiants chrétiens en France (1965–1970)* (Paris: Cerf, 1972).

Hervieu-Léger, Danièle, 'Le développement des communautés de base et leur contexte religieux en France', *Archives Internationales de Sociologie de la Coopération et du Développement*, no. 31, Jan.–June 1972, pp. 2–48.

Hervieu-Léger, Danièle (with Françoise Champion), *Vers un nouveau christianisme?* (Paris: Cerf, 1986).

Hervieu-Léger, Danièle, *et al.*, *Voyage de Jean-Paul II en France* (Paris: Cerf, 1988).

Hervieu-Léger, Danièle ed., *La religion au lycée. Conférences au Lycée Buffon 1989–1990* (Paris: Cerf, 1990).

Hervieu-Léger, Danièle, *La religion pour mémoire* (Paris: Cerf, 1993).

Hervieu-Léger, Danièle, 'Present-day emotional renewals: the end of secularization or the end of religion?', in William H. Swatos (ed.), *A Future for Religion?: New Paradigms for Social Analysis* (London: Sage, 1993), pp. 129–48.

Hervieu-Léger, Danièle, 'Religion, Memory and Catholic identity: Young people in France and the "new evangelisation of Europe" theme', in John Fulton and Peter Gee (eds), *Religion in Contemporary Europe* (Lewiston/Lampeter/Queenston: Edwin Mellen Press, 1994), pp. 125–38.

Hooykaas, R., *Religion and the Rise of Modern Science* (Edinburgh: Scottish Academic Press, 1973).

Huggson, Tom and Alan Trench, 'Brussels Post-1992: Protector or Persecutor?', in Mike Saks (ed.), *Alternative Medicine in Britain* (Oxford: Clarendon Press, 1992), pp. 241–9.

Hughes, Robert, *The Shock of the New* (New York: Alfred A. Knopf, 1980).

Hundley, Jane, 'Beauty in the New Age or the Power of Personal Presence', in Sondrad Ray (ed.), *How to be Chic, Fabulous and Live Forever* (Berkeley, CA: Celestial Arts, 1990), pp. 207–17.

Hunter, James, 'Subjectivization and the New Evangelical Theodicy', *Journal for the Scientific Study of Religion*, vol. 21, no. 1, 1982, pp. 39–47.

Illich, Ivan, *Limits to Medicine. Medical Nemesis: The Expropriation of Health* (London: Marion Boyars, 1975).

Inglehart, Ronald, *The Silent Revolution* (Princeton, NJ: Princeton University Press, 1977).

Irigaray, Luce, 'Egales a qui?', *Critique*, 480 (May 1987), pp. 420–37.

Irigaray, Luce, *Marine Lover*, trans. Gillian C. Gill (New York: Columbia University Press, 1991).

James, Marie-France, *Esoterisme, Occultisme, Franc-Maçonnerie et Christianisme* (Paris: Nouvelles Editions Latines, 1981).

Jameson, Fredric, *Postmodernism: Or, the Cultural Logic of Late Capitalism* (London: Verso, 1991).

Jandy, Edward C., *Charles Horton Cooley. His Life and His Social Theory* (New York: Octagon Books, 1969).

Jencks, Charles, *The Language of Post-Modern Architecture* (London: Academy Editions, 1977).

Jencks, Charles, *What is Post-Modernism?* (London: Academy Editions, 1986).

Jencks, Charles, *Post-Modernism: The New Classicism in Art and Architecture* (London: Academy Editions, 1987).

Jencks, Charles, *The Post-modern Reader* (London: Academy Editions, 1992).

Jones, W.T., *A History of Western Philosophy*, vol. 4, *Kant and the Nineteenth Century* (New York: Harcourt Brace Jonanovich, 2nd ed., 1975).

Kant, Immanuel, 'An Answer to the Question: "What is Enlightenment?"' (first published 1784), in Hans Reiss (ed.), *Kant's Political Writings*, trans. H.B. Nisbet (Cambridge: Cambridge University Press, 1971), pp. 54–60.

Katz, Jacob, 'Traditional society and modern society', in Shlomo Deshen and Walter P. Zenner (eds), *Jewish Societies in the Middle East* (Washington: University Press of America, 1982) (article first published in Hebrew in 1960), pp. 35–47.

Kearney, Richard and J.S. O'Leary (eds), *Heidegger et la question de Dieu* (Paris: Grasset, 1980).

Kellner, Douglas, 'Popular Culture and the Construction of Postmodern Identities', in Scott Lash and Jonathan Friedman (eds), *Modernity and Identity* (Oxford: Blackwell, 1992), pp. 141–77.

Kerr, Fergus, 'Simplicity Itself: Milbank's Thesis', *New Blackfriars*, vol. 73, no. 861, June 1992, pp. 305–10.

Kohn, Rachel, 'Radical Subjectivity in "Self Religions" and the Problem of Authority', in Alan Black (ed.), *Religion in Australia* (London: Allen & Unwin, 1991), pp. 133–50.

Kreeft, Peter, *Christianity for Modern Pagans. Pascal's Pensées, Edited, Outlined and Explained* (San Francisco: Ignatius Press, 1993).

Kristeva, Julia, *Powers of Horror*, trans. Leon Roudiez (New York: Columbia University Press, 1982).

Kristeva, Julia, *Nations Without Nationalism*, trans. Leon Roudiez (New York: Columbia University Press, 1993).

Kroker, Arthur and David Cook, *The Postmodern Scene* (New York: St Martin's Press, 1986).

Lasch, Christopher, *The Culture of Narcissism* (New York: W.W. Norton, 1979).

Lasch, Christopher, *The Minimal Self: Psychic Survival in Troubled Times* (London: Pan, 1985).

Lasch, Christopher, *The True and Only Heaven* (London: W.W. Norton 1991).

Lash, Scott, *Sociology of Postmodernism* (London: Routledge, 1990).

Lash, Scott, 'Genealogy and the Body: Foucault/Deleuze/Nietzsche', in Mike Featherstone, Mike Hepworth and Bryan S. Turner (eds), *The Body. Social Process and Cultural Theory* (London: Sage Publications, 1991), pp. 256–80.

Lash, Scott and Jonathan Freidman (eds), *Modernity and Identity* (Oxford: Blackwell, 1992).

Lash, Scott and John Urry, *The End of Organised Capitalism* (Cambridge: Polity Press, 1987).

Lash, Scott and John Urry, *Economies of Signs and Space* (London: Sage, 1994).

Latourelle, René, *Man and his Problems in the Light of Jesus Christ* (New York: Albe House, 1983).

Leeuwen, T.M. van, *The Surplus of Meaning. Ontology and Eschatology in the Philosophy of Paul Ricoeur* (Amsterdam: Rodopi, 1981).

Levenson, Michael, *Modernism and the Fate of the Individual* (Cambridge: Cambridge University Press, 1991).

Levinas, Emmanuel, *Otherwise than Being or Beyond Essence*, trans. A. Lingis (The Hague: Martinus Nijhoff, 1981).

Lewis, James and J. Gordon Melton (eds), *Perspectives on the New Age* (Albany: State University of New York, 1992).

Liebman, Charles S., 'The Reappropriation of Jewish Tradition in the Modern Era', in Jack Wertheimer (ed.), *The Uses of Tradition: Jewish Continuity in the Modern Era* (New York: Jewish Theological Seminary of America, 1992), pp. 471–7.

Lonegren, Sig, *Labyrinths: Ancient and Modern Uses* (Glastonbury: Gothic Image Publications, 1991).

Longley, Clifford, *The Daily Telegraph* (1 September 1995).

Luther, Martin, *Werke*, Weimarer Ausgabe 1883, III, Lectures on Romans.

Lyon, David, *The Steeple's Shadow: On the Myths and Realities of Secularization* (London: SPCK, and Grand Rapids: Eerdmans, 1987).

Lyon, David, 'A bit of a circus: notes on postmodernity and the New Age', *Religion*, vol. 23, no. 2, 1993, pp. 117–26.

Lyon, David, *Postmodernity* (Minneapolis: University of Minnesota Press, 1994).

Lyon, David, 'Jesus in Disneyland: the church meets the postmodern challenge', *ARC: The Journal of the Faculty of Religious Studies, McGill*, vol. 23, 1995, pp. 7–36.

Lyotard, Jean-François, *The Postmodern Condition: A Report on Knowledge*, trans. Geoff Bennington and Brian Massumi (Manchester: Manchester University Press, 1984).

Macey, David, *The Lives of Michel Foucault* (London: Vintage, 1994).

MacIntyre, Alasdair, *After Virtue. A Study in Moral Life* (London: Duckworth, 1985).

Mandrou, Robert, *From Humanism to Science, 1480–1700*, trans. B. Pearce (Harmondsworth: Penguin, 1978).

Manning, Phillip, *Erving Goffman and Modern Sociology* (Cambridge: Polity Press, 1992).

Marion, Jean-Luc, *Sur l'ontologie grise de Descartes* (Paris: Vrin, 1975).

Marion, Jean-Luc, *L'Idole et la distance* (Paris: Grasset, 1977).

Marion, Jean-Luc, *Sur la théologie blanche de Descartes* (Paris: PUF, 1981).

Marion, Jean-Luc, *Dieu sans l'être* Paris: Fayard, 1982 (trans. T.A. Carlson, *God Without Being*, Chicago: Chicago University Press, 1991).

Marion, Jean-Luc, *Prolégomènes à la charité* (Paris: la Différence, 1986).

Marion, Jean-Luc, *Sur le prisme métaphysique de Descartes* (Paris: PUF, 1986).

Marion, Jean-Luc; *Réduction et donation. Recherches sur Husserl, Heidegger et la phénoménologie* (Paris: PUF, 1989).

Marion, Jean-Luc, *La croisée du visible* (Paris: la Différence, 1991).

Marion, Jean-Luc, Special issue on *God Without Being*, *New Blackfriars*, vol. 76, no. 895, July/August 1995.

Marius, Richard, *Luther* (London: Quartet Books, 1975).

Martin, Bill, *Matrix and Line: Derrida and the Possibilities of Postmodern Social Theory* (Albany: State University of New York Press, 1992).

Martin, David, 'Towards eliminating the concept of secularization', *Penguin Survey of the Social Sciences* (Harmondsworth: Penguin, 1965).

Martin, David, *A General Theory of Secularization* (Oxford: Blackwell, 1978).

Martin, David, 'The secularization issue: prospect and retrospect', *The British Journal of Sociology*, vol. 41, no. 3, 1991, pp. 465–74.

Marty, Martin, *The Fundamentalism Project*, vols 1–4 (Chicago: University of Chicago Press, 1991–4).

McCutcheon, Allan, 'Generations, religion and the state: a cohort analysis of the newly unified Germany'; paper given at the International Sociological Association Conference, Bielefeld, Germany, 1994.

Mead, George Herbert, foreword to Charles Horton Cooley, *Human Nature and the Social Order* (New York: Schocken Books, 1964), pp. xxi–xxxviii.

Mead, Margaret, 'The modern study of mankind', in Lyman Bryson (ed.), *An Outline of Man's Knowledge of the Modern World* (Garden City, New York: Nelson Doubleday, 1960).

Megill, Allan, *Prophets of Extremity* (Berkeley: University of Califonia Press, 1985).

Mellor, Phillip A., 'Reflexive Traditions: Anthony Giddens, High Modernity, and the Contours of Contemporary Religiosity', *Religious Studies*, vol. 29, 1993, pp. 111–27.

Mellor, Phillip and Chris Shilling, 'Modernity, self-identity and the sequestration of death, *Sociology*, vol. 27, no. 3, 1993, pp. 411–31.

Melucci, Albert, *Nomads of the Present* (London: Hutchinson Radius, 1989).

Meskin, Jacob, 'Secular Self-Confidence, Postmodernism, and Beyond: Recovering the Religious Dimension of Pascal's *Pensées*', *Journal of Religion* (Oct. 1995), vol. 75, no. 4, pp. 487–508.

Milbank, John, 'The Second Difference: For a Trinitarianism without Reserve', *Modern Theology*, vol. 2, 1986, pp. 213–34.

Milbank, John, *Theology and Social Theory* (Oxford: Blackwell, 1990).

Milbank, John, 'The Name of Jesus: Incarnation, Atonement, Ecclesiology', *Modern Theology*, vol. 7, 1991, pp. 311–33.

Milbank, John, 'Problematizing the secular: the post-postmodern agenda', in Phillipa Berry and Andrew Wernick (eds), *Shadow of Spirit* (London: Routledge, 1992), pp. 30–44.

Miller, Jerome A., *In the Throe of Wonder* (Albany: State University of New York Press, 1992).

Miller, Thomas G., 'Goffman, Positivism and the Self', *Philosophy of Social Science*, vol. 16, 1986, pp. 177–95.

Morris, Thomas V., 'Wagering and the Evidence', in Jeff Jordan (ed.), *Gambling on God. Essays on Pascal's Wager* (Lanham, MD: Rowman & Littlefield, 1994), pp. 47–60.

Muchembled, Roger, *L'invention de l'homme moderne: Sociabilité, moeurs et comportements collectives dans l'Ancien Régime* (Paris: Fayard, 1988).

Newman, David, 'Spatial structures and ideological change in the West Bank', in David Newman (ed.), *The Impact of Gush Emunim* (London: Croom Helm, 1985), pp. 172–82.

Newman, David, 'Gush Emunim between fundamentalism and pragmatism', *Jerusalem Quarterly*, vol. 39, 1986, pp. 33–43.

Niebuhr, Richard, *The Responsible Self* (New York: Harper & Row, 1979).

Oliver, Kelly, *Reading Kristeva: Unravelling the Double-Bind* (Bloomington: Indiana University Press, 1993).

O'Neill, John, 'Religion and postmodernism: the Durkheimian bond in Bell and Jameson', *Theory, Culture and Society*, vol. 5, nos 2–3, 1989, pp. 493–508.

Parsons, Talcott, *Action Theory and the Human Condition* (London: The Free Press, 1978).

Pascal, Blaise, *Penseés*, trans. A.J. Krailsheimer (Harmondsworth: Penguin, 1966).

Perry, Michael, *Gods Within* (London: SPCK, 1992).

Pickering, W.S.F., *Durkheim on Religion* (London: Routledge & Kegan Paul, 1975).

Pine, Richard, *Brian Friel and Ireland's Drama* (London: Routledge, 1990).

Race, Alan, 'Orthodox Ripostes', *The Times Literary Supplement* (15 September 1992).

Radhakrishnan, S., 'Foreword' to Arthur Osborne, *Ramana Maharshi and the Path of Self-Knowledge* (Bombay: Jaico Publishing House, 1954), pp. xi–xii.

Ravitzky, Aviezer, 'Religious radicalism and political messianism in Israel', in Emmanuel Sivan and Menachem Friedman (eds), *Religious Radicalism and Politics in the Middle East* (Albany: State University of New York Press, 1990), pp. 11–37.

Reiff, Philip, *The Triumph of the Therapeutic: Uses of Faith after Freud* (London: Chatto & Windus, 1966).

Riddel, Carol, *The Findhorn Community* (Findhorn: Findhorn Press, 1991).

Rider, Jacques Le, *Modernity and Crises of Identity* (Cambridge: Polity, 1993).

Roberston, Roland, 'Humanity, globalization and worldwide religious resurgence', *Sociological Analysis*, vol. 46, no. 3, 1985, pp. 219–42.

Roberts, Richard, 'Transcendental Sociology: A Critique of John Milbank's *Theology and Social Theory*', *Scottish Journal of Theology*, vol. 46, 1993, pp. 527–35.

Rorty, Richard, 'Habermas and Lyotard on postmodernity', in Richard Bernstein (ed.), *Habermas and Modernity* (Cambridge, MA: MIT Press, 1985), pp. 161–75.

Rose, Gillian, *Hegel Contra Sociology* (London: Athlone, 1981).

Rose, Gillian, 'Shadow of Spirit', *Judaism and Modernity* (Oxford: Blackwell, 1992), pp. 37–51.

Rose, Nikolas, *Governing the Soul: The Shaping of the Private Self* (London: Routledge, 1991).

Roszak, Theodore, *Where the Wasteland Ends* (London: Faber & Faber, 1972).

Ruthven, Malise, 'Muhammad for our times', *The Guardian Weekly* (19 July 1992).

Sacks, Jonathan, *The Persistence of Faith* (London: Weidenfeld & Nicolson, 1991).

Sarup, Madan, *An Introductory Guide to Post-Structuralism and Postmodernism* (Athens, Georgia: University of Georgia Press, 1989).

Savage, Mike, James Barlow, Peter Dickens and Tony Fielding, *Property, Bureaucracy and Culture* (London: Routledge, 1992).

Schnall, David, 'An impact assessment', in David Newman (ed.), *The Impact of Gush Emunim* (London: Croom Helm, 1985), pp. 13–26.

Schneider, Louis and Sanford Dornbusch, *Popular Religion. Inspirational Books in America* (London: The University of Chicago Press, 1958).

Shafir, Gershon, 'Institutional and spontaneous settlement drives: did Gush Emunim make a difference?', in David Newman (ed.), *The Impact of Gush Emunim* (London: Croom Helm, 1985), pp. 153–71.

Sharot, Stephen, *Judaism: A Sociology* (Newton Abbot: David & Charles, 1976).

Sharot, Stephen, *Messianism, Mysticism and Magic: A Sociological Analysis of Jewish Religious Movements* (Chapel Hill: University of North Carolina Press, 1982).

Sharot, Stephen 'Israel; Sociological Analyses of Religion in the Jewish State', *Sociological Analysis*, vol. 52(S), 1990, pp. 63–76.

Sharot, Stephen, 'Religious fundamentalism: neo-traditionalism in modern societies', in Bryan Wilson (ed.), *Religion: Contemporary Issues* (London: Bellew, 1992), pp. 24–45.

Shilhav, Joseph and Menachem Friedman, *Growth and Segregation – The Ultra-Orthodox Community of Jerusalem* (in Hebrew) (Jerusalem: Jerusalem Institute for Israel Studies, 1985).

Shils, Edward, *Tradition* (London: Faber & Faber, 1981).

Silber, Michael K., 'The Emergence of Ultra-Orthodoxy: The Invention of a Tradition', in Jack Wetheimer (ed.), *The Uses of Tradition: Jewish Continuity in the Modern Era* (New York: Jewish Theological College of America, 1992), pp. 23–84.

Smart, Barry, *Postmodernity* (London: Routledge, 1993).

Smith, Houston, *Beyond the Post-modern Mind* (London: The Theosophical Publishing House, 1989).

Smith, Jonathan Z., *Map is Not Territory* (Chicago: Chicago University Press, 1993).

Solomon, Robert, *Continental Philosophy since 1750: The Rise and Fall of the Self* (Oxford: Oxford University Press, 1988).

Sprinzak, Ehud, *The Ascendance of Israel's Radical Right* (New York: Oxford University Press, 1991).

Stafford-Clark, David, *What Freud Really Said* (Harmondsworth: Penguin, 1985).

Steiner, George, *The Death of Tragedy* (London: Faber & Faber, 1961).

Sudjic, Deyan, 'In the steps of Hawksmoor', *The Guardian Weekly* (5 July 1992).

Taylor, Charles, *Sources of the Self* (Cambridge: Cambridge University Press, 1989).

Taylor, Charles, *The Ethics of Authenticity* (London: Harvard University Press, 1991).

The Church Times (23 July 1993).

The Church Times (26 May 1995).

The School of Esoteric Studies advertisment, *New Humanity* (February/March, no. 91, 1990), p. 10.

Thompson, E.P., *Witness against the Beast* (Cambridge: Cambridge University Press, 1993).

Thompson, Judith and Paul Heelas, *The Way of the Heart, The Rajneesh Movement* (Wellingborough: Thorsons, 1986).

Thompson, Kenneth, 'The secularization debate', in Peter Gee and John Fulton (eds), *Religion and Power, Decline and Growth* (London: British Sociological Association, Sociology of Religion Study Group, 1991), pp. 7–14.

Tipton, Steven, *Getting Saved from the Sixties* (London: University of California Press, 1982).

Toward a Global Ethic (Brussels: Union of International Associations, 1993).

Trump, Marla, *The Sunday Times* (13 February 1994).

Turner, Bryan S., 'Periodization and Politics in the Postmodern', in Bryan S.

Turner, *Theories of Modernity and Postmodernity* (London: Sage Publications, 1990), pp. 1–13.

Turner, Bryan, *Religion and Social Theory* (London: Sage, 1991).

Varga, Ivan, 'Modernity or pseudo-modernity? Secularization or pseudo-secularization: reflections on east-central Europe', in Richard R. Roberts (ed.), *Religion and the Transformations of Capitalism* (London: Routledge, 1994), pp. 231–47.

Veldman, Meredith, *Fantasy, the Bomb and the Greening of Britain* (Cambridge: Cambridge University Press, 1994).

Wallis, Roy, *The Elementary Forms of the New Religious Life* (London: Routledge & Kegan Paul, 1984).

Ward, Graham, 'Tragedy as subclause: George Steiner's Dialogue with Donald MacKinnon', *The Heythrop Journal*, vol. 34, 1993, pp. 274–87.

Ward, Graham, 'Theology and the Crisis of Representation', in Robert Detweiler (ed.), *Literature and Theology at Century's End* (Atlanta: Scholar's Press, 1994), pp. 131–58.

Ward, Graham, 'Marion's Postmodern Theology', in Phillip Blond (ed.), *Theology Before Philosophy* (London: Routledge, forthcoming).

Weber, Max, *The Protestant Ethic and the Spirit of Capitalism*, trans. Talcott Parsons (London: George Allen & Unwin, 1930).

Weber, Max, 'The social psychology of the world religions', in Hans H. Gerth and C. Wright Mills (eds), *From Max Weber: Essays in Sociology* (London: Routledge & Kegan Paul, 1961), pp. 267–301.

Webster, John, *Barth's Ethics of Reconciliation* (Cambridge: Cambridge University Press, 1995).

Weingrod, Alex, *The Saint of Beersheba* (Albany: State University of New York Press, 1990).

Westfall, William, *Two Worlds: Nineteenth Century Protestantism in Ontario* (Kingston and Montreal: McGill-Queen's University Press, 1991).

Willaime, Jean-Paul (ed.), *Strasbourg, Jean-Paul II et l'Europe* (Paris: Cerf, 1991).

Williams, Rosalind, *Dream Worlds. Mass Consumption in Late Nineteenth-Century France* (London: University of California Press, 1982).

Williams, Rowan, 'Postmodern Theology and the Judgement of the World', in Frederick Burnham (ed.), *Postmodern Theology* (San Francisco: HarperCollins, 1988), pp. 92–112.

Williams, Rowan, 'Hegel and the Gods of Postmodernity', in Phillipa Berry and Andrew Wernick (eds), *Shadow of Spirit: Postmodernism and Religion* (London: Routledge, 1992), pp. 72–80.

Williams, Rowan, 'Between Politics and Metaphysics: Reflections in the Wake of Gillian Rose', *Modern Theology*, vol. 11, 1995, pp. 3–22.

Wuthnow, Robert, *The Consciousness Reformation* (Berkeley: University of California Press, 1976).

Wuthnow, Robert, *The Struggle for America's Soul* (Grand Rapids: William B. Eeerdmans, 1989).

Index